'Tom Fort has devoted years of research to his subject and the result – as with all his writings – is both impressive and entertaining . . . the Fortian persona . . . makes him the Alan Bennett of the angling scene.' *Literary Review*

'Has all the elements of a Hollywood blockbuster, and then some . . . the story that Tom Fort tells demands the broad canvas of the big screen . . . it's got everything going for it: sex, exotic locations, a heartwarming saga of family values . . . The Latin name of this saline cheese straw is anguilla anguilla: so good they named it twice . . . It would be a pity if the story of the eel became the one that got away.' *Observer*

'This is a captivating study . . . Tom Fort is incapable of writing a dull sentence.' *Financial Times*

'Tom Fort tells the story of the eel in such a way that we cannot fail to share his passion . . . what an astounding story it is!' *The Tablet*

THE BOOK OF
EELS

TOM FORT

HarperCollins*Publishers*

HarperCollins*Publishers*
77–85 Fulham Palace Road,
Hammersmith, London w6 8jb

www.harpercollins.co.uk

This paperback edition 2003
1 3 5 7 9 8 6 4 2

A catalogue record for this book
is available from the British Library

isbn 0 00 711593 8

Typeset in Postscript Linotype Baskerville and Photina display
by Palimpsest Book Production Limited,
Polmont, Stirlingshire

Printed and bound in Great Britain by
Clays Ltd, St Ives plc

ACKNOWLEDGMENTS

My first thanks must go to the eel fishermen who gave so freely of their time in helping me: Brendon Sellick, Roger Castle, Dave Pearce, Paul and Charlie Wiley, Joe and Seamus Conlon, Kevin Johnston, John Quinn, Dick Langley, Jim Milne, Floyd Campfield and Larry Seaman. Thomas Nielsen enabled me to understand something of the murky world of glass eel fishing in France and Spain, while Father Kennedy was unstinting with his time and advice at Toomebridge, on Lough Neagh. Without the assistance of Carina Anderberg of the Danish Institute for Fisheries Research I would never have been able to follow the trail of Johannes Schmidt. In the same context, I owe a great deal to Jan and Inge Boetius, to Jurgen Nielsen of the Zoological Museum, Copenhagen, and to Soren Ellemann.

Without the generous help of Jim McCleave and Willem Dekker, I would not have begun to grasp the complexities of the eel's oceanic wanderings and its commercial exploitation in Europe. I am also grateful to Christopher Moriarty, Brian Jessop, Brian Knights, Anthony Knap, Alex Haro, and Dave Secor with assistance in matters of science. Chris Junker-Anderson opened my eyes to the rich eel heritage of the St Lawrence River, while John Casselman went to great lengths to ensure I was properly informed about its decline. Philip Lord of the New York State Museum put me onto the fishermen of Delaware River, while Thomas McGuane alerted me to the story of Larry Seaman and the eels of New York.

My brother Johnny was an invaluable companion on the Italian leg of the eel quest, and translated several passages from obscure texts. Another brother, Matthew, educated me in culinary aspects of the story. Massimo Cavalieri and Antonio Bosco were generous hosts in Comacchio.

Iain Naismith made the chapter about the Thames possible by allowing me to make use of his doctoral thesis on the subject, and I am hugely grateful to him; and also to Diana Cook, of the Richard Way second-hand bookshop in Henley-on-Thames, for providing that contact and lending me books which I could not afford to buy. Denys Tucker was a mine of information. I am also grateful to Nick Witchell, Kate and Bruce Lee, Liz Black, Alan Churchward, Jeff Carroll, Wayne Elliot, Guido Thillart, and Michael Brown.

Special thanks are due to my agent, Caroline Dawnay; and to my editor at HarperCollins, Susan Watt, who – as well as showing unwavering faith in me and my choice of subject – cajoled me into radical reworking of my material which greatly improved the finished article.

FOR HELEN

CONTENTS

PREFACE

It is a creature of mystery, the freshwater eel, with few admirers and fewer friends. Yet for as long as I have been stirred by rivers and lakes and the life within them – which is as long as I can remember – I have been intrigued by this extremely common, little known and little understood freshwater fish, the eel. While working on this book, that fascination became consuming, so that eels annexed my thoughts and infested my dreams. Whenever I crossed a bridge or glimpsed water from the road or a train, I tried to picture the dark, slender shapes hugging the mud. But the images were indistinct. It is easy to see, in the mind's eye, a salmon resting behind a rock, a trout sipping down an insect between two trails of green weed, a chub or barbel swaying in the current where the willow branches dip. With the eel, the best I could do was to say to myself, 'I know you're down there somewhere.' At night, however, they came into the open. They slithered through my sleep, backs green and brown, bellies yellow and pearly silver, snouts questing, tails undulating, a restless presence in my rest.

In writing this book, I have sought to share something of my own fascination, and to encourage some appreciation of this not-at-all-appreciated creature. I wanted to tell of its unusual physiology and highly individual life cycle, and to convey my own wonder at its uniquely extended and perilous travels. I wanted to celebrate the quality of its flesh and its high reputation among chefs. I wanted to follow it, as far as I could, into its world. Most of all, I wanted to leave a record of the co-existence of our two species – how, as the eel has gone about obeying its biological commands, we through studying its patterns of behaviour have exploited it while doing it no harm.

There is a temptation in every age to see its changes as a taking of the wrong path, a turning away from values of proven worth and to prophesy doom. And it is true that hindsight often reveals the rage and despair in those prophecies to have been exaggerated, if not unwarranted. So maybe I am wrong – I hope so – in fearing that we are losing something irreplaceable as the dislocation between our consumer society and the world around it grows wider and more fixed.

It is not that we actively seek to corrupt or destroy it. It is that, not understanding how it works, we do not know what we are doing. We clamour for more living space and ease of travel, so the countryside is devoured by houses and roads. We require electricity to power our conveniences, so we build dams that destroy river ecosystems. We are told until we come to believe it that it is our right to have cheap food, so our farmland is despoiled and our livestock mutated into freaks. Then, suddenly, we wonder: where are the skylarks, where are the hedges, where are the water meadows and the water voles and the cod and the salmon and the whales? Where did BSE come from, and foot-and-mouth? And how is it that we – the richest, best-educated, most sophisticated society in the history of our planet – seem so powerless to mend our ways?

Fish and fishermen are early casualties. Fishermen take

what the waters provide, and when they cease to provide, the fishermen cease to exist. For as long as I can remember I have been a lover of fish, and I have tried to educate myself about their world. But for me it is an amusement, albeit a consuming one, a part of my life; whereas for fishermen it is a way of life and a matter of survival. For thousands of years the eel has been hunted and eaten because it is available and because it is good to eat. There are still a few eel catchers left, the last of a long line. When they are gone, and the sons they hoped would take their place decide that life must have more to offer than attending on eels, the relationship will be over.

For reasons of convenience as well as personal preference, I have largely confined myself to dealing with the two Atlantic species: the European eel, *Anguilla anguilla*, and the American eel, *Anguilla rostrata*. This is not because the dozen and more other species in the world are uninteresting or undocumented. But to attempt to do justice to the entire genus would require a work of Proustian proportions, and run the risk of forfeiting the attention of even the most sympathetic of readers. In retrospect I am acutely aware of things I didn't do, or couldn't, which I wish I had. For instance, I wish I had been better as an eel catcher, and I wish very intensely that I could have looked into that strangest of birthplaces and graveyards. But there is only so much one man can do – even for an eel.

ONE

My eel

I did not care for biology lessons. The classroom was dark and cold, the air still and musty, smelling of feet and adolescence and old dissections. One gowned pedagogue after another would stand before us, droning on about photosynthesis or cell structure or some such stuff. Occasionally we would be given slices of an apple to cut up. Along the corridor was the school museum, which contained – among a mass of mouldering and moulting examples of the taxidermist's art – a cat with two heads and a duck with four legs. But I cannot remember our studies ever embracing animals, alive or stuffed. I can remember nothing beyond diagrams on the blackboard and bits of browning apple on my desk.

If only the fusty old fool had told us the story of the eel! It would have roused us from our preoccupation with our spots and blackheads, our gnawing and constant hunger, our almost equally disturbing anxieties as to whether we were likely to end up as homosexuals. But if he knew it, he kept it to himself, together with all the other marvels of the world about us. Consequently, as a boy, I remained ignorant of the veiled drama of this creature's life. But I did, at odd moments, encounter the fish itself. On holidays, my brothers and I used to wander the high, nameless becks and burns of Lakeland and western Scotland, with fishing rods and tins of worms. There were always trout in these wild little waters: fierce, hungry fellows eager to dash at a bait and sweet just out of a frying pan. Very infrequently, the resistance to the lifting of the rod point was stronger than usual, and from the bubbly pool would emerge, not the spotted trout of desire, but something the length and colour of a black bootlace, and the thickness of a hosepipe, corkscrewing itself in mid-air with unnerving vivacity.

Such captures were not at all welcome. It is not easy to subdue a tangle of eel, hook, and slime-strewn line when one is balanced precariously on a rock in a rushing stream without the basic necessities for eel control: two free hands (at least), a newspaper or rough cloth, a sharp knife, a flat surface. No one who has not grappled with a live eel can have any conception of how impossible it is to hold it. The experience was likened by one Victorian wag to attempting to detain a pig by the tail 'when it has been well soaped'.

I hope we did not abuse those little upland eels too much. There would have been profanity, and there may, I fear, have been some stamping upon them, perhaps even some kicking to assist them in their return to the water (they were far too small to be worth eating). Certainly there was no rejoicing over their capture. There are anglers who pursue eels with intent, but we were not among them.

However, there have been occasions when I have been grateful to the eel. Many years ago I went with my eldest brother to Loch Lomond in Scotland, the home of enormous pike which were rumoured – falsely – to be easily caught. At a village on the shore we asked the first man we met where the best place was to engage with these monsters. He hired us his boat, and directed us to a shallow, reedy bay – a place which, it transpired after we had fished it for a week, was favoured by the pike for their spawning, which had taken place two months earlier, and at no other time. So we caught no pike. But every now and then we found a bite-sized chunk missing from our herring baits, and, once we had worked out what was going on, we had some fun with the eels. However one does not travel four hundred miles to catch three-quarter-pound eels, so the experience was not repeated.

With the same brother and a friend I once took a boating holiday on the Fens. It was roastingly hot, and the water was like warm soup. Most fish will not feed in such conditions, but eels like them. One close and still night, I had left a little dead gudgeon out as bait, with my rod propped up against the rail, while we played poker and drank beer in the cabin. We were interrupted by the sound of line whizzing off my reel. I beat my way through the moths dancing in the cabin light to my rod, which was in the act of disappearing over the side. I grabbed it, and struck. After a few minutes of heaving, a huge eel broke the surface, thrashing in the beam of our torch. Somehow we netted it and somehow I killed it, as we had an idea it would provide relief from our diet of tinned baked beans and frankfurters. But I wanted to weigh it first, and we had no scales. A day later, in intense heat, we reached St Ives, where I bought a set of scales. My specimen weighed four and a quarter pounds, which is a big eel, and its body was as thick as my forearm. However, when I cut off its head, I was assaulted by an overpowering stench of decomposed entrails, and I hurled it back into the green water.

Holidays at my great-aunt's house at the southern end of Coniston Water in the Lake District offered more opportunities to dabble with eels. The property was close to where the River Crake leaves the lake for Morecambe Bay and the sea. A little way down the river was a deep, still, black pool, fringed by reeds and spotted with bright green lily pads. It was a mysterious, slightly unnerving place, but powerfully suggestive of eels. In the evenings we would row down and lay night-lines, baiting the hooks with worms or the heads of perch we had caught in the lake. We would return in the early morning, when the mist was rising in curls over the black mirror of water. The lines came in with blobs of eel slime clinging to them. Sometimes there was a living resistance, and beneath the boat you could make out the pale belly of an eel twisting in the darkness. But these were always small, and more trouble than they were worth once we had finished sorting out the tangles. Once, though, my eldest brother caught a decent-sized specimen on rod and line. He killed it and chopped its head off, and left the corpse in a white enamel bowl outside the front door. When he returned a few minutes later, the bowl was empty. A general search was ordered, and the headless eel was eventually found half-way down the path leading to the water.

Many years later I was invited, with my friend Stephen, among others, to fish for trout on the River Test in Hampshire, which is perhaps the most famous trout river in the world. Generally one does not fish for eels on the Test any more than, having been invited to play golf at Carnoustie or St Andrews, one would delay teeing off to look for mushrooms. Our host's face registered puzzlement when we appeared brandishing eel-fishing gear and asked if we could hunt for worms in his manure heap.

Sitting beside a pond waiting for the questing eel to find one's bait is a slow business. But stalking them is stirring sport. You must look in the shaded places, where the water curls around the base of a willow, where you may spot a still, narrow head among the roots. Or you may make out a slender shape at the edge of a patch of green, a tail waving in imitation of the weed. Your little bunch of worms must land well upstream from the eel, a distance nicely calculated so that the current brings it to within a foot or two of the fish's sensitive nostrils. Then – assuming the eel does not take fright and flee – a period of high excitement ensues. If the water is clear enough, you may see the tail quiver and the head move forward until your worms are no longer visible; then feel the line tremble between your fingers. As you tighten a touch, the sensation of munching transmits itself. You strike, lift the furiously writhing creature out of its element before it has time to wrap its tail around some root, lay it on the grass and consider its fate.

All that broiling July day Stephen and I hunted eels. The

little ones we put back, the better ones – a pound or so – we consigned alive to a bucket. Our host reappeared, baffled, but happy that we were happy. Stephen lit a fire, then took the eels, stabbed them through the back of the head, nailed them to the door of the fishing hut, and, having made an incision around their necks, took a pair of pliers and with one smooth downward motion stripped off the slimy skins. The flesh beneath was blue-silver, dry and firm. Within a couple of minutes they had been gutted and tossed upon a piece of chicken wire laid over the fire, where they spat and sizzled as the fat ran out. Our host joined us again, peered momentarily at the trails of slime on the fishing hut door, and politely refused to take a fillet in his fingers. We were not so inhibited, and the warm evening air was suffused with the savour of eel meat and exclamations of epicurean delight.

In general, however, the eel favours the night. As darkness falls on the lake, it stirs. There is light at the surface, the light of the night sky, reflected gleams picked out by the ripples, enough to make out the shadows of the reeds and the trees, the trails left by the ducks, the hills dimly still, upside-down. But go down, and the darkness asserts itself. There, unseen, the creature is hunting. It glides across the bottom, its pale belly stroking the mud. Its body is serpentine, its slenderness belying its muscled strength. It slips sinuously through the tendrils of weed in its path, and they do not stir.

Its eyes are pebbles of black on the side of its pointy snout. They are not needed for this business. In front of each eye is an oval panel crammed with sensory devices to guide it on its trail. In front of them is a wide, thin mouth, opening and closing on the thousand and one nourishing organisms going about their obscure little lives in that obscure world. Most are minute and it is a night's work to swallow enough of them to keep the creature from being troubled by hunger after it retires to its hideout with the rising of the sun. But sometimes, with a snap, it will take a whole little fish, which will satisfy it for two or three days. And once in a while it might find the fish too big to be swallowed whole. Then it fastens its little teeth into the meat, and spins on its own axis until a mouthful is torn free.

It is a creature of secret places, and its ways are discreet. It hides in the mud, under stones and beds of weed, in the roots of trees, in the holes left by voles and in the crevices of lock gates and old bridges. By daylight you are likely to search for it in vain, unless the water is unusually clear, in which case you may discern that snout protruding from a shadow, that tail waving below a patch of weed. But you may be sure that it is there, somewhere; in this lake and every other lake, in every river great and small, every rivulet and streamlet, pond, dyke, ditch, mere, everywhere from harbours and the estuaries of rivers up to the farthest-flung trickle.

It hunts by night and it travels by night. The extraordinary journeys that occupy the first and last stages of its life are undertaken away from our seeing eye. And in between, when it is never further away from us than the nearest piece of water, it keeps itself to itself. Were you minded to look, you could find it anywhere from Iceland, around Scandinavia, through the Baltic, down western Europe to the northern coast of Africa as far east as the Suez Canal; and on the other side of the Atlantic from Greenland and Labrador to the Gulf of Mexico and Venezuela. Millions of people live within a bicycle ride of its home and know nothing of it. Even those moved to investigate its secrets find them extraordinarily hard to crack. There are mountains of learned papers dealing with the most recondite aspects of the eel's physiology and behaviour, but while much is now known, many mysteries remain.

What we do know about this extremely common creature stretches credibility. I am well aware that the same is said of many of the inhabitants of the world about us. 'Isn't that amazing?' we exclaim at our television sets as the professional haunter of rainforest or tropical reef lays bare the means by which some furry tree-dweller secures its foodstore or some gristly mollusc ensnares its prey. But the fate of tiny hedge beasts and flashing reef fish, the birds of marsh and moor, even the soft-eyed, warm-blooded mammals of the sea, does not directly affect our lives, because they do not figure in our diets.

We like to think that we know most things about the animals we have admitted to our food chain (although, as BSE demonstrated, never enough). Through studying their habits we have subjugated them to our ends. We have learned to make them bigger, leaner, more fertile, not fertile at all – anything to suit our convenience. We rearrange the genetic composition of cows to equip them with udders so huge they cannot walk. We mutate the chicken into a beakless, shackled, egg-producing machine. We imprison pigs in the darkness, and make monsters of them. We cram the silver salmon – born to roam the seas – into cages, feed them on the processed flesh of other fish treated with dye to make their flesh pink, dose them with cocktails of virulent chemicals to discourage sea lice from eating them alive, then try to convince ourselves that we are giving ourselves a 'natural', 'healthy' form of nourishment.

But, although the flesh of the freshwater eel has been prized ever since Mesolithic man first loped through the forest to the water's edge and stabbed down his three-pronged spear on its twisting form, the species has never been enslaved. It is true that in Japan the eel has been reared in captivity since the late nineteenth century, and that eel farming has been taken up on an extensive scale in the Far East and in several European countries. But, despite all the efforts of skilled geneticists, it has proved impossible to persuade the eel to breed in captivity. So those who would continue to enjoy its sweet, immensely nutritious flesh depend on the creature's own capacity to renew itself.

Regrettably, those places where the eel's exceptional calorific and culinary qualities continue to be properly esteemed do not include my own country, where, over the past half-century or so, it has disappeared from the list of dietary staples. An edition of Mrs Beeton's cookbook of the 1930s included recipes for eel soup, jellied eel, boiled eel, stewed eel and fried eel. Twenty years later Constance Spry considered the fish worthy only to be potted into a paste. The contemporary equivalent of those two ladies, Delia Smith, has nothing to say on the subject, beyond allowing smoked eel to be 'almost on a par with smoked salmon, in my opinion'. In general, we British no longer eat any freshwater fish, with the exception of rainbow trout, which are reared in cages and fed on pellets made from other fish and taste of the squeezings from old dishcloths. A limited domestic market for eels does survive though, kept alive by the surviving eel and pie shops in east London and the eastern suburbs, the jellied eel stalls, and a small but growing smoked eel sector.

Matters are very different in Continental Europe. To this day, the ritual of Christmas Eve in traditional Italian households includes a dish of *capitone arrostito* – roasted eel. The Dutch adore them smoked, and have developed a significant eel-farming industry to satisfy their appetite. The Germans love big eels, stewed or smoked. The Danes have an ancient tradition of eating them, as do the Swedes, the Finns, the Belgians and the Swiss. Several of the great restaurants of France continue to offer complex testimonials to the qualities of the eel, and it is cherished by those most fervent of fish-eaters, the Spanish and the Portuguese.

The eel may be fried, roasted, grilled, broiled, boiled, steamed, stewed, smoked, pickled. Whatever the method, the characteristics of the white flesh are its sweetness and its richness. Jane Grigson wrote: 'I love eel . . . Sometimes I think it is my favourite fish. It is delicate but rich, it falls neatly from the bone.' For Grigson, its culinary apotheosis was Monsieur Pasteau's *matelote d'anguille*, which she held to be the chief reason for visiting the town of La Chartre-sur-le-Loir, the little Loir whose waters help feed the great Loire, the foremost French eel river. Another English writer, Quentin Crewe, paid his homage in the village of Passay, on the edge of the great Lac de Grand-Lieu near Nantes, where he questioned one of the last of the traditional eel fishers, Monsieur André Baudray, about his methods, and savoured Madame Baudray's *matelote*, eel stewed for two hours in red wine, with Málaga grapes and prunes from Agen.

*   *   *

The eel is – of course – a finned, cold-blooded vertebrate which breathes through gills; in other words, a fish. But its habits, and, more particularly its appearance, set it apart from other fish. Its shape is against it, for – although we have learned that it is right to love, or at least tolerate, snakes – the serpentine form still taps into deep-rooted instincts of revulsion. Take into account the eel's muted colouring, its snoutiness, its thick coat of viscous slime, and its convulsive writhings when it is removed from its element into ours, and you have a creature with a tricky image problem. Add to that its entirely false reputation as a scavenger of decomposed flesh, and a smattering of biological data – the toxicity of its blood (sufficient to kill a dog), its hermaphroditism, its unnerving capacity to continue squirming after what one callous biologist referred to as 'skin removal, brain destruction and sectioning of the posterior nervous system' – and you have a demon of the watery sphere.

Usually, the mere mention of its name is enough to provoke a shudder of revulsion, and the suggestion of an encounter with a living specimen is liable to bring on an attack of the vapours. Even among anglers, who cherish water and most things that live in it, its reputation is low. This prejudice is attributable partly to the eel's looks, and partly to its habit of taking baits intended for other species, and the terrible mess that tends to ensue when it does so. The writer and poet Patrick Chalmers, a generally genial and tolerant soul, displayed this unthinking antipathy to the full when he described a tussle with an unwanted eel: 'I offered it, with a shudder, my new bait . . . the eel came sinuously to it . . . it opened a yellow and reptilian mouth . . . the ghillie looked at the eel as though it was the Accuser of the Brethren . . . He beat it to death . . . he kicked the corpse into a whin bush.'

Even the greatest and wisest angler of my lifetime, the late Richard Walker, became a barbarian when dealing with eels. In his book *Still-water Angling*, first published in 1953, he alleges – quite baselessly – that 'ducklings, moorhens and even cygnets are pulled under screaming' when big eels are about. Having offered some serviceable advice on how to catch them, he deals at some length with a greater challenge – subduing them:

> You have to assault the eel . . . the best plan is go for the brute bald-headed, armed with a newspaper, a stick and a stout knife. First, try to get the eel to roll itself up in the newspaper . . . this is your chance to get it a blow with the stick, either on its nose or about three inches from its tail . . . you can stick the knife through it just in front of the pectoral fins, aiming to sever its vertebrae; this kills it . . . Since eels are so inimical to every other kind of fish, and even to wildfowl, it is probably best to kill every one caught.

It is curious that a man with such tender feelings towards carp and roach should have considered any fish deserving of treatment more in keeping with a Quentin Tarantino movie than 'the contemplative man's recreation'. But Walker's complete ignorance of the eel's eating habits – and consequent brutality – were widely shared. The eel's status as an inferior form of fish life legitimised the use of any method, the cruder and more barbaric the better. Francis Francis, the chief angling expert of the high Victorian era, recommended 'sniggling' for them, a technique requiring the use of a stick of ash, alder or hazel with a length of cord tied to one end. At the other end, said Francis, a 'large darning needle' should be 'lashed on crossways', with a worm threaded over it. The bait having been taken, the sniggler should wait for the fish to swallow worm and needle, then give a slight pull to turn the needle 'across his gullet'. Thus attached, the wretched creature was 'easily captured'. Even more amusing was the technique referred to by Francis as 'stichering', in which 'an old sickle . . . roughly toothed' was tied to a twelve-foot pole, and employed to levitate eels from the drains of the water meadows on the bank. 'An unskillful sticherer,' says Francis with lumbering humour, 'will sometimes chop off his neighbour's ear or poke out his eye, which doubtless lends excitement to the sport.'

As I have mentioned already, I have caught one big eel in my life. But, to be honest, I did not appreciate at the time what a thing I had done. That was more than thirty years ago, when four-pound eels – indeed eels of all sizes – were much more common than they are now. I wanted very much, in the course of researching and writing this book, to catch or at least do battle with a big eel; to have a monster eel story of my own to tell.

But big eels are like the elders of any species. They have not become big by being foolish and impetuous. They do not take a bait readily, and on the occasions they do, the tackle must be strong and the angler resourceful, to coax them into the net. The pursuit of big eels demands a considerable commitment in time. Nor is that time likely to be packed with incident. The eel specialist must be prepared to sit as still as a sleeping heron, for nights on end (for big eels are generally nocturnal feeders), beside some still, black pond, mere or canal, sustained during the vigil by inner strength and quiet passion.

There are groups dedicated to this unusual form of self-denial. I once heard the secretary of the National Anguilla Club – an organisation dedicated to studying and conserving eels, as well as angling for them – being interviewed on the radio about his calling. He had the air of a mystic about him as he talked, quietly and soberly, about his obsession and the demands it made of him; of the countless hours he had spent, watchful, unmoving, waiting for the buzz of his electric bite alarm, for the rustle of line disappearing from his reel into the blackness before him, for the upward sweep of his rod and the heavy, living resistance somewhere in the depths. He revealed, as if it were a trivial matter, that he had spent an entire season after eels without, as he put it, 'banking a single specimen'. There was a pause while the interviewer digested this. 'Some people, Jim [or whatever his name was], might say that you were completely mad.' 'Some people have indeed said that to me, Nick,' replied the eel man in untroubled tones.

Myself, I own that I do not have that kind of dedication. Moreover, it was the thought of having caught the monster that appealed to me more than the actual catching. I was not entirely comfortable with the mental picture of myself alone, in the dark, the water at my feet lashed to a froth by a thing almost as long as me and as thick as my leg, jaws agape. So I began to modify my ambitions. I realised that a leviathan was almost certainly beyond me, and that I should be prepared to settle for eels of manageable proportions caught by any reasonably humane means. One thing I was firm about: avoiding the night. Unlike the eel, I am not a nocturnal creature, and all my experiences of fishing at night – encompassing being washed away on a Thames millstream, being stranded by the receding tide on the shores of a remote Scottish sea loch and standing on a brother's favourite trout rod – had been unsuccessful and generally unhappy. I am at ease with dusk, as long as some pale gleam from the departing sun flickers on the surface, and I can manage the twilight that precedes dawn. But it is my strong opinion that the 'witching time of night' is best left to the bats and the badgers.

I was anxious to try an ancient and humane method in which worms and worsted are wound into a ball which is lowered into eel territory and raised once the prey's teeth become properly entangled. These days its practitioners are rarely met. But Jim Milne, an old fisherman from Epney on the Severn who showed me how elvers – or baby eels – were caught, had done a good deal of it in times past, and at the mention of it his hunter's interest perceptibly quickened. He spoke of paddling quietly across the sandbanks where the eels foraged, of the insistent nibbling at the squirming ball, of eels by the half-hundredweight, eels by the barrel. I said I would provide the worms. Jim promised the boat and the expertise. That was in April. By early September – prime time for patting, as Jim called it – wiser and more cautious counsels had prevailed in the Milne household. My suspicion was that Jim's wife, Ruth, was more than a little reluctant to see her octogenarian husband adrift on those capricious waters with a tyro such as myself, and in such a cause.

I would have tried spearing, although it hardly belongs in the code of angling and is entirely illegal. But, as far as I could ascertain, most of the eel spears were in museums or on collectors' walls, and the spearers in the ground. My thoughts turned to nets. One of the most effective ways of taking eels is by using a train of connected mesh funnels known as fyke nets. These strings of traps, linked by walls of netting, are not baited, but are placed at an angle to the routes taken by eels as they roam in search of food. The theory is that the eel follows its way through the funnels until it reaches the last, known as the cod end, from which there is no escape except the way it came, a manoeuvre generally beyond eelish intelligence. I had seen fyke nets in use on the Thames Estuary, and I felt that I might be able to manage them myself. The obvious place to try was Coniston, where what had been my great-aunt's lakeside house could be rented through her family. I booked it for the following August, and plotted the attack.

I approached the Environment Agency for permission to use fyke nets. 'This is a most unusual request,' said the lady at the Agency's office in Penrith. But she was helpful, and I received a lengthy document authorising me – subject to a multiplicity of conditions – to use nets for one week 'for research purposes'. So, one brilliantly sunny late summer's day, I went to Morecambe to borrow Dick Langley's gear. I drove along the seafront from the north, with the unbroken line of hotels and boarding houses on one side, and the grey mud and the grey sea on the other. Holidaymakers strolled up and down the promenade, enjoying the warmth. But to me nothing, not even such a gorgeous day, could disguise the down-at-heel dinginess of this most unappealing of seaside resorts. 'People always come back to Morecambe,' Dick Langley said with a throaty laugh. 'They can't believe what they saw the first time.'

In normal circumstances, Dick makes a typically erratic fisherman's living, catching eels, bass, codling and other species out in the bay. He has a licence to fish for elvers in the rivers running into the bay, and to take eels from various lakes and tarns. But these were not normal circumstances. Foot-and-mouth disease had swept through Lakeland. The fields were empty, the grass long and lush, the farmers out of sight. The only work was cleansing the farms, and Dick was one of those doing it, making better, regular money than the eels could ever provide. 'Every cloud and all that,' he commented with a tight, humourless smile. He had many friends among the farmers and shared in the tragedy that had blighted the fields and fells.

I spent three days as a Coniston eel fisher. The weather was benign and, in the absence of wind and with the help of my brother Matthew on the oars, it was surprisingly easy to feed the stack of netting over the stern of the boat so that it lay stretched out on the bottom. I used two strings of nets, which were held in place by metal weights attached to either end. At one end there was also a buoy, a piece of white polystyrene that was reassuringly visible from our landing stage.

At first we were very excited. Matthew and I speculated gloatingly about the scale of the catch, and discussed how we would dispose of it. He is a food writer and an exceptionally accomplished cook, and I was keen for him to work his way through some of the classic eel dishes; perhaps starting with the *matelote d'anguilles* before progressing to something more intricate, perhaps *anguille durand*, eel stuffed with pike and poached in a *mirepoix bordelaise*. We need not have worried. The total harvest from the exertions of three days was three small eels, a host of tiny perch, and two or three miniature pike. I was bitterly disappointed. Dick Langley said he had heard dark tales of the south end of the lake being fished out by a family of rogues and poachers from Flookburgh, a few miles away. When I suggested to the lady at the Environment Agency that the dearth of eels might warrant investigation, she replied that their 'sampling' showed there was a healthy population, and intimated that I had been either unlucky or – more probably – inept.

Chastened, I had one hope left. I have a friend called Chris Yates, a tall, slender, bony, softly and slowly spoken, balding, impoverished father of four, who is a remarkably skilful fisherman and a remarkably talented chronicler of the joys and absurdities of the angler's life. Chris's speciality is catching huge carp (he used to hold the record, a mighty fish of fifty-one pounds), and he had told me that his current favourite carp lake contained something else: enormous eels. He had taken them up to four pounds while carp fishing, and there were tales, he said, of giants, of fish straightening out cod hooks in the night, of quantities so vast that they had been netted and fed to the dogs. I very much liked that touch – fed to the dogs.

Chris's carp lake is shaped like a fat sausage, and is concealed by ancient woods of oak and beech in a valley in Wiltshire. The place is called Fonthill, a name still tinged with notoriety on account of the extraordinary follies of one of its owners of old, William Beckford (curiously enough a previous proprietor, the second Earl of Castlehaven, who was executed in 1631 after being convicted at a trial of his peers of sodomy). The lake was already here when Beckford inherited the estate and an immense (though often exaggerated) fortune on coming of age; as was a mansion built by his father on a scale so overwhelming in its lavishness that it was dubbed Splendens. Beckford disliked it and had it flattened, preferring to commission the fashionable architect of the day, James Wyatt, to build him a sham Gothic abbey with a soaring octagonal tower at its centre. Close by, he had another lake dug, so that he could view his abbey reflected in moonlight, an obligatory experience for those of extreme Romantic inclination.

Poor Beckford! Had he taken up fishing and been sent to a good school, something might have been made of him. As it was, his father died when he was young and his mother kept him at home, spoiling him grotesquely. The wayward and precocious youth developed into a wayward and precocious young man, given to wandering around Europe behaving badly. He achieved sudden fame at the age of twenty-four with the publication of his Oriental fantasy *Vathek*, which he is reputed to have written – in French – in three days and two nights. Subsequently, his reputation ruined by the almost certainly unfounded accusation that he had debauched an aristocratic youth, Beckford lived a generally sad and solitary life at Fonthill, shunned by his neighbours and society at large. The building of the abbey and its tower, and the shaping of the grounds to a suitably poetic echo of Paradise, took twenty years, and consumed the greater part of Beckford's wealth. He sold Fonthill to a Scotsman,

John Farquar, a gunpowder millionaire known, on account of his personal habits, as Old Filthyman. Three years later, in 1825, Wyatt's tower fell down, and a few months later Farquar died of apoplexy. Beckford himself lived – in reduced but by no means straitened circumstances – for another twenty years, but did not revisit Fonthill.

History hangs heavy over the place, and so did the weather the day of my visit. It was mid October, late in the year for eels, but extraordinarily warm, with grey cloud pressing down on the valley, suffusing the still air with damp. They were conditions that might have been tailored for the occasion. To begin with, Chris and I fished at the shallow, northern end where, he maintained, the big eels were supposed to hunt. Apart from a certain eeliness in the air, which may have been auto-induced, we met no sign of them. Several large carp passed by, tracing spearheads on the surface, and Chris caught a handsome trout on his bunch of maggots. The shadows lengthened and deepened as dusk crept in. Chris said we should try a deep hole by the dam, an infallible spot. And, sure enough, just before half-past seven, with full darkness almost on us, I felt a chewing at my worms, struck, and felt my eel. After a brief tussle, Chris scooped his big net under the fish's silvery belly and lifted it up. It was not large, maybe a pound or so, hardly a cause for elation. But I felt mildly relieved to have had something, and in gratitude we unhooked it and let it depart in peace.

Later, in the local pub, the Beckford Arms, I met the source of the Fonthill eel stories, the estate's former keeper. It was true – they had fed fish from the lake to the dogs, as an alternative to rabbits. And there had been eels among them, although the great majority were perch. And it was true about the cod hooks. The keeper's brother-in-law, who hailed from some cod-blessed seaside place, had put night-lines out, and in the morning they had been retrieved clogged with slime, with the hooks straightened out – but never an eel still on the end. The keeper himself used to spear eels from the bridge at the top end of the lake and sell them locally. But his motives appeared to have been entirely commercial, and he neither ate eels himself nor had any lively interest in them. Having waited in vain for some stirring account of monsters slain or glimpsed, wildfowl engulfed, wanderers met by night wriggling through the fields, I finished my second pint and left the pub. Outside, the night was still warm and heavy with moisture. It was a night made for eels, and I wished with a fierce, futile intensity that we had stayed by the lake and fished on into the darkness.

TWO

A dainty dish

In a good season – that is to say, in times past – Brendon Sellick would catch plenty of eels. But you wouldn't call him an eel fisherman, just a fisherman; and you would not mistake him for anything else. There cannot be many of his sort left anywhere, and in his immediate vicinity there are just him and his son, who helps him out on the mudhorse. This unusual mode of conveyance is essential to Brendon's way of fishing. Indeed, without it there would be no fishing. And I doubt that, when he is gone – he is in his late sixties, and has been at it for more than fifty years – there will be any fishing.

Brendon's cottage, and the ramshackle shed from which he sells his catch, are set back a little way from a defensive barrier raised in 1939 to discourage any German landfall at Bridgwater Bay in Somerset. On the map, the bay is a bulge of blue on the southern side of the Severn Estuary. A mile or two to the east of Brendon's place, it is fed by two lethargic channels leading from the damp and reedy flatland of Sedgemoor, the rivers Parret and Brue. Beyond is the once fashionable resort of Burnham on Sea, where pleasure-seekers took to the waters – and may do so still – even though the bluest of skies is needed to disguise their brown colour. The mighty tides that sweep up and down the estuary dictate a ceaseless, shifting balance of power between the sea and the banks of sludge and silt laid there over the ages by the rivers of the marshes. When the tide is out, the water is reduced to a channel so distant that it appears in danger of being obliterated altogether. Mud is in the ascendant, a sticky, glistening, quaking, grey expanse, streaked with lines of greasy, soapy rocks. It is a world of its own, requiring special techniques from its residents and visitors. The wading birds do nicely, and so does Brendon on his mudhorse.

Although he is a fisherman, he has no boat. His nets are fixed in the mud, strung out along lines of blackened stakes arranged at angles across the routes favoured by the fish as they move in to forage with the rising tide. At the height of the tide, when the bay is filled, the nets are invisible. As it recedes, the stakes appear like watery sentinels, until it is time for the mudhorse. Some of the nets can be reached on foot, but others – generally the most productive – cannot. So Brendon lies face down on the mudhorse – a low wooden platform on runners, resembling a toboggan – and with his hands and feet propels himself across the flats, plucking the catch as he goes.

There are eels, flounder, dabs, whiting, a multitude of shrimps, the occasional bass, the very occasional salmon. It is an extraordinarily simple, not to say primitive, way of fishing, no different in its essentials from that carried out along this coast for centuries (remains of medieval fixed nets have been found at Minehead, not far away). It is the kind of fishing that has absolutely no place in the modern world; its 'inefficiency' providing enough for the fisherman's own needs and a modest surplus to sell or barter, and no more. Brendon Sellick does it because, in the world he was born into, you did what your father did, unless compelling circumstances intervened – and his father was a mudhorse man. But times had changed, as he explained to me in his piping burr. The nature of the revolution was, for him, illustrated by his last holiday – a three-week cruise with his wife to Egypt, Israel and the Greek islands. 'Dad wouldn't have believed it,' he said, hardly seeming to believe it himself. The idea that the son of a Sellick who had cruised the Greek islands would be content to eke out a living gliding over the mud of Bridgwater Bay on his belly, extricating flapping fish from nylon netting, was clearly absurd.

To my disappointment, I did not see the mudhorse out of its stable. When I visited Brendon, the tides were too small to expose the more distant nets. So I followed him on foot, in waders. To our left, half a mile away, was the huge, squat, concrete mass of Hinckley Point nuclear power station, with the low line of the Quantock Hills behind. Every so often the screech of the gulls was drowned out by the roar of steam being released from one of the massive chimneys. Brendon told me that before Mrs Thatcher's time, someone had had the idea of utilising the warm water from the power station for an experimental eel farm. A million pounds was invested, and the eels did very well, growing large and – according to Brendon – slightly blue. They were taken off by tanker to Germany, until the order came from on high – Brendon thought from Mrs Thatcher herself – that Hinckley Point was to be sold off, which meant no more money was to be frittered away on fattening blue eels for Germans. 'I liked her,' Brendon mused. 'She turned the country round, you know. But that was a shame about the eels.'

We sloshed along the accessible nets. In the last, their beaky little heads stuck through the mesh, were two smallish eels, the only ones. 'It's been a terrible year for them,' Brendon lamented. 'Terrible. I don't know why, haven't a clue. Not enough eels, I suppose.' We talked about the migration. 'And they say it comes all the way from – what do they call it? – the Sargasso, and then all the way back again. Amazing, innit?' I wondered if he believed 'them'. He told me that one day before the war, his father had caught a sturgeon in the nets weighing nearly a hundred pounds. 'Seven foot long it were. Amazing. No, I've never seen another one.'

Back in his shed he filleted a cod for me, and packed up a bag of juicy, freckly shrimps. Chickens wandered through the clutter of nets, dilapidated lobster pots, perished rubber boots and plastic bags, helping themselves to fragments of shrimp scattered on the floor. Brendon thought he would have the eels himself, stewed then left to cool so a jelly formed around the chunks. 'I likes 'em,' he said with relish. 'Mind, there's not many does.'

When Brendon has eels in any quantity he sells them to Michael Brown, a former journalist, long-distance walker and elver fisherman now turned eel smoker. This is the eel in a socially acceptable form, with head, slimy skin and awkward bones removed: a moist, rich, flavoursome and manageable fillet, made more delicious still with a dab of sauce made from the horseradish growing in the fields around. Brown's smokery is housed in an outbuilding on a farm deep in the Somerset Levels, a mile or two from the ruins of noble Muchelney Abbey, where a millennium ago the monks received six thousand eels a year from their fisheries. Next to it is a little restaurant where you may eat eel warm from the smokery, with boiled potatoes. A fyke net is strung from the ceiling, and on the wall is a testament from one Ernie Woods to the huge eels of Chard Reservoir, which 'barked like dogs'.

Another of Michael Brown's suppliers – as unlike Brendon Sellick as a bass is a flounder – is a former teacher at Christchurch Grammar School in Dorset, Roger Castle. Whereas Sellick is no more than vaguely curious about eels and enjoys telling tales about their unaccountable habits, Castle has long been gripped by the strange architecture of their life cycle, and has carried out a long, unfinished investigation into it. He was born in Poole and as a boy lived on a boat in Poole Harbour, a prosaic name for a considerable inland sea now encircled in the clasp of suburban sprawl, but still – with its creeks, channels, islands and mudbanks endlessly swept by the restless incoming and outgoing of the sea – a wild and lonely place demanding respect, even from those who know it well.

Castle took a degree in physical education and biology at

Loughborough University and wrote a learned paper called 'The Life History of the European Eel' for his general science course. Aside from a scholarly reworking of the standard accounts of the eel's life cycle and migrations, it contains an interesting account of the eels of Poole Harbour which – back in the 1950s – were present in enormous abundance (Castle talks of being able, on warm summer evenings, 'to catch the fish as fast as you can get a line to them'). He deduced that the harbour eels comprised a resident saltwater population, sustained at a high density by an inexhaustible supply of small crabs, shrimps and prawns, and worms.

In the 1970s the buoyant price for adult eel stimulated a concerted assault by local fishermen on the Poole eels. Roger Castle became involved, although he encountered fierce animosity from the locals when they could spare the time from hauling in the eels. The fishing was completely uncontrolled, and after a few years catches plummeted. Somewhat bruised by his experiences, Castle sought more peaceful pastures. He began fishing the two rivers that debouch into the harbour at Christchurch, the Avon and the Stour. These are like two cousins from branches of a family very much divided in their fortunes: the Avon much the more refined, draining much of Wiltshire and flowing in a stately fashion through Hampshire, once – though no more – one of England's premier salmon rivers; the Stour slow and sluggish, murky and reedy, ambling its way through the eastern part of Dorset, never much of a river for salmon and now without them altogether, but renowned for its pike and perch. Both rivers were good hunting grounds for the eel, and using fyke nets through the summer, shifting from one location to another (for they soon become alert to the predator in their midst), Castle was able to satisfy his yearning for involvement with eels and to contrive for himself a useful income. In the early 1990s he persuaded the Bournemouth and West Hants Water Company to let him install an eel trap, or rack, at Longham on the Stour. He was thus able to extend his season into late autumn by catching the cream of the harvest, the silver eel.

When not in use, Castle's eel rack – which resembles a giant fire grate – is tucked up underneath a brick outhouse built over part of the river's flow. On those moonless autumn nights when the eels are wont to run, it is lowered into position, and the sluice gate upstream adjusted to increase the volume of water through it. It is a most ingenious and impressive apparatus, even though on the night I inspected it, only one eel came in. Nor was Castle much more successful with the fyke nets he had set on the Avon a couple of miles away. It was late in the year, and he suspected that the unusually high water levels of the previous weeks had sent the silvers on their way when he was unable to work his trap. Either that, or – for their inscrutable reasons – they were waiting.

He was filled with gloom about the creature's prospects. Over the past ten years he had experienced a steady decline in catches – noticeable on the Avon, steep on the Stour. Castle believed the spread of toxic silt beds had fouled the mouth of the Stour, persuading the incoming elvers either to choose the cleaner, more alkaline flow of the Avon, or to stay in the estuary.

Roger Castle is the only eel fisherman on the Stour

and Avon. He is proud of that singularity, and of the knowledge and understanding of this most enigmatic of fish which he has accumulated as a professional fisherman. As a consequence he is apt to be impatient with those – the fishery officers of the Environment Agency – who issue his licences, restrict his freedom to operate, and question his experience. More than that, he is fearful for his eels; fearful that, having been the only eel fisherman, he will be the last – not because it is a tough and demanding occupation, although it is, but because there will be no eels left.

As with so much else, it was the Greeks who first found the words to sing the praises of the eel. The curiosity of their intellectuals – most notably Aristotle – about the creature's life cycle clearly reflected an established epicurean enthusiasm. In Aristophanes' *The Archanians*, the hero Dicaeopolis, upon learning that a smuggler has secured for him fifty of the succulent eels of Lake Copais, bursts forth: 'O my sweetest, my long-awaited desire.' In another of his plays, a sausage seller shouts: 'Yes, it is with you as with the eel-catchers; when the lake is still they do not take anything, but if they stir up the mud, they do; so it is with you when you disturb the state.'

In about 330 BC, a Sicilian Greek known as Archestratus wrote a popular satire on the hedonism of the age called *The Life of Luxury*, in which he referred to the eel as 'the undisputed master of the fishmonger's stall' and noted that 'the eels of the Strymon River and Lake Copais have a formidable reputation for excellence thanks to their large size and wondrous girth'. Archestratus essayed a feeble joke about eels being more valuable than gods – 'since prayer is free and at least a dozen drachmas is required to secure an eel' – before paying this tribute: 'All in all, I think the eel rules over everything at the feast and commands the field of pleasure, despite being the only fish with no backbone' (another translation has this as 'no scrotum' – my ancient Greek is inadequate to resolve the matter).

Another shadowy figure from those distant days, Agatharchides of Knidos, alleged that the Boeotians held the fat eels of Lake Copais in such reverence that they turned them into demi-gods, putting crowns on them and offering prayers. According to Alexandre Dumas's *Le Grand Dictionnaire de Cuisine*, 'the Egyptians placed eels on a par with the gods . . . they raised them in aquariums, whose priests were charged with feeding them with cheese and entrails.' (An American anthropologist, Albert Herre, who worked in the Philippines in the 1920s, found a 'well-developed' eel cult among the Lepanti Igorots who lived near Mount Mougoa. They kept sacred eels in pools, which were fed daily on rice and sweet potatoes by devotees who sang songs of praise as they went about their work.)

All the peoples of the ancient world ate eels, with the exception of the Jews, who were forbidden on the erroneous grounds that it was of the company 'that hath not scales . . . and shall be an abomination'. The place of the eel in Roman affections was savagely mocked by Juvenal, who alleged – most unfairly – that they fed on sewage:

Now comes the dish for thy repast decreed
A snake-like eel of that unwholesome breed
Which fattens where Cloaca's torrents pour
And sports in Tiber's flood, his native shore.

According to the legendary Roman epicure, Marcus Gavius Apicius, six thousand eels were served at various feasts marking the triumphs of Julius Caesar. They were supplied by Gaius Hirrius, whose fishponds were so famously productive that – mainly on account of them – he was able to sell his estates for the fabulous sum of four million sesterces. (Of Apicius and his gluttonous excesses, *Chambers Biographical Dictionary* records: 'It is said that when he had spent £800,000 upon his appetite and had only some £80,000 left, he poisoned himself to avoid the misery of plain diet.' Being informed that the prawns of Libya were even larger and more luscious than those available in his native Campania, Apicius is said to have sailed straight away for Tripoli; and on discovering that the report was false and the prawns were no better, to have sailed home again.)

'It is agreed by most men,' wrote Izaak Walton in the first edition of *The Compleat Angler*, published in 1653, 'that the Eel is a most dainty dish. The Romans have esteemed her the Helena of their feasts, and some the queen of palate pleasure.' Walton cautioned against overdoing it, quoting Solomon: 'Eat no more than is sufficient, lest thou surfeit.'

But flesh of such richness and flavour can be difficult to resist. The pre-eminent Irish eel expert, Christopher Moriarty, speculated that Henry I of England, who, according to the account of the chronicler Henry of Huntingdon, died from eating lampreys 'contrary to the instructions of his physician', might in fact, given a general confusion between the two species, have been gorging on eels.

One who certainly succumbed to an extravagant anguillo-philia was the wretched Simon de Brie of Tours, the puppet Pope Martin IV installed by Charles of Anjou in 1281. He did not last long, dying four years later – much to his patron's inconvenience – from an excess of Lake Bolsena eels, which he favoured stewed in Vernaccia wine. One of Simon's epitaphs viewed his fate from the celebratory perspective of his prey: 'Gaudent anguillae, quia mortuis hic jacet ille qui quali morte excoriabit eas.' His punishment was to be dispatched to Purgatory, where Dante spotted him:

> . . . e quella faccia
> di la da lui, piu che l'altre trapunta,
> ebbe la santa Chiesa in le sue braccia:
> dal Torso fu, e purga per digiuno
> l'anguille di Bolsena e la vernaccia

> (. . . and that visage
> beyond him, more shrivelled than the others,
> held the Holy
> Church within its arms; from Tours sprang he
> and by fasting purges
> the eels of Bolsena and the sweet wine).

Another possessed of a fierce and notorious passion for eel flesh was the Holy Roman Emperor, Charles V. Having spent thirty years vying with the King of France, Francis I, as to who should be master of Europe, Charles famously abdicated and retired to the monastery of Yuste in the Spanish province of Estramadura, where he kept a close eye on his son and successor, Philip II, and was tormented by gout and gluttonous yearnings. The great American historian of Spain, William Hickling Prescott, wrote of Charles:

> In the almost daily correspondence [with the Secretary of State] there is scarcely one letter which does not turn on the Emperor's eating or his illness. It must have been no easy matter for the secretary to preserve his gravity in the perusal of dispatches in which politics and gastronomy were so strangely mixed together. Fish of every kind was to his taste, as indeed was anything that in its nature or habits approached to fish. Eels, frogs, oysters occupied an important place in the royal bill of fare. Potted fish, especially anchovies, found great favour with him. On an eel-pasty he particularly doted.

How the world-weary, gouty Emperor would have relished an eel dinner with Izaak Walton, whose favourite recipe – presented with lip-smacking relish – makes something of a nonsense of his call for self-restraint:

> First wash him in water and salt; then pull off his skin below his vent or navel, and not much further: having done that, take out his guts as clean as you can, but wash him not: then give him three or four scotches with a knife; and then put into his belly and those scotches sweet herbs, an anchovy and a little nutmeg grated or cut very small and mixed with good butter and salt; having done this, then pull his skin over him all but his head, which you are to cut off, to the end that you may tie his skin above that part where his head grew, and it must be so tied as to keep all his moisture within his skin: and having

done this, tie him with tape or packthread to a spit and roast him leisurely, and baste him with water and salt till his skin breaks and then with butter: and having roasted him enough let what was put in his belly, and what he drips, be his sauce.

One of the chief attractions of the eel was that, in an age when most fish and meat was of necessity preserved in salt, it was readily obtainable fresh, if not actually alive. When Henry III celebrated St Edward's Day in October 1257, it is said that fifteen thousand eels were provided for the feast. On a more modest scale, when Bishop Hales of Coventry and Lichfield called his sixty guests to the table for the Feast of the Assumption on 15 August 1461, they were served with two salmon, two chub (a dubious choice – Walton called the flesh 'not firm but short and tasteless'), three pike, four perch, half a dozen dace and trout, and two dozen each of grayling and eels.

Although Walton's recipe was ornate and clearly intended for special occasions, the abundance of eels, the length of their season, the ease with which they could be kept alive for lengthy periods, and their range of distribution, made them a dietary staple – at least for the English and much of Continental Europe. Londoners, famously, took them to their hearts, inventing the eel pie and jellying in their honour. Perhaps surprisingly, eighty or so eel and pie shops still do business in the East End and outlying districts – although these days the contribution to turnover from the old cockney favourite, stewed eel and 'liquor' (green parsley sauce), is pretty negligible. Some of the families involved in the trade – the Cookes, the Kellys, the Manzes – go back to Victorian times, when eel was cheap and plentiful. The

Reverend David Badham, a Victorian curate and authority on mushrooms, insects and fish, described the thriving trade in his book *Ancient and Modern Fish Tattle*:

London ... steams and teems with eels alive and stewed; turn where you will and 'hot eels' are everywhere smoking away, with many a fragrant condiment at hand to make what is itself palatable yet more savoury ... For one halfpenny a man of the million may fill his stomach with six or seven long pieces and wash them down with a sip of the glutinous liquid they are stewed in.

The affinity between the capital and eels went back many centuries. Shakespeare's Fool invokes it as he chatters to Lear: 'Cry to it, nuncle, as the cockney did to the eels when she put them in the paste alive; she rapped them o' the coxcombs with a stick and cried "down, wantons, down".' At about the same time that assiduous recycler of other men's work, Gervase Markham ('a base fellow', Ben Jonson called him), included a recipe for eel pie in his brantub of domestic counsel, *The English Hus-Wife*, advising that it be cut up, combined with 'great Raisons' and onions, and placed in a coffin or pie dish. By the time Dr William Kitchiner published his *Apicius Redivivus*, or *The Cook's Oracle*, in the early 1800s, the ingredients had multiplied to include parsley, sherry, shallots and lemon, all to be hidden beneath a dome of golden pastry. 'It is a great question debated for ages on Richmond Hill,' Dr Kitchiner reported, 'whether the pie is best hot or cold. It is perfect either way.'

The only European city to rival London in its love of eels was Naples. Mr Badham included this description of the Neapolitan fish market on Christmas Eve:

The dispersals of this delicacy occupy either side of the Toledo from end to end and there display the curling, twisting snake-like forms of their slippery merchandise. Some, suspended over the booths, wriggle around the poles to which they are attached; others, half-flayed to demonstrate the whiteness of their flesh, undulate their slimy coils by thousands in large, open hampers . . . Others are fizzing and spluttering in the midst of hot grease in huge frying pans. Every man, woman and child carries home eels for breakfast, dinner, supper. Every Scotchman who chanced to find himself in the midst of such a scene will learn to hate and recoil from a Church which sanctions such an abomination as food.

The French, too, revered their eels. A cookery book of the seventeenth century, *Le Cuisinier Français*, gives a bewildering array of recipes, including eel stuffed with whiting and mushrooms and braised in brandy and white wine, eel served with fish *veloutée* and crayfish *coulis*, and eel sliced and larded with anchovy fillets. The most illustrious of all French gastronomes, Jean-Antoine Brillat-Savarin, included a charming eel story in his best-known work, *The Philosopher in the Kitchen*. A horse dealer named Briguet, having made a decent fortune in Paris, returned to his home village of Talissieu, in the Chambéry region, where he married a woman previously employed as a cook to the notorious Mademoiselle Cheverin, 'once known to all Paris as the Ace of Spades'. It was the custom in the diocese that included Talissieu for the parish priests to dine together once a month to discuss ecclesiastical matters. When it was the turn of the curé of Talissieu to host the dinner, he – having been presented by a parishioner with a three-foot eel 'taken from the limpid waters of the Seran' – asked Madame Briguet to work her culinary magic with the fish. She gladly agreed, confiding that she had a little box containing 'certain condiments' given to her by her former mistress, the Ace of Spades. The dish was prepared, the guests sat down. 'It looked magnificent and smelt delicious. Words could not be found to express its praise. It disappeared, body and sauce, down to the last particle.'

As the evening wore on the proceedings became increasingly convivial. 'The reverend men were stirred in an unaccustomed manner. Their conversation took a ribald turn . . . and was entirely given to the sweetest of the deadly sins.' Next morning they were all thoroughly ashamed of themselves, and blamed Madame Briguet's eel for their loose tongues. 'I have inquired in vain after the nature of the condiment,' Brillat-Savarin concluded. 'The artist herself pleaded guilty to serving a highly spiced crayfish sauce, but I am convinced she was not telling me everything.'

Across the Channel, the English yielded nothing in their enthusiasm. Parson Woodforde of Weston Longville in Norfolk recorded in his diary his keen appreciation of the occasional 'fine string of eels' from his local miller, and would have them stewed in milk or rolled in seasoned flour and fried in clarified butter. Another clergyman of literary inclination, Richard Barham, author of the *Ingoldsby Legends*, had firm views:

If you chance to be partial to eels
then – *credo experto* – trust one who has tried –
have them spitch-cock'd or stewed – they're too oily
when fried.

Spitch-cocking (or spatch-cocking) is the Anglo-Saxon method of grilling, in which the eel is split lengthways, and the backbone removed, the two halves then being placed over or under the heat. A more intricate version has long been practised in Japan, where it is known as *kabayaki*. The classic mode of preparation requires that the eel be pinned through the head – alive – to a wooden board, slit open along the back with one cut, opened out for the backbone and guts to be removed, then cut into twelve-centimetre lengths. Bamboo or metal skewers are threaded through the flesh to restrain it from curling when cooked. Boiling water is poured over the fillet, after which it is lightly steamed, then grilled over charcoal, the grilling being interrupted three times for the meat to be dipped in a soy sauce.

The passion of the Japanese for this delicacy is unbounded. The first written record of *kabayaki* dates back to the thirteenth century, and the eel occupies a place of enormous importance in the complex relationship between the Japanese and their food. The standard book on the subject, Isa Matsui's *The Eel*, published in 1972, runs to 737 pages, of which more than a hundred are devoted to eel dishes, the eel in literature, religion and legend, and other cultural associations. It is reckoned that today more than a hundred thousand tons of eel are consumed annually in Japan – ten times as much as in all the other eel countries of the world put together. The scale of this demand, and the inability of the long-established Japanese eel-farming sector to meet it, has promoted an explosive growth in the international trade in live eels, some aspects of which will be examined later.

The Japanese fascination with the eel continues to extend far beyond the pleasure it provides skewered and grilled.

Shohei Imamura's film *The Eel*, which was joint winner of the Palme d'Or at the Cannes festival in 1997, is a dark, enigmatic reflection on that fascination, in which the feelings of the protagonist for his pet eel act as a counterpoise to other forces leading him to murder and redemption. It is difficult to imagine any European or American director of Imamura's stature choosing to occupy himself with a celluloid meditation on a creature so lacking in conventional box-office appeal.

THREE

By diverse means

The men who caught the eels to satisfy the great and the greedy generally kept quiet about their ways and means. Their traces have to be dug for in the mud left by floods, sifted from ancient and unreliable chronicles, ferreted out from the documentation accumulated in dusty heaps as human society acquired the habit of minuting its mundane transactions. They do not amount to much: a sieve-full of old fish bones, a scattering of flint flakes from prehistoric eel spears, the record of dealings between the monastery's financial obedientiary and fisherfolk required to pay their dues in scaly form. But they tell some sort of a story.

Several millennia before Aristotle took out his pen of split reed and scratched the first observations and speculations about the lives of eels on his papyrus sheet, men who lived by water had worked out what they needed to know and had fashioned ways to lay hold of an elusive but reliable source of nourishment. They knew that through the summer eels fed and might be caught on bait; that with the coming of autumn they made their way downriver; that in winter they hid in the upper layer of mud where they dozed.

A glimmering of how some of our prehistoric ancestors lived their short, arduous lives has been provided by archaeological finds around the northern end of what, to this day, remains the most abundant wild eel fishery in Europe, Lough Neagh in Northern Ireland. These are some of the earliest known human settlements, going back to the time when the sun first rose on something resembling communal life, almost nine thousand years ago. The oldest is at Mount Sandel, situated on the lower Bann, the river that connects Lough Neagh to the sea and acts as a gateway for inward and outward migration.

At Mount Sandel, at Toome Bay – where the Bann leaves the lough – and at one of the river crossing points, Newferry, quantities of fish bones have been unearthed together with flakes from implements of stone, bone and flint surmised to have been fishing spears or parts of fish traps. These fragments were recovered from deposits of ash contained within layers of diatomaceous earth laid down by the seasonal flooding of the areas along the river between 6000 and 1000 BC. In 1951 a worked wooden harpoon was found at Toome and later dated to 5725 BC. More revealing was the discovery, between Newferry and

Toome, of a line of wooden stakes connected by wicker-work – unmistakably a four-thousand-year-old precursor of the skeagh, or fishing weirs, still used on the Bann to intercept eels.

It is likely that these Mesolithic hunters moved up and down between the lough and the sea, occupying and deserting camps according to the dictates of the seasons. There is evidence that Mount Sandel was used in autumn and winter, while Newferry would have been uninhabitable in winter because of flooding. Around 3000 BC the first Neolithic farmers arrived in the area and the two groups probably coexisted in passable harmony for some time, the older concentrating on the specialised demands of hunting and fishing, trading their captures for tools of pol-ished stone, pots and other modern conveniences manufac-tured by the newcomers. Gradually the distinctions between them would have faded anyway. And it is inconceivable that anyone – be they Mesolithic, Neolithic or the Celtic-speaking Iron Age pastoralists who came later – would have neglected the inexhaustible food source represented by the salmon and eels which swarmed up and down the Bann.

In Continental Europe, the exploitation of the eel would have evolved on much the same lines. Remains of pre-historic traps – in the form of stakes and woven fences – have been found on the Danish coast where the sil-ver eels exit into the North Sea. Pieces of spears made of bone and horn have turned up all over Scandinavia and as far east as Poland. In central France, close to the Vézère, one of the main tributaries of the Dordogne, a carved cylinder of stone was found in the cave of La

Madeleine, showing a human, two horses, and a creature which looks a lot more like an eel than anything else. Wherever our prognathous forbears found themselves beside still or moving water, they would have worked out that eels were good to eat, plentiful, and ever-present; and would have made nets, pots, traps and hooks to catch them.

In general the interest of the ancient scribes in the eel was biological and culinary. The one authority to show an interest in how the fish was caught, rather than in the mystery of its origins or qualities on the table, was a Roman of Praeneste, Claudius Aelianus, who, in the second century AD, compiled a collection of contemporary curiosities entitled *De Natura Animalium*. This included an account of a queer method of eel fishing supposedly employed on the river Eretaenus (where they are 'of very great size and far fatter than those from any other place'):

> The fisherman sits upon a rock jutting out . . . or else upon a tree which a fierce wind has uprooted and thrown down close to the bank . . . The eel fisherman seats himself and taking the intestines of a freshly slaughtered lamb, he lowers one end into the water and keeps it turning in the eddies; the other end he holds in his hands, and a piece of reed, the length of a sword handle, has been inserted into it. The food does not escape the notice of the eels, for they delight in this intestine. The first eel approaches . . . and fastening its curved, hook-like teeth, which are hard to disentangle, continues to leap up in its efforts to drag it down. When the fisherman realises from the agitation that the eel is held fast, he puts the reed to his mouth and blows down it with all his

might, inflating the intestine very considerably. And the downflow of breath distends and swells it. And so the air descends into the eel, fills its head, fills its windpipe and stops the creature's breathing. It suffocates . . . and this is a daily occurrence, and many are the eels caught by many a fisherman.

Aelian was a notoriously credulous soul, but it is worth pointing out that his book also contains a reference to fly fishing for trout, as practised by the Macedonians, which subsequent investigation has shown to be – almost certainly – authentic and reliable. Whether the same can be said of his eccentric and laborious eel-fishing technique is, perhaps, open to doubt.

After Aelian, a literary curtain descends for several centuries. Fishing for eels by more efficient means than suffocating them through a hollow reed certainly continued. For instance, archaeologists digging in the remains of the town of Oldenburg in Schleswig-Holstein – which stood beside a lake – found that more than half the fish bones thrown out by the residents between 650 and 900 AD came from eels. It is a matter of regret that no one troubled to record how the fishermen of Oldenburg – or anywhere else – came by their eels, but the silence is characteristic of the times. It was broken only by that indispensable if erratic illuminator of Anglo-Saxon ways, the monk Bede of Jarrow, who credited Saint Wilfrid (or Wilfrith) – at various times Abbot of Ripon, and Bishop of York, Hexham and Leicester – with having saved the South Saxons from famine in the late seventh century: 'The people had no skill in fish-catching except only for eels . . . The Bishop's men used the eel nets . . . and with the help of Divine Grace caught 300 fish.'

It is to Bede that we owe the traditional derivation of the name of that ancient centre of virtue and learning situated in the heart of the eel's watery realm in eastern England: 'Ely is in the province of the East Angles, a county of about 600 families in the nature of an island enclosed with marshes or with waters, and therefore it takes its name from the great plenty of eels taken in those marshes'.

Anyone who has read *Waterland*, Graham Swift's black and tortuous Fenland tale of love, betrayal, incest and madness, will have obtained some idea of the entwining relationship between those who lived beside those still, green, weedy waterways and the slippery creatures hidden within them. The smell of the place, of mud, decomposing reeds and weeds, and fish, which suffuses Swift's narrative would have been a lot stronger in Bede's time and over the succeeding centuries, before the marshes were drained and brought to heel; when the lives of the people of the Fens were lived on, in and surrounded by water, and they owed their obeisance to their ecclesiastical overlords in the abbeys and monasteries which had arisen on the few knobs of dry land. There is a roll of their names in one of the early texts, the *Coucher Book of Ely*: 'Henry son of Osbert de Walpole, Hugh Wade, Henry Dale, Moyses, Roger Fot, John Gubernator . . . 14,500 eels paid on the first Sunday in Lent.'

They are good, sturdy Fenland names, men adept at spearing, netting and trapping the eels that slithered in such profusion across the soft mud at the bottom of those count-less ditches and dykes and meres and infinitely slow-moving rivers. There are more, listed in the *Ramsey Cartulary*, the foundation charter granted in 970 by King Edgar: Alfgar of

Hilgay and Hugh of Wiggenhall, altogether 'seven fishermen and their seven assistants and seven little ships'. The charter mentions among the properties owing dues, the manor of Welles 'which was of profit to the abbey solely on account of its render of eels; 20 fishermen gave 60,000 eels every year for the use of the brethren.' The monks of Thorney Abbey were similarly well provided for, Bishop Aetholwold having endowed them – at a cost of twenty-one pounds – with the fisheries 'surrounding the villages of Wyllan and Eolum . . . and 16,000 eels were captured there each year.'

Bishop Aetholwold may well have been alert to the merits of eels, since – as a young man, before his elevation to the see of Winchester – he had been dean at Glastonbury, which was the greatest of all the religious houses and commanded another eel stronghold, the equally flat and damp Somerset Levels. He was a strict and unbending Benedictine, and forcibly imposed Benedictine doctrines – among them a powerful interdict against the eating of meat – on a number of institutions. Such a prohibition would have been less burdensome at Glastonbury than in some other places. As early as 670, the monastery's abbot, Beorhtwald, was granted by King Cenwalh of Wessex the rights to the fishing at Meare on the dark and torpid Brue river. Some time later a building known as the Fish House was built at Meare, whose walls still stand. Glastonbury's chief fisherman resided there, organising a regular supply of eels, tench, carp, pike and roach for the monks. For seven hundred years and more Glastonbury reigned supreme among the religious institutions of England, until Thomas Cromwell contrived the execution of its last abbot, Richard Whiting – 'The Abbot of Glastonbury is to be tried at

Glastonbury and also executed there with his complycys . . .
see the evidence be well sorted and the indictments well
drawn,' read his directions on the matter – and the noble
buildings and their treasures were wrecked and looted and
lost for ever. Whiting's head was placed on the abbey's walls;
and the quarters of his body were displayed over the gates
of Wells, Bath, Ilchester and Bridgwater. There would be
no more dishes of eels for the monks of Glastonbury, nor
for those of neighbouring Muchelney and Athelney, whose
charters also referred to marshland fisheries yielding eels by
the thousand.

Long before Glastonbury fell victim to a complaisant king
and his hatchet man, strict observance of St Benedict's ban
on meat-eating had faltered and faded away. But by then
the taste for freshwater fish, and the methods of catching
and preparing them, had been thoroughly absorbed into the
fabric of life, with the Church – as so often making a virtue
of self-interest – providing the organising impetus. However
avid those monks of Fenland and Somerset may have been
for their portions of eel stewed and boiled, they cannot
possibly have consumed them in the numbers recorded in
those dusty old scrolls. It follows that they, or – more likely
– the officers of the monastery, traded in them.

Towards the end of the Middle Ages, the technology
developed on the Continent for the construction and maintenance of stews and fishponds was greedily embraced by
the piscivorous aristocracy and religious orders of England.
The principles were laid down in the mid-sixteenth century
by the learned Bishop Janus Dubravius of Olmutz, in his
De Piscinis et Piscium, but were certainly in circulation much
earlier than that. All over England holes were dug in the

grounds of princely houses, abbeys and monasteries, filled with water, and stocked with carp, tench, bream, pike and eels. Prior William More of Worcester left a detailed record of his care of monastic stewponds at several locations. Between 1518 and 1524 he put six thousand eels into the ponds – no minor enterprise, given that they had to be caught somewhere and transported live.

In general, however, the eel was so abundant and ubiquitous that it was much less trouble to catch it in its chosen natural habitat than to raise it in captivity. The records of this endeavour are sparse and, in themselves, not enormously exciting. The remains of a Saxon fish weir have been dug up at Colwick, on the Trent in Nottinghamshire, which is assumed to have been used to trap migrating eels, since the *Domesday Survey* refers to all twenty-two 'piscaria' on the Trent being for eels. The *Luttrell Psalter*, which dates from the fourteenth century, shows basketwork traps of green willow or osier placed in a mill race to catch silver eels. (They were known as kiddles, possibly the origin of the phrase 'a pretty kettle of fish'.) Evesham Abbey was but one of many monastic institutions which maintained such traps as of right. Its stations, at two mills on the Avon, are said to have yielded two thousand eels a year.

Men used bait to catch eels in the summer and intercepted them with fixed traps in the autumn. They also speared them whenever the opportunity presented itself but mainly in the winter, when fresh fish were hard to come by, and the eels had retired to holes in the mud, where their heads might be spotted by the practised eye and their bodies either impaled on a single prong, or – more often – jammed between two or three serrated prongs arranged like a fork. A late-fifteenth-century manuscript of heraldic bearings, *Shirley's Book*, displayed the Harding arms with a chevron gules between three eel spears. John Guillim's *A Display of Heraldrie*, which appeared in 1610, described how spears were used:

> . . . for the taking of eeles, which being (for the most part) in the mudde cannot be taken with Net or any other Ginne: which gave occasion to the invention of this Instrument, a long staffe being set in the socket thereof, and so to strike into the depth of the mudde and by means of the Barbes of this Instrument they detain as many as come within the danger of.

In the previous century, the first great English antiquary, John Leland, referred to Langport market in Sedgemoor being full of 'peckeles, as they call them, because they take them in those waters by pecking an eel speare in them when they lie in their beds.'

The method was employed all over Europe until comparatively recently. Eel spears were still being made in the small Danish town of Skyum until thirty years ago; and Dr Christopher Moriarty records how commercial eel spearing continued on the mudflats at Rosslare, in south-east Ireland, into the 1960s, when tidal changes resulted in the eel grounds being buried by sand. An account of spearing on Ullswater, in north-west England, is contained in James Clarke's *Survey of the Lakes*, published in the late eighteenth century:

> Two or more persons go in a boat on a summer morning, from three till six o'clock. One gently moves the boat by the margins of the lake, whilst

the other looks. He no sooner sees one than he sticks it with an eel spear and by this method great numbers are sometimes caught.

A rather more vivid description is found in a book called *The Practice of Angling Particularly as Regards Ireland*, which was published in 1845. It was the work of James O'Gorman, a well-known resident of the town of Ennis, of whom the *Limerick Chronicle* reported on his death that 'he was the most expert angler in Clare and a devoted admirer of the gentle Izaak Walton.' O'Gorman saw the locals at work on a nearby lake:

> When the rushes grow up there is a regular flotilla of spearmen. A man stands on his bundle, poking before him with his long-handled spear. When he takes an eel he bites his head between his teeth, and then strings it up with a needle on a long cord. Anything so hideous as the appearance of these fellows, their faces begrimed with blood and dirt, can hardly be imagined.

'These fellows': that is as close as we get to knowing them. They were Irish bog peasants, marshmen, fenmen, men of the waterside, plying their skills in remote, damp places, at dusk, through the night and at dawn, keeping themselves to themselves, not caring much to share their secrets with outsiders, certainly not the sort to take a pen and write it down. As Andrew Herd has pointed out in his revelatory history of fly fishing, *The Fly*, we bookish types inevitably view the early development of 'country pursuits', whether it be fishing, bee-keeping, wildfowling, hunting or apple-growing, through the distorting lens of books. We are apt to forget that, in a world nine tenths of whose population could not read or write and to whom the printed word meant and mattered nothing, the process of discovering, learning, advancing, and refining was taking place out there in the field, far away from the desks and fireplaces of literary folk.

Thus, men who lived by rivers with trout in them and found they were good to eat, discovered at least two thousand years ago that they might be conveniently caught on a tuft of fur and feather arranged to look like an edible insect, with a hook concealed beneath it. When Aelian described how those Macedonians of old lured their speckled fish, he was not reporting a technological breakthrough but merely dropping in, by accident, on an established tradition. In the succeeding centuries, men – shepherds, woodcutters, herdsmen, pastoralists, poachers, charcoal burners – went on catching trout on artificial flies, all the time refining the technique. They did so, not to amuse themselves, but as one small part of their strategy for survival – a strategy which did not extend to sitting down by the light of a candle at the end of another long, hard day, and taking up pen, ink and parchment to make a record for the enlightenment of generations to come.

They were silent, these fishermen, for centuries. But they fished, cast their flies in the mountain streams of the Balkans, the Alps, the Pyrenees, and on the slower, weedier lowland rivers – anywhere trout thrived and ate insects. As they did so, they made their traditions, their own unwritten folk history. Eventually the first stirrings of a European civilisation were felt, and society began to aspire to something beyond conquest, defending itself and feeding itself, and became alive to the notion that there might be more to life than merely the striving to continue it. Music, painting and literature burst forth. Games, played in one form or another for centuries, were celebrated and codified. And someone, charmed by the way fly fishermen contrived to catch trout, wrote some of it down; and some time later Caxton's fellow pioneer of the printed book, Wynkyn de Worde, attached the anonymous *Treatyse of Fysshynge with the Angle* onto the end of a hotchpotch of other texts covering the amusements available in the countryside. From that publication, at the end of the fifteenth century, subsequent writers dated the birth of the 'history' of angling.

The humble eel received short shrift in the *Treatyse*, being labelled as 'a quasy [i.e. liable to case nausea] fysshe, a ravenour and a devourer of the brode [fry] of fysshe.' As a consequence of these shortcomings, the eel is bracketed with the pike as 'behynde all other to angle', the one method – grudgingly suggested – being to drop a 'grete angyll twytch or mennow' [earthworm or minnow] into a hole and await developments. Thus, from the start, the eel was expelled to the ghetto of the piscatory world, as being wholly unworthy of the notice of educated men in search of sport. The eel was left to those who had learned from their fathers, as their fathers had from their fathers, about its usefulness. This extended far beyond its role as food. From its skin they made hinges for doors, membranes for filtering liquids, and flexures for flails. The skin had protective qualities, too. The men and women of the Fens made garters of it and swore that they helped keep off the ague, a constant threat in those dank climes. Strips of skin were dried in the sun, greased with fat, placed in a linen bag stuffed with thyme, lavender and marsh mint, then buried under the peat for the summer, before being dug up, greased again, polished with a smooth stone and declared ready to be tied around Fenland legs.

Thomas Boosey, in his *Anecdotes of Fish and Fishing*, quotes another, more specialised application for the eel:

> If you would make some notorious drunkard to loathe and abhor his beastly vice, and for ever after to hate the drinking of wine, put an eel, alive, into a wide-mouthed bottle with a cover, having in it such a quantity of wine as may suffice to suffocate and strangle the eel; which done, take out the dead eel and let the party whom you would have reclaimed, not knowing hereof, drink of that wine.

The generations of eel men learned of its habits, and handed down their knowledge: where and when to lay traps, cast bait, stick spears; the influence of the seasons and the moon. Theirs was a closed world, and they had no need to write any of this down, even if they could. But they did have to talk to each other. And that is all that is available to the outsider – the varied vocabulary of eeling.

Thus, on the Severn, in Kent and in Lancashire, the eel spear was known as a shear or shar, in Wiltshire as a sticker, in Humberside as a stang or stang gad, in Yorkshire as a dilger, in Fenland as a pritch, in the Borders as a glaive, glave or gleve. That other favoured method, used for centuries all over the British Isles and Continental Europe, in which a ball of worms woven into a looped length of worsted or wool was lowered into a likely eel haunt, and sharply raised when its motions suggested the entanglement of teeth is, in the English translation of Friedrich Willem Tesch's dense and scholarly study, *The*

Eel, rendered as naring. On Sedgemoor it used to be known as clotting – a term employed in several other eel regions – or rayballing. Variants include patting, tatting, totting, sniggling, snigging, bobbing, bebbing, babbing, bubbing and broggling. Permanent traps for intercepting migrating silver eels were kiddles, or – much later, and particularly on the Thames – bucks. Terms for movable, baited pots included grig, putcheon, hive and wheel.

To the naked eye, the American eel, *Anguilla rostrata*, is no easier to distinguish from its European cousin, *Anguilla anguilla*, than a citizen of Milwaukee from one of Birmingham or Düsseldorf. They look the same, they behave the same, they taste the same, and for centuries they were prized for the same reasons. In his study of one of the Native American peoples of Maine, *Penobscot Man*, the ethnologist Frank Gouldsmith Speck included an eyewitness description of a fishing party at work in the early years of the twentieth century. It happened in August, when the berries of the poke bush are at their most toxic, before the eels stir on their quest for the sea. Five families of Penobscot came to the river; men, women and children. For two days they dug the roots of the Indian turnip that grew wild along the streams and in damp places. They mashed the roots and the pokeberries into a pulp on flat rocks, which ran purple with the juice. When they had enough, they spread out along a mile of river. At a signal they waded into the water, casting the pulp across the surface and stirring up the muddy bottom with sticks. As the poison took effect, the Penobscot were driven ashore, where they applied plantain leaves to soothe their inflamed skins and waited.

> Torpid eels began to appear upon the surface, and before an hour had passed the surface was spotted with the bodies of dead and dying fish, which floated belly up. The children of the party, having recovered from their hurts, were forced to enter the water and bring the fish ashore, where they were skinned and salted by the women. After this the eels were placed upon dead limbs and laid in the sun for two days. Then they were hung up in a tent and smoked until there was no drip from the suspended bodies.

It was the way of the Penobscot to avail themselves of everything the shores and hinterland provided. In the spring they netted alewives, shad, salmon and sturgeon. They planted corn, beans and potatoes to be harvested in late summer. In June they came down to the sea to hunt seals and porpoises, and to gather eggs, baby seabirds, clams and lobster. In October they took to the woods, setting traps for muskrat and hare. They feasted at Christmas, then hunted moose and caribou, and later otter and beaver.

The eel had three seasons: summer, fall and winter. In summer they trapped them in baskets of woven splints, and poisoned them. In winter they speared them through holes in the ice, using a weapon eighteen or twenty feet long with outer prongs of hardwood and a central one of bone, later iron. And in between, when the silver eels made for the ocean with the coming of autumn, it was time to man the weirs. Up to a dozen families would camp at the places where the traps had been maintained by generations past. They made fences of willow and brush running downstream at an angle from each bank. Where the fences met, three trays of willow rods, ten feet long by seven wide by a foot deep, were fixed, one on top of the other, the rods spaced so that the biggest eels were caught in the top and the smallest in the bottom. Somewhere close at hand a pit was dug and lined with salt, into which the eels were thrown to rid themselves of their slime and die.

The highly nutritious flesh of the American eel was a staple in the diet of the Penobscot as it was for their neighbours, the Micmacs of Nova Scotia. Archaeologists have found an encampment at the southern end of Kejimkujik Lake in Nova Scotia, which dates back five thousand years and which they believe was used for seasonal eel fishing. Indeed all the Native American tribes scattered across the virgin lands of New England and the basin of the St Lawrence had reason to be thankful for the eel and to study its habits.

Although their territories lay towards the northern limit of the species' range, the immensity of the St Lawrence – its mighty tidal displacement, the tens of thousands of miles of suitable habitat it offered – made it the greatest wild eel river system in the world. Its abundance of fish – not just eels, but salmon, sturgeon, shad, alewives and others – dumbfounded the first white settlers. The possibility that it could ever be exhausted or cease to provide could not have crossed their minds, or the minds of those who lived from it.

A riddle confronted the Jesuit missionaries who were dispatched to Canada during the seventeenth century to spread the Word of God in territories claimed by France – generally on rather tenuous grounds – as conquests. The land they called New France had clearly been shaped by God and provisioned by Him on the most lavish scale; yet was inhabited and enjoyed by people for whom it could not possibly have been intended since they were not even aware of His existence. It was evidently their duty to annexe it spiritually in the name of the Christian God, just as it was the duty of the military to do so temporally in the name of the King of France. But at least some of them had the wit to realise that the manner in which the 'savages' and 'barbarians' lived from the land and the water had an ordained appropriateness about it, however inscrutable the divine purpose might be; and had the sense to observe without condemnation, and to learn.

The process of annexation initiated by Samuel de Champlain when he founded Quebec in 1608 was problematic enough, the writ of France being in practice restricted to a scattering of well-guarded settlements on or near the St Lawrence River. The spiritual mission, begun by Franciscans in 1615 and subsequently pursued with typical energy and zeal by the Jesuits, was at least as hazardous and strenuous. The fathers endeavoured to spread the Word among the Abenakis of Acadia (now Maine); the Montagnais and lesser tribes of the lower St Lawrence; the Huron and their enemies the Iroquois; the tribes beyond Lake Huron, including the Beaver and the Cree; and the Sioux who lived along the Mississippi. They strove and suffered. Some were captured and tortured, many died. Sometimes they were listened to, often they were chased and harried. Sometimes they baptised.

However limited the success of the Jesuits – and the

matter is complex and controversial – and whatever view we may take of the pursuit of the missionary principle among native peoples, there is reason to be grateful to those fathers of the black gown who laboured so heroically so far from home. In the form of the celebrated *Jesuit Relations*, the written records of their missionary work compiled by successive superiors in Quebec to be sent back to the headquarters of the order in Paris, they left an amazingly detailed and revealing commentary on the alien world into which they had been delivered. Although the ostensible purpose of the *Relations* was to keep the order informed about the progress of the mission, a great deal else found its way into their narratives. Indeed, one suspects that – as the fathers settled themselves in their birch-bark wigwams deep in the boundless wilderness, surrounded by people they necessarily regarded as godless primitives – they often found it easier to describe the wonders of the land and the extraordinary customs and practices of its inhabitants than to give a wholly objective account of how well they were doing.

The first of the Jesuit missionaries was Father Pierre Biard, who was sent on the orders of Henri IV to the settlement of Port Royal, on the coast of Acadia. Although the native Micmacs seem to have paid little heed to him, certain aspects of their way of life clearly made a favourable impression on him. 'Never had Solomon,' he wrote, 'his mansion better regulated and provided with food than are these homes and their landlords. But then a greater one than Solomon has made them.' Father Biard ate seal – 'as good as veal' – and bear – 'which is very good'. The inshore waters and streams swarmed with herring, smelt, salmon, sturgeon and eels 'good and fat'. 'Anyone who has not seen it could scarcely believe it,' he marvelled. 'You cannot put your hand in the water without encountering them.'

The Acadia mission was a failure, and Biard, who had actually arrived in 1611, the year after Henri's assassination, was captured by English raiders, eventually making his way back to France. In 1632 French rule over Canada was confirmed by treaty with England, and a Jesuit mission was established in Quebec under the leadership of Father Paul le Jeune. Over the next ten years le Jeune composed and compiled ten *Relations* for his superior in Paris, Father Jacquinot, who responded to the growing public interest in the New World by having them published. Le Jeune had taken the trouble to learn something of the language of the neighbouring Montagnais, and studied their way of life. It is clear from the attention he gives the subject that the eels of the tidal St Lawrence, and of the lakes and rivers feeding into it, represented a crucial source of food:

> In regard to eels, they fish for them in two ways, with a weir and a harpoon. They make the weirs very ingeniously, long and broad, capable of holding five or six hundred eels. When the water is low, they place these upon the sand in a suitable and retired spot, securing them so they are not carried away by the tide. At the two sides they collect stones which they extend out like a chain or little wall . . . so the fish, encountering the obstacle, will readily swim towards the mouth of the net. When the sea rises it covers the net; then, when it falls, they go and examine it. Sometimes they find there are one or two hundred eels . . . When the sea is rough many of them are taken; when it is calm, few or none.

The fishing with harpoon, or spear, took place at night:

> Two savages enter a canoe – one at the stern, who
> handles the oars, and the other at the bow, who, by
> the light of a bark torch fastened to the prow, looks
> around searchingly for the prey, floating gently along
> the shore of this great river. When he sees an eel,
> he thrusts his harpoon down . . . There are certain
> ones who will take three hundred in one night . . .
> It is wonderful how many of these fish are found in
> the months of September and October. It is thought
> that this great abundance is supplied by some lakes
> in the country further north, which, discharging their
> waters here, make us a present of this manna.

Other brothers used the same term to convey what
struck them as the miraculous nature of this supply. Franco
Bressani, who preached among the Huron in the 1640s and
1650s, spoke of the eel as 'a manna exceeding all belief'. One
or two men, he claimed, could catch five or six thousand in
a night, which – smoked or salted – could be kept all winter
and 'are much better than any eels in France'. 'To tell the
truth,' he enthused, 'this country is the Kingdom of water
and of fish.'

The fishing methods observed by the first pioneers, traders
and missionaries – and described in such careful detail
by Father le Jeune – had been in use for many centuries before they came. A Canadian archaeologist, Chris
Junker-Andersen, carried out an examination of a midden
uncovered at an Iroquois seasonal camp on a creek close to
the northern side of the St Lawrence, near the present-day
town of Morrisburg. Radio-dating of carbon showed the
camp to have been in use for at least four hundred years,

up to the time the Iroquois – for reasons still not wholly understood – vanished from the St Lawrence valley at the end of the sixteenth century. Peaks of activity occurred in the middle of the twelfth century, towards the end of the fourteenth, and in the middle of the sixteenth. Study of the fauna remains indicated that the diet of the Iroquois using the camp included ten species of freshwater clam, four of turtles, nine of snails, at least sixteen of birds, more than twenty of mammals, and twelve of fish. The single most common vertebrate was *A. rostrata*. Chris Junker-Andersen believes the camp was established specifically to exploit the migration of the silver eel, and that its occupation would have been generally restricted to the fall. While some eels were consumed there and then, most would have been dried and smoked and transported elsewhere, to be eaten over the winter. Smoked eel, like biltong in southern Africa, would have been ideal travelling food.

When the first French explorer of Canada, Jacques Cartier, sailed up the St Lawrence in 1535, he encountered Iroquois along the upper reaches and commented on their reliance upon smoked fish, including eels, to survive the winter. By the time Champlain revisited the area, the Iroquois had been supplanted by their traditional enemies, Algonquian-speaking tribes such as the Weskanini and the Montagnais (or Innu). But the exploitation of the eel by age-old means continued throughout the St Lawrence system as far as the western end of Lake Ontario, where the Niagara Falls presented a barrier insuperable even for this assiduous traveller. It embraced groups of tribes divided by ancient enmities: Iroquois, Huron, Algonquian. And, as Junker-Andersen has demonstrated, even Huron people living along Lake Huron's Georgian Bay – well beyond the limits of eel distribution – habitually travelled east in order to take part in seasonal fishing.

The establishment of the first colonial settlements along the eastern seaboard presaged a struggle between the great European powers – England, France and Holland – which would consume the 'kingdom of water and fish' along the St Lawrence and across the virgin lands to the south and south-west for a century and a half. By the agencies of warfare and disease, this struggle brought catastrophe to those who inherited it. If any of the invaders or their descendants had moral qualms about the holocaust unleashed upon the Native Americans, they generally kept quiet about them. In the case of the French and the Dutch, the paramount consideration in dealing with the Indian tribes was trade, particularly in furs; for the English it was to obtain land for settlement. Both came with the impregnable assumption that the indigenous people were not really human, and that to exploit, trick, slaughter and dispossess them was to secure for the true inheritors of the earth what was rightfully theirs. But, although it was customary to deride the 'savages' for their brutish habits, aspects of their way of life – in particular their genius for hunting and fishing – often aroused a genuine, if condescending, wonder.

Travellers' tales of the marvels and terrors encountered in this wilderness were – however fanciful or incompetently written – immensely popular. One notably inept example was an account published in 1751 by John Bartram of a journey up the Susquehanna in Pennsylvania, through the lands of the Onondaga, to the Oneida River and Oswego on the shores of Lake Ontario. On the Susquehanna, Bartram found the Indians 'cut a stick about three foot long and as thick as one's thumb, they split it about a foot down, and when the eel is gutted, they coil it between the sides of the stick and bind the top close, which keeps the eel flat, and then stick one end in the ground before a good fire.' Further north, on the Oneida, Bartram met Onondagas of genial disposition:

> These Indians were very kind to us ... In the morning they catched some stout eels and a great fish two feet [sic] long, it was round and thick, they strike them with long slender shafts 18 or 20 feet long, pointed at the end with iron ... the two splints of wood spreading each side directs the point into the fish, which at a great depth would otherwise be difficult to hit.

Eel fishing was evidently of great importance to the Onondaga, one of the Iroquois peoples spread across the lands to the south of Lake Ontario who together formed the political confederation known as the Hotmonshonni, or League of Five Nations. Two years after Bartram's book appeared, two German missionaries, David Zeissburger and Henry Frey, were entertained by an Onondaga chief called Otschinachiatha. He told them about his fishing weir, explaining that 'each one has his own place where he is allowed to fish and no one is permitted to encroach ... A chief is appointed to each fishing place, and he has his people who belong to him.'

The two brothers went downstream from Lake Oneida, until they came to a weir which 'quite closed the river', where a number of Onondaga were fishing. An opening through the obstruction was made on the orders of Chief

Hatachsocu, and the travellers were given some dried eels in exchange for flour. They reached the Seneca River and another weir 'where there were also Onondagas, who were very friendly and gave us eels.'

A nineteenth-century traveller, Christian Schultz, reported that eels were found in Lake Oneida 'in the greatest abundance and are the finest and largest that I ever saw.' Schultz described the weir constructed below the outflow from the lake, and the setting of the basket at its apex:

> I was present when one of the baskets, which had been set overnight, was taken up; it filled two barrels and the greater part of the eels weighed from two to three pounds each. I have always been prejudiced against eating eels on account of a rancid taste ... but, being prevailed upon to taste of these, I must declare that I have never before tasted any fish so delicious, without excepting even the salmon. A family who live at the outlet of this lake depend almost entirely on this eel fishery. They salt down about forty barrels a year, and find a very ready sale for them at ten dollars a barrel.

The Native Americans were the great catchers and consumers of the freshwater eel, and with their expulsion from the major waterways and general decline, interest in exploiting the species waned. There were pockets of aficionados – witness a ditty quoted in the official *History of the Town of Windham in New Hampshire*, published in 1883:

> From the eels they formed their food in chief
> And eels were called the Derryfield beef
> It was often said that their only care

And their only wish and their only prayer
For the present world and the world to come
Was a string of eels and a jug of rum.

But, broadly speaking, as the United States developed into a city-based society, the habit of eating freshwater fish withered. With the development of the rail network, almost all the population centres located within the eel's distribution range became accessible to supplies of fish from the sea, which were regarded as being tastier and generally more appealing.

The same thing had already happened in England. The railway lines crept to every corner of the land, enabling the ports to dispatch fresh sea fish anywhere and everywhere. In the course of the nineteenth century the middle classes abruptly forsook the mundane flavours of carp, tench, pike and eels, and they have never returned to them. And within a couple of generations the economic and social chains which had tended to anchor age-old traditions in their particular regions began to give way to new, more potent forces. Thus, the narrator of Graham Swift's *Waterland* – son of a Fenland lock-keeper and eel-catcher – becomes a teacher in Greenwich. The life of the eelman was associated with slime and fish smells, toil, unsociable hours, uncertain and meagre incomes. As regional diversity was eroded by upward mobility and creeping social homogeneity, so those quaint old ways were lodged in the museum of folk memory, to be sighed over nostalgically as belonging to a past which – as it recedes ever further from view – seems, at sentimental times, somehow quieter and less troubled.

Nowadays, glistening on the supermarket counter under the watch of staff in striped aprons, bogus boaters and regulation disposable gloves, are fish hoovered up by factory ships from every distant ocean of the world; beheaded, betailed, scaled, filleted, spirited across continents to be laid on beds of sparkling ice. To this generation, brainwashed into believing that the only good food is food cleansed of any vestige of its mucky history, the slithery eel comes with an image deficiency so acute as to disqualify it from polite society. The wonder is that there are any English eel fishermen left at all.

FOUR

Genesis

The New Zealand Maoris, for whom the two species of freshwater eel indigenous to the North and South Islands have been dietary staples since they arrived from Polynesia twelve hundred years ago, accounted for the creation of the fish with this story: Tuna (the eel) dwelled in a heavenly stream in the land of Nukutawhakawhaka, where he amused himself by tormenting the two wives of Maui Tikitiki when they came to bathe. Maui commissioned Haeri to catch Tuna, whereupon he chopped the troublesome eel-god in two. One half fell into the sea and became the conger, and the other into the Muriwaihoata River, where it became the freshwater cousin.

Biologists prefer a more gradualist version. Recent DNA

research carried out in Japan suggests that eels evolved between sixty and a hundred million years ago, and that the ancestral species was based in the western Pacific, near present-day Indonesia. Some time in the Eocene or Oligocene epoch, perhaps thirty to fifty million years ago, this primal species split into two groups. One, from which the several Pacific breeds are descended, stayed pretty much where it was. The other dispersed far to the west on the global equatorial current that swept across the Tethys Sea separating the North American and Eurasian continents from Africa, South America and India. According to the Japanese hypothesis, the westerly group must have reached the palaeo-Atlantic before the Tethys Sea closed in the middle to late Oligocene, about twenty-five million years ago. Some time later – perhaps ten million years ago – this group divided between an Atlantic contingent *(Anguilla anguilla* and *Anguilla rostrata)*, and the African and Australasian species *(Anguilla mossambica* and *Anguilla australis)* which dispersed south. As the two halves of America came together, the eel was distributed around the North Atlantic by a developing oceanic gyre, or circular current system. But no such delivery system existed further south, which explains why there are no freshwater eels anywhere in the South Atlantic.

So the eel is an ancient creature and a primitive one. But its primitiveness does not mean that it is simply made, only that it was perfectly made in the earliest times. In fact its sensory equipment is so complex as to defy analysis, even now. Scientists who have spent lifetimes dissecting eels and studying their habits still do not have any clear idea how – for example – they find their way across the vast expanses of the ocean to their breeding grounds. The Irish poet, Seamus Heaney, was stirred by the mystery. In 'The Return', he wrote:

> Who knows if she knows
> her depth and direction;
> She's passed Malin and
> Tory, silent, wakeless,
> A wisp, a wick that is
> Its own taper and light
> Through the weltering dark.

This is a creature whose life cycle might have been designed to confound and amaze. Its partiality for seclusion has made it possible to believe almost anything about it: that it was engendered from the mud or its own slime or from the action of sunlight on dew or from the backside of a particular beetle; that a whistled love song might lure it to the water's edge to couple with a lustful snake; that it was in the habit of slithering into the fields to feed on peas and turnips, and would take refuge in haystacks when the weather turned cold; that drinking wine suffused with fragments of its skin might turn a drunkard into a teetotaller and facilitate the repositioning of the vagina; that the illicit wives and bastard children of priests were saved from disgrace by taking its form.

It is easy to scoff at the absurdities of Aristotle, Pliny, Oppian, old Izaak Walton, Gesner, Albertus Magnus and the rest of the gang of credulous souls. But what if the clock had stopped a century ago with the puzzle of the creature's origins unsolved? Imagine some crackbrain coming up with this proposition: that it is born of an egg in a sac of oil suspended above the prodigious depths of the strangest sea on earth; that, as a sliver of tissue no thicker than the nail on my little finger and half its length, it embarks on a three-thousand-mile journey across the Atlantic Ocean; that having completed that journey it changes its appearance so thoroughly that it was as if a sheep had turned into a goat; that having been a sea fish it turns into a freshwater fish; that it ascends whichever river takes its fancy and makes its home a mile or three hundred miles from the sea, and disappears from sight for the next ten or fifteen or forty years; that one dark and stormy night in autumn it forsakes that home and retraces the route of its infancy – turning back into a sea fish on the way – until it reaches that marine forest that was its birthplace; that there it mates with others of its kind gathered in that one place from all the thousand thousand waters of Europe; and dies. It's not difficult to picture the shaking of scientific heads, the sceptical smirks, to hear the murmurs of disbelief.

In 1862 one of the lesser London publishing houses, G. Shield of Lower Sloane Street, issued at a price of two and sixpence a little book by one David Cairncross, the son of a farmer in Forfarshire and subsequently chief engineer and manager at a factory in Dundee. Dedicated to the president, vice-president and members of the Blairgowrie Angling Club, it is entitled *The Origin of the Silver Eel*. It is one of the two or three most peculiar volumes I have come across in thirty years of collecting and inspecting books about fish and fishing.

The frontispiece consists of two illustrations. The upper is of a small eel, conventional in appearance apart from two prominent ears. The lower, captioned 'The Beetle in the act of Parturition', shows an odd-looking coleopterous insect lying on its back, with its six legs in the air and two attachments resembling curly hairs emerging from its backside. The text begins with a lengthy apologia for the author's lowly origins and lack of formal education – hence his reliance on his 'old trusty copy of *Bailey's Dictionary*' – before delivering its defining statement, the fruit of sixty years' enquiry, which is that 'the progenitor of the silver eel is a small beetle'.

A little later Cairncross tells the story of this discovery: how, at the age of ten, his curiosity was aroused by finding a number of 'hair eels' in an open drain; how, even at this tender age, he was unable to credit the claim made by his friend that these had fallen from the tails of horses while they were drinking and had been brought to life by contact with water; how his suspicions were aroused by the presence of a number of dead beetles at the bottom of the drain; how, twenty-two years later, while working in his garden in Dundee, he observed a beetle making its way to a little pool and delivering two baby eels a quarter of an inch long before expiring; how, nine years after that, a beetle gave birth to a brace of eels in his well, which eventually – after a lengthy disappearance – grew quite normally; how the matter was finally settled when he took a 'hair eel' left in the well by a beetle, placed it in a glass tube and watched it, over a period of six months, develop eyes and fins until 'it was fairly formed and trying to get out of the tube'.

As corroboration, he relates how he met two local farmers who were perplexed by the presence of quantities of silver eels in a ditch on their land. Cairncross investigated, found several of the beetles, and informed the farmers that these insects were the parents of the eels. 'They believed me,' he records, 'and rejoiced in the solution of the mystery.'

The first part of this very short book deals with the generation and habits of eels, ending with a chapter discussing 'Parallelism between the Bee and the Eel-Beetle' and 'Parallelism between the Toad and the Eel-Beetle'. The second of these cases is especially revealing: 'the one alters its form from fish to that of quadruped, to live on land; and the other alters its from that of an insect to that of a fish to live in water.' Cairncross pauses briefly to record an affectionate tribute to his pet toad, Oberon – whose passing at the age of six left his owner 'as sorry as I afterwards was for my favourite dog' – before devoting the second half of a very odd book to a ragbag of disappointingly conventional tips on angling.

Perhaps the oddest thing about it is how its author persuaded anyone to publish it. Did not Mr Shield of Lower Sloane Street have suspicions about an author who maintained that an insect could give birth to a fish? It is evident that the objection must have been raised by someone, for Cairncross attempted to silence anonymous scoffers by referring to the tree-grafter who coaxes an ash to grow from an elm. 'Could not the Great Creating Gardener,' he asked grandly, 'graft a foreign nature onto that of an insect?'

My purpose in dwelling on *The Origin of the Silver Eel* – apart from its curiosity value – is that it illustrates in the most extreme form a tendency initiated when Aristotle first considered the freshwater eel in the fourth century BC – to treat this fish as a freak of nature. The inability of eel watchers over two millennia to work out what this most secretive of creatures was up to legitimised a rich stew of far-fetched theorising. The joke, of course, is that the truth, when at last it was uncovered, was at least as extraordinary as almost any of the theories (though not, perhaps, Mr Cairncross's).

Aristotle studied the mystery of the eel twelve hundred years before the Scottish beetle man, and did very much better. Perhaps he shared his countrymen's passion for eating them; certainly something moved him to treat them with some thoroughness in his *Historia Animalium* and *De Partibus Animalium*. Basing his observations on the River Strymon, in northern Greece, Aristotle noted that the eel fed mainly at night 'on his own species, on grass, on roots, on any chance food found in the mud'; and that in autumn the adults went down to the sea 'at the time of the Pleiades, because at this period the water is troubled and the mud raised up by the contrary winds.'

Aristotle believed the eel to be neither male nor female, which, considering its hermaphroditic tendencies, was not so wide of the mark. He challenged the view that gender might be distinguished by the size of the head: 'When people rest duality of sex in the eel on the assertion that the head of the male is bigger and longer, and the head of the female smaller and more snubbed, they are taking duality of species for duality of sex.' It is remarkable to find the same error – that the females are broad-headed and the males narrow-headed – being endorsed as a scientific fact by the respectable British naturalist, Sir Herbert Maxwell, in 1925!

It is true that Aristotle's version of the eel's genesis was totally wrong. He said they came, not from pairing or an egg, but from 'the entrails of the earth'. This expression was subsequently distorted to justify the charge that Aristotle thought eels were generated 'spontaneously, from mud', which was represented as a most comical example of the ancients getting things wrong. The pre-eminent French expert on eels, Louis Bertin – who was professor of herpetology and ichthyology at the Museum of Natural History in Paris until his death in a car crash in 1956 – defended the great polymath. In his splendidly scholarly yet accessible book, *Eels: A Biological Study*, Bertin translated Aristotle's Greek as 'worms of the earth' rather than 'intestines or entrails', and suggested that he may have been referring to eels coming from worms or larvae contained within mud, rather than the mud itself; or even to elvers.

Whatever Aristotle's shortcomings, they were modest compared with those of Pliny the Elder. Pliny – who perished in the eruption of Vesuvius in AD 79 and thought caterpillars were born of dew drops – said in his *Natural History* that eels reproduced themselves by rubbing their bodies against rocks: 'from the shreds of skins thus detached come new ones.' A century later, the poet Oppian of Cilicia was equally, though more excusably, fanciful:

> Strange the formation of the eely race
> That knows no sex, yet loves the close embrace.
> Their folded lengths they round each other twine
> Twist amorous knots and slimy bodies join;
> Till the close strife brings off a frothy juice,
> The seed that must the wriggling kind produce
> That genial bed impregnated all the heap
> And little eelets soon begin to creep.

Elsewhere in the five books of his *Halieutica*, Oppian

described the strange nuptials of the Roman eel and the snake. The reptile – 'odious and lustful' – makes his way to the water's edge, where – having vomited forth his fatal poison to make him 'gracious and amiable' – he whistles a love song. The Roman eel darts towards the shore; the snake throws himself into the foam. 'Their mutual desire is satisfied. They are together. Panting with pleasure the female draws the snake's head into her mouth.' At the completion of this ecstatic coupling, the snake returns to the place where he deposited his poison and re-absorbs it. But, says Oppian, should anyone by some mischance have recognised the stuff and got rid of it, the snake – overcome by shame – will bang its head against the stones until it dies.

For the next thousand years no one wrote anything poetical, scientific or speculative about the eel's origins, although they were surely hunted, sold, bartered, battered, broiled, grilled, drooled over, esteemed and discussed as they were in Aristotle's day. So, in considering what men thought about where this favoured delicacy came from, it is necessary to leap the centuries. That prodigious medieval savant, Albertus Magnus, Count of Bollstadt, was clearly interested in eels, recording, among various stories, that in the exceptionally bitter winter of 1125 a number of them left the water as it froze to take refuge in a haystack, where the frost eventually killed them. Wisely, perhaps, the erudite Albertus avoided the knotty question of how eels were born, and it was not until the sixteenth century that several lively minds returned to the subject that had foxed Aristotle. The fruits of their speculations were distilled by Izaak Walton in *The Compleat Angler* and used by him as a cloak to shroud his own ignorance.

Walton is maddening in his inconsistencies. In one paragraph of his chapter on eels he refers quite soberly to the sight of elvers running a river near Canterbury, the little eels 'about the thickness of a straw . . . as thick on the water as motes are said to be in the sun', before appearing to approve the notion that eels come either from the dew or 'the corruption of the earth'. This, he asserts bafflingly, 'appears to be made possible by the barnacles and young goslings bred by the sun's heat and the rotten planks of an old ship, and hatched of trees.'

With his readers still trying to digest this nonsense, Walton – just two paragraphs on – declares that 'the eel is bred by generation . . . her brood come from within her . . . I have had too many testimonies of this to doubt the truth of it myself.' He concludes, mysteriously: 'If I thought it needful, I might prove it, but I think it is needless.' Among the other authorities quoted by Walton in his medley of invention, folly, plagiarism and sound sense, are the Swiss sage Conrad Gesner – who thought pike were bred from a special form of vegetation known as Pickerel Weed – and Rondeletius, otherwise Guillaume Rondelet, a physician from Languedoc who wrote a book about sea fish and is said to have died from eating too many figs.

Of all these scholars, only the last seems to have taken the trouble to find things out for himself instead of depending on the fallible testimony of others. It was Rondeletius who first observed that adult eels go down to the sea and never return – a tendency attributed by Walton to their fondness for the taste of salt, which also, in his view, explained why 'powdered [i.e. salt] beef is a most excellent bait to catch an eel'!

* * *

Long after Walton, discussion in England of the eel and its habits continued to be characterised chiefly by ignorance and credulity. In Italy, by contrast, enquiries were pursued more rigorously. No more than eight years after the publication in 1676 of the expanded edition of Walton's marvellously vital but scientifically primitive *Compleat Angler*, a scholar of Tuscany, Francesco Redi, produced a groundbreaking work, *Osservazioni degli Animali Viventi negli Animali Viventi*. It was, as the title (*Observations of Living Animals in Living Animals*) suggests, primarily a treatise on parasites. But Redi – a physician to the Medici, poet and letter-writer, who proved that maggots came from the eggs of flies rather than being spontaneously generated – included this remarkable passage about the freshwater eel:

> I can affirm, following my long observations, that each year, with the first August rains and by night when it is most dark and cloudy, the eels begin to descend from the lakes and rivers in compact groups, towards the sea. Here the female lays her eggs, from which, after a variable time depending on the rigours of the sea, hatch elvers or young eels which then ascend the fresh waters by means of the estuaries. Their journey begins about the end of January or the beginning of February, and finishes generally about the end of April.

This represented a considerable leap forward from guesswork about the possible influence of sunshine on slime or drops of dew. Francesco Redi, by researching the matter thoroughly for himself, worked out the shape of the story.

He also demonstrated the fallaciousness of the popular belief that eels were viviparous – which is to say that they carried their young in a developed state. He proved that the microscopic worms found inside adult eels – which were assumed to be its young – were no more than parasites.

A century after Redi, Carlo Mondini, professor at the University of Bologna, announced that he had located the genitals of the female eel. He likened them to a frilled ribbon, and found they extended the length of the abdominal cavity, beyond the anus. Subsequent investigations by one of the most distinguished of all Italian scientists, the physiologist and natural historian Lazaro Spallanzani, shed more light – and deepened the mystery.

In the late 1780s Spallanzani left his base at the University of Pavia to make a leisurely journey in search of knowledge. He went to Elba and Venice and into the Apennines, studied volcanic activity at Vesuvius, Etna and Stromboli, enquired into the origins of basalt and coral, and researched techniques of swordfishing. And he came to the lagoon of Comacchio, on Italy's northern Adriatic coast, which was then and had been for centuries Europe's greatest eel fishery. He spent several months there and observed the mass migration of the silver eels to the sea. There could, he felt, be but one explanation:

> The constant efforts of the eels to escape from their prison, this persistency in trying to surmount all the obstacles they meet, this obstinacy in letting themselves be caught rather than turn back, this movement of a blind instinct which carries them to a sojourn in the sea as soon as they are fully

> grown, can only result from a need as lively as
> it is imperative. And what is there more press-
> ing, more irresistible than the propagation of the
> species?

This was well deduced. But there was a flaw. It was clear to Spallanzani what the mission of the eels was. And – thanks to Mondini – he knew where the equipment was, at least in the female. But where was the ammunition? Where were the eggs? Spallanzani – described by Pasteur as 'one of the most able physiologists with which science has been honoured, the most ingenious and the most difficult to satisfy' – was flummoxed. He calculated that over the previous forty years, 152 million Comacchio eels had been cut open to be salted, without a single pregnant one being found. He examined and re-examined Mondini's 'frilled organs', poring over globules that his predecessor claimed were ovaries, but all to no avail. He admitted defeat, while urging his successors on: 'This problem, far from discouraging us, must excite our utmost efforts.'

The quest did indeed continue, and within a hundred years of Spallanzani's death several links in the reproductive chain had been identified. Biologists at the University of Trieste had the clever idea of searching for the male sex organs in smaller eels. The discovery of these – ribbons looped rather than frilled, as in the female – was announced in 1874 by the museum's director, Szimon Syrski. But without the presence of either sperm or ova, the identification of the sexual organs was of limited value. How did they work, and when, and where?

A clutch of Europe's important men of science took up

the challenge, and fierce was the competition between the centres of learning. Professor Claus of Vienna University, Professor Siebold of Munich University, and Professor Virchov of Berlin University all commanded their students to hunt down the secrets of the eel. Among them, famously, was Sigmund Freud. In 1876 he was dispatched by Claus from the Institute of Comparative Anatomy in Vienna to a new experimental station in Trieste, with orders to subject Syrski's work on eels to the closest scrutiny. Having faithfully sliced his way through four hundred dead eels, Freud published his 'Observations on the form and fine structure of the looped organs of the eel considered as testes', in which he described how he had found what might have been an immature testicle; or might not. Freud, who had been hoping for a brilliant discovery to make his reputation, felt very much let down by eels, and came to the view that the many hours he had spent disentangling portions of their entrails had been wasted. After the riddle of the eel's gonads, the exploration of the human psyche and the identification of the castration complex must have seemed comparatively straightforward.

At length the frustrations and failures of this slimy-fingered fraternity of competing sleuths were brought to a close by a sensational discovery. In 1897 an Italian biologist, Giovanni Battista Grassi, astounded the community of eel watchers by announcing that he and his assistant at the University of Messina in Sicily, Salvatore Calandruccio, had caught in the turbulent straits separating the island from the Italian mainland a male *A. anguilla* whose gonads were swollen with sperm. As a result of this and another equally extraordinary discovery by the two men the previous year

– of which more shortly – the entire picture of the eel's sex life was transformed.

While Italy led the way, with assorted Poles, Austrians and Germans valiantly labouring to keep up, England floundered in ignorance, the few enquiries that were undertaken being characterised not by common sense and scepticism but by a willingness to believe the eel capable of almost anything. Admittedly there were limits. The seventeenth-century preacher and ecclesiastical historian Thomas Fuller recorded the story that 'when the priests would still retain their wives in spite of what the Pope and Monks would do to the contrary, their wives and children were miraculously turned into eels.' 'I consider it a lie,' concluded Fuller severely.

In his anthology *Fish, Fishing and the Meaning of Life*, Jeremy Paxman included, under the title 'A True Story about a Big Eel', an extract from a late-eighteenth-century compendium, Taylor's *The Wonders of Nature and Art*. It tells of how a company of soldiers quartered near Yeovil in Somerset were called out to investigate reports that a large creature was helping itself to hay from a farmer's barn; which, when shot with a musket, proved to be an eel so enormous that eight horses were required to drag it to a house, where, upon being hacked up and roasted, it discharged an 'inundation of grease so prodigious that it was running out of the keyhole and door.'

We will allow that as a leg-pull. But what are we to make of the highly respected Edward Jesse, friend of William IV and deputy director of royal parks and palaces, in whose *Gleanings from Natural History* appeared a sober account of eels quitting a pond near Bristol, climbing a tree on its banks, slithering along branches overhanging a conveniently placed stream, and dropping into the moving water? 'A friend of mine who was a casual witness of this process,' wrote Jesse, 'assured me that the tree appeared to be alive, and the rapid and unsteady motion of the boughs did not appear to impede the progress of the eels.'

This example of scientific observation was published in the 1830s. Not long before, Dr George Shaw, the joint founder of the Linnaean Society, the Keeper of the Natural History section of the British Museum and the author of a number of more or less well-informed papers about the wonders of nature, offered his opinion that the eel 'may be considered in some degree connecting the fish and the serpent world together.' He mocked the 'errors of the ancients and even some of the moderns' as being 'too absurd to be mentioned in the present enlightened period of science', before stating that eels carry 'eggs and ready formed young at the same time'.

Even that most energetic and celebrated of Victorian naturalists, Frank Buckland, was confounded by the eel. Buckland was an extraordinary mixture of eccentric, genius and mountebank, who lived in the midst of a menagerie of beer-swilling monkeys, meerkats, rats and hares, regarded firing at cockroaches with benzine from a syringe as a sport on a par with shooting rabbits, and whose father claimed to have eaten part of Louis XIV's heart. In his *Familiar History of British Fishes*, published in 1873, Buckland stated as fact that eels deposited their eggs in inshore waters. He added: 'The roe of the eel is exceedingly minute, and is often taken to be simply fat. I once, and once only, found some young eels hatching out. This was on the rocks at the entrance to Guernsey Harbour.' Buckland was supported by his contemporary, Jonathan Couch (a well-known amateur naturalist who served as vicar of Polperro in Cornwall for sixty years and was the grandfather of the poet and storyteller, Sir Arthur Quiller-Couch). Couch, in his *History of British Fishes*, maintained that 'their spawn is deposited in harbours chiefly . . . where it is scattered loosely in the sand.'

The failing of these English ichthyologists was that they were amateurs, self-trained enthusiasts, unfamiliar and impatient with the rigours of scientific enquiry, all too eager to leap to false conclusions on the basis of second-hand testimony. It is typical of the half-baked condition of knowledge that Thomas Boosey should have credited William Yarrell – the founder of this dynasty of laymen – with having 'laid to rest the *vexata question*' by tracing the eels 'down to the brackish water whither they go, generally but not universally, to spawn.'

To be fair to Yarrell, he did explode the nonsense about eels carrying their young fully formed, by examining the female sex organs, of which he gave a sound description: 'Two long narrow sacs extending one each side of the air-bladder . . . puckered or gathered in along the line of junction . . . the free or floating edge thrown into creases or plaits like a frill.' Yarrell was working from drawings executed only a few years after Mondini's discovery of the female sex organs by the great surgeon and natural historian, John Hunter.

It was another of the very few trained scientists among

this gallery of self-appointed experts who came closest to guessing the truth. Sir Humphry Davy, who died in 1829, is credited with the discovery of sodium, magnesium and strontium, and the invention of the miner's safety lamp. He was a keen angler and naturalist, and pondered the life cycle of the eel, considering the riddle of its birth 'one of the most abstruse and one of the most curious in natural history, and – though it occupied the attention of Aristotle and has since been taken up by some of the most distinguished naturalists – is still unsolved, though I trust it will not remain so much longer.' Davy – writing some years before Yarrell or Jesse – offered a startling speculation: that eels 'deposit their ova in parts of the sea near deep holes'.

It is in keeping with England's record in eel research that in 1925 – three years after the full and accurate account of the creature's life cycle had been published, in English, in scientific journals throughout the civilised world – Sir Herbert Maxwell should have publicly credited the triumph to Giovanni Battista Grassi, the wrong man. But although Grassi did not solve the mystery, he was a pivotal figure. In Italy his lasting claim to fame – reflected in the Institute in Rome which bears his name – was the part he played in the campaign to eradicate the scourge of malaria from the European mainland (both he and the American, Robert Ross, claimed to have identified the deadly partnership between the disease and the mosquito – it is typical of Grassi's career that it should have been Ross who got the Nobel prize). But much earlier, in the late 1880s, he had secured a position at the new Institute of Oceanography in

Messina, which was fortuitously placed for the investigation of *A. anguilla*.

The Straits of Messina divide Calabria and Sicily and, at the time of the equinoctial tides, great upsurging currents sweep into the bottleneck from the marine abysses to the north and south, regularly depositing a harvest of deep-sea fishes on the beaches. Among these had been noted as early as the 1850s a flat, transparent creature with a body shaped like a willow leaf and a tiny head with round black eyes and a pair of jaws armed with a few jagged teeth. In a German classification of the Apodes, it was listed as a separate species of sea fish, and given its own Latin name – *Leptocephalus brevirostris*, which is literally translated as 'thin-head short-nosed'. No one suspected it of being anything other than one more, not at all remarkable, marine creature.

But Grassi and Calandruccio, who found thousands of these black-eyed slivers of tissue, became interested. They began to suspect that they must represent the larval stage of some other fish. They knew that in such cases there was invariably a close correlation between the number of muscle segments, or myomeres, along the back of the larva and the number of vertebrae in the finished article. They established that the average complement in the thin-head was 115, and they set about making a match. They found it in *A. anguilla* and nowhere else. The European freshwater eel has an average vertebrae count of between 113 and 117, with 115 much the most common. This was enough for a working hypothesis: that these fragile larvae thrown up from the marine depths were the children of the humble eel found in every lake and river in Italy.

In 1896 the Reports of the Royal Academy of Rome contained sensational news from Messina. Not only had Grassi and Calandruccio confirmed that hypothesis by observing and recording the metamorphosis of thin-head into eel in their aquarium, they had also found in the sea one of the creatures in the process of metamorphosis – a semi-larva, half thin-head, half eel. And hardly had these revelations been digested when the two Italians were back, with their capture in the sea of a sexually mature male eel.

It was understandable – although unfortunate for him – that Grassi should have believed that the chain was now complete, and that he was entitled to claim the laurels. He had been able, he said, 'to dispel, in the most important points, the great mystery which has hitherto surrounded the reproduction and development of the Common Eel.' He summed up his findings thus:

> The abysses of the sea are the spawning places of the Common Eel. Its eggs float in the sea water . . . Eggs which are, according to every probability, those of the Common Eel are found in the sea from January to February. I am inclined to believe that the elvers ascending our rivers are already one year old.

Behind the passionless language – the idiom conventionally employed by one scientist modestly sharing with his colleagues across the world his advancement of the great cause binding them all – Grassi was bursting with nationalistic pride. He, a scientist of the new nation, had cracked the riddle that had defeated great brains for more than two millennia. The story of the eel, one of the most remarkable life cycles in the natural world, belonged to Italy.

Alas for Giovanni Battista Grassi and his pride! In his

haste to claim the prize, he had overlooked the one enormous, fatal flaw in his account. Why, if the eel spawned in the abyssal depths of the Mediterranean, were all the thin-heads found in the Straits of Messina fully grown and either on the point of metamorphosing into elvers, or in some cases already doing so? Why, out of the host of specimens delivered to Grassi and Calandruccio, had there been none in the earliest stages of their infancy? With hindsight the implication of this deficiency seems blindingly obvious. But at the time no one thought of challenging the thesis riding so proudly on the back of the spectacular Italian triumphs. Grassi was hailed as the man who had settled that tricky matter of the eel. Secure in that reputation – as he thought – he went on to grapple with the malarial mosquito. By the time he returned to the eel, his triumph – so effortfully gained and thoroughly enjoyed – was wrecked beyond hope of repair.

FIVE

Searching

It did not take long for the first cracks to appear in Giovanni Battista Grassi's version of the birth of eels. In the early summer of 1904 a Danish research vessel, the *Thor*, was carrying out investigations in the North Atlantic on behalf of the International Council for the Exploration of the Sea, known as ICES. The purpose was to find out more about the breeding areas of important eating fish, such as cod, whiting, plaice and herring, and a fine-mesh net was used to recover the eggs and larvae of the various species. In May an *A. anguilla* thin-head seven and a half centimetres long was captured in a trawl near the surface of waters to the west of the Faroes – the best part of two thousand miles from the creature's supposed birthplace in the Mediterranean. Among those on board the *Thor* was a young Danish scientist called Johannes Schmidt, whose brief was to pinpoint the spawning grounds of cod. He studied the larva, and something stirred in his agile mind.

Insofar that a story about a fish can have a human hero, Johannes Schmidt is that hero. He was the man who located the spawning grounds of the European freshwater eel in an area of the far south-west of the North Atlantic ocean known as the Sargasso Sea. It was a discovery that should be counted one of the triumphs of modern scientific enquiry and Schmidt achieved it through an exceptional combination of sound science, elastic and imaginative thought, leadership, luck, and a determination truly eel-like in its obstinacy. Of equal importance in the context of this narrative was the manner in which he set about ensuring that he, and he alone, received the credit; thereby establishing an unbreakable association between his name and the solution of the mystery.

Johannes Schmidt was born in 1877. His father, Ernst, was employed as manager of an estate not far from Copenhagen called Jaegerpris, famous for its rare plants. The family lived there and, after Ernst's death, when his son was seven, retained a house that remained a refuge for Johannes all his life. His paternal great-grandfather was Christian Schmidt, a botanist who served as inspector of the Royal Gardens. His mother, Camilla, was of Greek origin, and it was from her that he inherited his strikingly Mediterranean looks. Her brother, Johannes Kjeldahl, was a celebrated professor of chemistry at the University of Copenhagen, where Johannes enrolled in 1894 to study medicine and natural science. Schmidt's official biography speaks of him standing out 'among the more light-hearted Danish students, with his penetrating eyes, dark hair, and intense concentration. He spoke little and took no part in class banter, but worked extremely hard.'

Botany was Schmidt's first enthusiasm and at the age of twenty-two he joined an expedition to study the flora of what was then the Kingdom of Siam. In those early years Schmidt extended his botanical work to embrace the sea. He studied and published papers on planktonic algae, the influence of external agents on the leaves of maritime plants, and the *cyanophycae* of Iceland, and secured a position as a biologist with ICES. Thus it was that he was on board the *Thor* when that significant thin-head was landed.

Schmidt's definitive account of his work on the European eel was completed in 1921 and read to the Royal Society of London in 1922 and published the following year. Reading it, one would not guess that he had been no more than a junior member of the research team on the *Thor*; or that the project had been directed – not by him – but by a distinguished Danish oceanographer of the previous generation, Dr C. C. Johannes Petersen. There is no reference to Petersen at all, beyond mention of the fact that the thin-head was taken in a 'Petersen's young-fish trawl'; although in a much earlier, interim report on his eel investigations, Schmidt was more generous, crediting Petersen as director of the first *Thor* voyage, and praising him for having arranged for the same vessel to be equipped with 'the most modern apparatus' for a second research trip.

Schmidt never disclosed whether, before that fortuitous

encounter in the grey waters of the North Atlantic, he had ever had any interest in the habits of *A. anguilla*. He was, however, extremely quick to recognise the significance of the capture, and to make the appropriate representations – even if his explanation of how Denmark came to seize the baton from Italy, and how he came to challenge the work of Giovanni Battista Grassi, is imprecise in the extreme: 'Owing to various circumstances,' he wrote, 'it came about that Denmark, a country where eel fishing is a specially important industry, was accorded the task of prosecuting the investigations further, and it fell to my lot to take charge of the work.'

The *Thor*'s second cruise, in 1905, took her south from Icelandic waters. This time there was a single purpose, to find more thin-heads. The little nets devised by Petersen to capture small marine organisms were dipped along the Norwegian coast and in the North Sea, without result. *Thor* sailed around northern Scotland, and in May small numbers of larvae were found to the west of the Hebrides, over deep water but in the surface levels. Numbers increased further south – seventy were taken in one haul in the mouth of the Channel. In Schmidt's mind, the most significant factor was that almost all the thin-heads were fully grown, at about seven and a half centimetres, but had not begun metamorphosing. There were no specimens in the North Sea, the Baltic, along the Norwegian coast, or along the Channel. 'I was able to conclude,' Schmidt wrote in italics in his 1922 Royal Society paper, 'that all the eels of Western Europe come from the Atlantic.'

This was, to put it mildly, a sweeping assertion to make on the basis of such limited research, and is worth noting that at the time Schmidt was much more circumspect. But he certainly sensed that Grassi's thesis was beginning to tremble, and he pressed on. 1906 saw the *Thor* further south, in the Bay of Biscay. Again, fully grown thin-heads were encountered in abundance, over depths as great as fifteen thousand feet. None of those caught in spring and early summer had begun metamorphosing, whereas by autumn most had. Moreover, those of the first category – presumed to be younger – were found further to the west, over the deeper water. A pattern was emerging. Schmidt now had sound reasons for believing that the thin-heads were coming from the west.

It was time to take the argument closer to Grassi's home waters. Through the winter of 1908/9, and through the summer of 1910, the *Thor* puffed her way around the waters to the west of Gibraltar, and through the Mediterranean itself. In 1912 Schmidt's partial hypothesis was published in the journal *Nature* under the title 'The Reproduction and Spawning-places of the Freshwater Eel'. Of his conclusions, the most penetrating was that 'the spawning places must lie in the Atlantic beyond the Continental Slope, and that they must be in the North Atlantic.' The most contentious was that 'the eel does not spawn in the Mediterranean at all.'

This was a frontal assault on Grassi. Schmidt said that the Italian's 1896 paper 'was certainly responsible for the general belief that the spawning grounds were to be found there.' In fact a close reading of Grassi's work reveals that he never claimed the Mediterranean as the exclusive breeding ground, even if he did little to contradict that impression. Grassi wrote: 'It is not true that *leptocephali* are limited to Messina . . . at Messina there are special currents which tear up the deep sea bottom ... which everywhere else is inaccessible.' Schmidt presented his evidence: that the thin-heads were smaller and more numerous at the western end of the Mediterranean, near Gibraltar; that they were bigger and fewer the further east the nets were cast; that there were no larvae east of Italy. What he neglected to mention in his eagerness to strike at Grassi was the size of his sample. This was not publicly disclosed until fifty years after Schmidt's death, in a painstaking review of his original work undertaken by the Danish biologist Jan Boetius and a colleague from Cambridge University, Edward Harding. They found that a derisory total of forty-five larvae had been caught in the whole of what Schmidt referred to grandly as 'the third stage of the solution of the eel problem'. Boetius and Harding described the sample – with extreme restraint – as 'a very small material on which to base the conclusion that tiny larvae simply cannot be found in the Mediterranean.'

In his final version of 1922, Schmidt – surely aware that his Mediterranean data was sparse to the point of worthlessness – skated over that part of the research. In reality, it had never been necessary to inflate it as he had, for as early as 1910 he had been furnished with evidence which – although he would doubtless have preferred to find it himself – served to confirm every strand of his hypothesis, and to inflict a mortal blow on that of his Italian rival.

A Norwegian vessel, the *Michael Sars*, had been commissioned by the Scottish oceanographer, Sir John Murray, to undertake a comprehensive survey of the North Atlantic. The distinguished band of marine biologists on board was led by Dr Johan Hjort, a highly respected authority on deep-sea life. In a report on the cruise published in *Nature*, in

1910, Hjort disclosed that among the hundreds of *leptocephali* of various species taken in the pelagic tow-nets and trawls had been forty-four offspring of the European freshwater eel. Twenty-three of them had been taken in the northern sector, all of which were more than six centimetres long, and about half – those found over Scotland's Continental Slope – were in the process of metamorphosis. This merely confirmed Schmidt's own findings. It was the location of the other captures – and above all the size of the specimens – that must have had him hopping with excitement. The remaining twenty-one thin-heads were all caught to the south and west of the Azores, two thousand miles from European shores. They ranged in size from six centimetres down to four centimetres, much the smallest yet found. And the further west they were taken, the smaller they were.

The inference was clear, and Johan Hjort had no hesitation in making it. 'As a provisional working hypothesis,' he wrote, 'I should be inclined to regard the Continental Slope as the area where the transformation of the larvae takes place, and the southern central part of the North Atlantic as the probable spawning area of the eel.' But Hjort had a notable caution: 'So long as the eels have not been discovered the spawning area must also be considered an unknown.'

Schmidt knew how vital the finds were to his cause. They sent him scurrying to the recesses of the Zoological Museum in Copenhagen, where, gathering dust on some neglected shelf, was a collection of assorted *leptocephali* deposited half a century before by a Captain Andrea (described by Schmidt as a 'zealous collector of pelagic fauna'). He found three specimens of freshwater eel larvae in Captain Andrea's old jars, of which two were *A. anguilla*. Of these the smaller was forty-one millimetres, the same as the smallest taken by the *Michael Sars*. The difficulty for Schmidt was that these thin-heads of identical size had been caught fifteen hundred miles apart – one to the south-west of the Azores, Captain Andrea's near Madeira. Even so, the shape of the story was now clear. The further south and west, the smaller the thin-heads were. If he could find the place where they were as small as they could possibly be, he would be on top of the breeding grounds.

Schmidt was acutely aware that he needed more evidence, and that the only way to get it was to secure a suitable vessel and fund it himself. But for the moment no ship was available, and he was forced to seek help elsewhere. He approached the owners of Denmark's shipping lines and persuaded them to have their skippers sailing North Atlantic routes pause every now and then to dip one of his pelagic trawls. This haphazard programme began in 1911, but the catches were meagre. Nevertheless Schmidt took comfort from the capture of the smallest thin-head recorded thus far – thirty-four millimetres – well to the south and west of any previous find.

His 1912 article for *Nature* was presented as a review of the current state of play. But there was a more personal sub-text. A fuller version of the paper was originally submitted to the Royal Society of London. But – in what the eminent zoologist Charles Tate Regan was to describe in his obituary of Schmidt as 'an extraordinary rebuff' – the Society rejected it on the grounds that Grassi's work on the subject 'was considered sufficient'. According to Tate Regan, Schmidt was 'greatly astonished' by this decision. It is reasonable to assume that he was enraged and wounded as well, and that this explains the determination evident in his article in *Nature* to discredit Grassi and sink the Italian's version of the eel story beyond hope of recovery.

In this Schmidt was largely successful. But Grassi did not take his overthrow lightly or with good grace. He accused the Dane – with ample justification, as was to become clear seventy years too late – of not trying hard enough to find younger thin-heads in the Mediterranean. For Grassi, just as with Schmidt, nationalistic pride was at stake. 'I have called attention,' he protested, 'to the inadequacy of a thesis according to which our eel would not in reality be ours, but would have originated in the Atlantic Ocean.' In 1913 Grassi published his monumental monograph on the *Metamorphosis of the Muraenoids*, in which he persisted in his view that *A. anguilla* spawned in the depths of the Mediterranean. But Grassi – who for years had been complacently receiving the plaudits of the scientific community – was on the ropes. In its review of his work, *Nature* concluded that 'Schmidt has the advantage.'

Wholly ungenerous to his rival, Schmidt did at least acknowledge Hjort's 'very important discovery' (interestingly, Hjort paid tribute to the 'excellent Danish investigations planned by Dr Johannes Petersen and carried out by Dr Johannes Schmidt'). Schmidt elegantly conceded the defective state of current knowledge:

> We have not yet attained to the full solution of the exceedingly difficult eel problems, but the steady progress of the last twenty years is full of promise for the future. We cannot say exactly where the eel spawns, though the Sargasso Sea is perhaps the

principal spawning region, but continuing collections and investigations of the currents *will assuredly lead to the discovery of the eggs and earliest larvae* . . . [my italics] Altogether the whole story of the eel and its spawning has come to read almost like a romance, wherein reality has far exceeded the dreams of phantasy.

Schmidt now endeavoured to press home his advantage over Grassi. In his last pre-war paper 'On the Classification of Freshwater Eels', Schmidt referred to the Italian with unmistakable scorn, mocking his rival's suggestion that the reason no small thin-heads had been caught in the Mediterranean was that 'at greater depths the conditions of life may perhaps be more favourable to the larvae, rendering them better able to avoid capture.' Schmidt gives the impression of someone restraining himself, with difficulty, from shouting: 'I repeat . . . that the reason these growing stages were easily discovered in the Atlantic but not, despite my continued efforts, in the Mediterranean . . . is purely and simply this: that they do not exist in that sea because the eel does not spawn in the Mediterranean.'

Johannes Schmidt's dynamism, clarity of thinking and single-mindedness had made the eel story Danish property, and it was generally assumed that its final solution lay in Denmark's – i.e. Schmidt's – hands. In 1903 he had married Ingeborg Kuhle, daughter of the chief director of the Carlsberg Brewery, and seven years later he was appointed director of the prestigious physiological institute funded by the brewery. He exploited his position and growing international reputation to good effect. In 1913 a

Copenhagen shipping company made available to Schmidt a fast schooner, the *Margrethe*, which – unlike the *Thor* – was capable of crossing the Atlantic.

She sailed in August, taking a course south-west from the Faroes to the Azores, then on to the Sargasso Sea. In all 714 European thin-heads were caught, and twenty-four American. As she reached the Sargasso, the numbers increased and the size decreased, confirming Schmidt's hypothesis. But the great majority were between thirty-five and forty-five millimetres long, hardly any smaller than the specimens he already knew about. Over the central Sargasso, he did catch a modest number of between twenty and twenty-five millimetres long – and one of seventeen. But they did not differ significantly from specimens taken earlier in the summer, a little to the north and west, by one of the Danish ships whose help Schmidt had enlisted.

Schmidt must have been disappointed. But, characteristically, he turned the results to invaluable effect. He remained convinced that he had been in the right place, and decided that it must have been at the wrong time, and that spawning must have taken place several months before.

Disaster followed. In December the *Margrethe* ran aground in the Virgin Islands and was wrecked. The precious collections of *leptocephali* were saved, but Schmidt was forced to abandon his plan to resume operations in the target area the following spring. However, he did continue to receive a trickle of specimens from the transatlantic steamships, two of which – taken in May 1914 over the central and deepest part of the Sargasso – were a mere nine millimetres long. Schmidt was more certain than ever that this location, 26°N 54°W, was the place.

Later that year war broke out. Several of the steamships which had assisted Schmidt were sunk by German submarines, and the collecting of thin-heads came to a standstill. It was to be five years before the immense depths of the still, blue Sargasso would be disturbed by the little nets again.

During those years Schmidt prepared for the triumph he knew was within his grasp. He was well aware of how close he must have been when war broke out; and the one consolation of that enforced suspension was that no one else could go sailing across the Atlantic either. But he was mindful, too, that it would not be easy to convince the sceptics, to educate the uneducated. He surely chewed over that humiliation inflicted on him by the so-called men of science of the Royal Society. And if he required a further reminder of how reluctant some people were to abandon the error of their ways, it was supplied by his ageing but indomitable Italian adversary, Giovanni Battista Grassi.

Grassi had evidently spent the war years smarting from his humiliation at the hands of the Dane, and longing for redress. He continued his efforts to find infant thin-heads in the Mediterranean, without any success. Undeterred, in 1919 Grassi published his final contribution to the quest which intermittently had exercised him for so long, 'Nuove Ricerche sulla Storia Naturale dell' Anguilla'. Although Grassi claimed admiration for Schmidt's 'really efficacious and fruitful work', his text is drenched in bitterness. He lashes out at ICES for preferring the 'certainty' furnished by Schmidt to his own 'mere conjecture': 'I can but drop my head and smile, just as I drop my head and smile when he [Schmidt] lards his memories with claims of priority which are as base as they are unfounded.' Again, Grassi affirmed his belief that somewhere in his own, damnably unforthcoming sea, adult eels of Italian parentage were doing what had to be done to stock Italian rivers with Italian infants. But by now no one outside Italy had any interest in Grassi or his discredited views – not even to the extent of seeing his study translated into English. Schmidt had no need to respond publicly. But we may be sure that he noted the refusal of his old antagonist to lie down and observe a decent silence.

Schmidt knew he had to supply facts, certainties. There was no room here for assumptions and deductions and pleasing propositions. And herein lay his difficulty. Doubtless he dreamed of uncovering the final proof, of finding adult eels in the act of mating or, at least, of recovering the eggs before they hatched. But Schmidt knew the location, knew what tremendous and improbable good fortune would be required for his little nets, dropped into that colossal mass of water, to be working at the right depth, the right spot, the right moment. He could not depend on such a stroke of luck, could not afford even to hope for it. He had evidence pointing one way and one way only, and he would obtain more evidence. But that evidence could only be circumstantial, and its very nature would raise as many questions as it answered. Johannes Schmidt knew that. He knew his eels. But he also knew that, to achieve his purpose, he had to supply those answers and bury those questions.

The strategy Schmidt devised was bold, simple, and – according to the traditional standards of scientific enquiry – not wholly scrupulous. He did not seek to test his hypothesis, but rather to present evidence that supported it, while ignoring or obscuring that which did not and to disguise that distortion. Publicly, he defined his aim thus: 'I perceived that if the problem were to be solved in anything like a satisfactory manner, it would be necessary to ascertain, not only where the youngest larvae were to be found, *but also where they were not*' (my italics). In saying this, he was subscribing to the conventional procedure for testing a hypothesis. But in fact Schmidt made no such effort. He did not try to ascertain where the tiniest thin-heads were absent; and he then pretended that he had.

In the early spring of 1920 the 550-ton schooner *Dana* – provided courtesy of the East Asiatic Company of Copenhagen – set sail from Gibraltar for the western Atlantic. Her captain's orders were simple: to follow Johannes Schmidt's orders. There were no other competing interests, and everyone knew what had to be done.

The vessel made straight for the Sargasso Sea, and there followed a course around and between the locations where the smallest thin-heads had been recovered by the *Margrethe* and the steamship *Samui*. Good numbers of larvae were captured straight away. On 8 June, 29°N 60°W, Schmidt and his crew netted more than thirteen hundred thin-heads, many of them between seven and ten millimetres long, and the great majority at depths between fifty and a hundred metres. On 27 June, a little way to the south-west, they took almost eight hundred specimens with one haul of the nets. 'The contents,' recorded Schmidt, 'presented a remarkable sight. This one haul gave us a greater number than had hitherto been obtained in the whole course of any expedition . . . it affords us a clear idea of the enormous quantities in which the young larvae are present.'

Schmidt suspected that he had again missed the spawning time, since the thin-heads, while smaller than any previous recovered, were not at their viable minimum. The next year, 1921, *Dana* set out earlier, reaching the target area in February. The first catches – in February and March – were sparse. But on 12 April, at 26°44′N, 51° 25′w, they began finding thin-heads in numbers, some as small as five millimetres in length. Keeping a course centred on 27°N 59°w, they came upon larvae everywhere, the vast majority of them less than twenty millimetres long. The tiniest of all, at five millimetres, were retrieved in mid April at locations that had been fished without result three weeks earlier. Given what little is known about the very earliest stages of larval life, it seems likely that Schmidt missed the hatching by a day or two at most, and possibly only hours.

One can only guess at the keenness of his disappointment. But there was comfort too. The second voyage of *Dana* had provided plentiful confirmation of the conclusions which Schmidt had reached many years before, and which he was setting down in their definitive form even before the vessel reached home. Of equal importance was that nothing had been found that could be used to cast doubt on those conclusions.

In late July Schmidt gave orders for *Dana* to set sail for home. Vexed though he must have been by the realisation that he had come so close to laying hands on absolute proof, he still had what he wanted. Within an area the shape of an egg held horizontally between twenty-five and thirty degrees north, and fifty-five and sixty degrees west, he had found an enormous abundance of thin-heads so young that they must have been on top of their birthplace. The circumference of the egg had been defined – not by the presence or otherwise of the new-born thin-heads – but by the course the ship had followed. Nevertheless Schmidt had decided. It was time to tell the world that this was the spawning ground of the freshwater eel.

On the night of 2 February 1922 Johannes Schmidt's paper, 'The Breeding Places of the Eel', was read to that same Royal Society of London which, ten years earlier, had spurned its predecessor. Early the next year *Nature* published a concise summary of his findings, and a few months after that the Royal Society paper reached print. In 1924 Schmidt delivered a slightly amended version in the form of a lecture to the Smithsonian Institute in New York, which published it the following year. In essence, though, what was to be hailed as 'Schmidt's classical theory' achieved its authoritative expression in the Royal Society paper.

Extending over almost thirty large pages, and accompanied by several plates, it is an impressive piece of work by any standards – and by those of the genre, it is an indisputable masterpiece, a tour de force. The presentation of the argument is marvellously clear, the progression of logic forcefully maintained. It does not talk down to its audience, but nor does it assume they are experts on the subject – merely that they possess a high degree of intelligent appreciation. The use of English is sure-footed, the style easy in its rhythms. It is almost incredible that it should have been written by a foreigner (almost all Schmidt's 126 original papers were composed in English – he had realised long before that a mastery of what had become the international language of science would be crucial to the acceptance of his work).

Schmidt's purpose was to silence doubters before they could open their mouths. To achieve it, he had decided to present what he must have known perfectly well was no more than a sound hypothesis as fact, as a narrative of events. In this, his outstanding opportunity to win over his fellow scientists, he must answer not just the one great question – the location of the spawning ground of the freshwater eel – but all other major questions as well. This he did in his conclusion in which he refined, distilled, and synthesised the whole argument into an affirmation intended not to persuade or provoke, but to convince: to send that distinguished audience away in no doubt that they had heard the final word.

His approach is evidenced from the very first word of the title. By using the definite article, Schmidt gives notice that this is to be much more than a mere proposition, an explanation of available data. He offers himself not as a scientist who has constructed a plausible elucidation of limited information, but as an explorer returned from charting a previously unknown land. He does allow his subject to retain one significant secret, admitting that after leaving the European coastline 'the last trace of the eel is lost . . . how long the journey lasts, we cannot say.' But uncertainty is promptly swept away: 'We now know the destination sought: a certain area situated in the western Atlantic, north-east and north of the West Indies. Here lie the breeding grounds of the eel.'

From that statement, Schmidt proceeds to more facts:

> Spawning commences in early spring, lasting to well on in summer. The tiny larvae, seven to 15 millimetres in length, float in water layers about 200–300 metres from the surface, in a temperature of about 20 Centigrade. The larvae grow rapidly . . . and in their first summer average about 25 millimetres in length. They now move up into the uppermost water layers, the great majority being found between 50 and 25 metres, or even at the surface itself. During their first summer they are found in the Western Atlantic (50 degrees longitude West). By their second summer they have attained an average length of 50–55 millimetres and the bulk are now in the central Atlantic. By the third summer they have arrived off the coastal banks of Europe, and are now fully grown, averaging about 75 millimetres, but still retaining the compressed leaf-like form. In the course of the autumn and winter they undergo the retrograde metamorphosis which brings them to the elver stage, in which they move in to the shores and make their way up rivers and watercourses everywhere.

Swiftly and elegantly, Schmidt dealt with the awkward problem posed by the American eel, *A. rostrata*. So close is the resemblance between these cousins that to be sure which you are dealing with, it is necessary to administer a mortal blow, remove the backbone, and count the vertebrae. Between 102 and 110 means it came from the western side of the Atlantic. 111 to 119 means it came from the eastern. Such an examination is a delicate business when it involves dealing with adult eels in the laboratory. Identification from larvae no more than ten millimetres long is, to quote Schmidt's restrained words, 'a very lengthy and laborious business, especially on board a small vessel at sea.' Nevertheless specimens of *A. rostrata* had cropped up in sufficient numbers in the Sargasso Sea to make it clear that they, too, must breed there or thereabouts. The puzzle was to work out how the two species disentangled themselves. How did these hosts of minute and feeble thin-heads milling around in their billions in the Sargasso manage to sort themselves out so that those descended from eels with an average of 107 vertebrae in their backs populated the seaboard to the west, and those born of eels with 115 vertebrae went east? Schmidt's solution was beautiful in its simplicity – that the American thin-heads were concentrated slightly to the west, were born earlier and grew faster, and were thus able to complete their shorter and less arduous migration within a year.

To provide visual reinforcement for his story, Schmidt devised a masterstroke. It is a chart of the North Atlantic, squared by lines of latitude and longitude. On it are superimposed four egg-shaped ellipses. The smallest, defined in a thicker line than the others and about the size of a thrush's egg, is the breeding area itself. It has the numeral 10 beside it, to indicate the maximum size of the thin-heads found within it. The next oval, a little larger, is the limit for fifteen-millimetre larvae, the next for those of twenty-five millimetres, and the largest – extending to 43°N 18°W – for those of forty-five millimetres. Intersecting the four eggs are three open arcs in dotted lines, organised on the same principle, indicating – in an area closer to the American coast – the incidence and size of the American thin-heads encountered in the various searches of the Sargasso. According to

Schmidt's chart, the southernmost limit to the occurrence of thin-heads is the twenty degrees latitude line. Beneath it Schmidt printed the words: NO LARVAE.

It is difficult to do justice in words to the beguiling simplicity of the diagram. It makes the thrust of the argument clear to the dullest intelligence, and has the subliminal effect of containing it, as it were, within the ellipses, and thus settling it beyond challenge. For his article in *Nature* Schmidt refined the chart, leaving out the curves dealing with the American thin-heads, highlighting the 'breeding area' with its own shading, adding a fifth outer line reaching to Europe to indicate limits for unmetamorphosed larvae, and supplying a thick strip along those European, near-Eastern and African coasts with eel populations. Given the degree to which it illuminates the 'classical theory', it is small wonder that versions of the figure have been reproduced in virtually every subsequent treatment of the eel story.

One wonders what the august members of the Royal Society made of what they had heard and seen; what the murmurings were in the cloakroom as they buttoned their overcoats, adjusted their mufflers, put on their hats and set off along The Strand that February night. They must surely have been intrigued by the solution to such an enduring mystery and impressed by the manner of its presentation. I hope they were stirred, too – even moved – by the truly extraordinary nature of this creature's life and wanderings.

As for the great detective who had brought this chain to the light and made sense of it, the taste of success must have been very sweet. Yet Schmidt remained aware that the crowning triumph had eluded him. He still dreamed of finding the eels as they mated, of scooping up from those cobalt waters that first stage of life, the bridge between the sexual act and the tiniest thin-heads – the fertilised eggs. He had come so close in April 1921, taking thin-heads as small as pine needles, possibly only hours old. He had to try again. In the spring of 1922 a new *Dana* – a converted trawler equipped as a research ship and this time funded by the Danish government – was criss-crossing the designated breeding grounds. Just as before, large numbers of very small thin-heads were retrieved, one just four millimetres long. But, just as before, no eggs, no mature eels, no proof. And, just as before, no attempt made to search below 20°N or to the east.

Schmidt must have realised that it was time to move on, to extend his range. His name had become synonymous with the 'discovery' of the eel's spawning grounds. His work had brought prestige to his country, and cemented his position as one of its outstanding men of science. There was little more that he could do with *A. anguilla*; little more that that most slippery customer could do for him.

In 1925 he published the second part of his 'On the Distribution of the Freshwater Eels throughout the World', covering the Indo-Pacific species (part one, dealing with the Atlantic eel, had appeared as long ago as 1909). The following year he took *Dana II* to Australia and New Zealand to investigate their eels. Two years later, on 14 June 1928, *Dana II*, again under Schmidt's direction, sailed out of Copenhagen at the start of a long-planned and much-trumpeted circumnavigation of the world. Eel matters played a comparatively small part in this oceanographical epic; nevertheless Schmidt was able to extend his studies of tropical species and add significantly to his vast collection. In the course of these years he wrote detailed papers on the Australasian eels – deducing persuasively and probably correctly that they bred in a deep warm-water basin, not dissimilar to the Sargasso Sea, off Vanuatu. He also located the spawning grounds of the tropical eels of Indonesia off the east coast of Borneo.

Dana II returned to Copenhagen on 30 June 1930, where Schmidt received a welcome appropriate to a national hero. The immense task of sorting through and classifying the collections brought home was still in its early stages when, towards the end of February 1933, Johannes Schmidt died suddenly and unexpectedly. He was fifty-six. Tate Regan's lengthy and laudatory obituary for the journal of ICES said he had suffered from heart trouble for years and was unable to withstand an attack of influenza. The British zoologist said the news had still come as a shock: 'Only last November he was in London, and after a Royal Society Club dinner, delighted those present with an account of the migrations of the cod from Greenland to Iceland and back again.' Tate Regan described Schmidt as 'dark, good-looking, youthful and intellectual in appearance . . . a charming companion . . . unlike some men of science always ready to tell what he was doing and what he hoped to achieve, but in a quiet and modest way.' A tribute in *Nature* referred to him as 'one of oceanography's outstanding leaders . . . a man of quite exceptional charm, with a genius for friendship.' To his disciple, Louis Bertin, he was ever 'the illustrious Johannes Schmidt'. Bertin dedicated his own fascinating and learned book about eels to the memory of the Dane, and honoured him by never deviating from his word.

Schmidt never revisited his classical theory. But in the last year of his life, reviewing *Dana II*'s circumnavigation and his previous researches, he did allude in extreme terms to the contention upon which the whole structure was founded. 'We have been able to settle conclusively,' Schmidt wrote, 'that they [the newly hatched larvae] are found in an area to the north-east of St Thomas [in the Virgin islands] and south-east of the Bermudas, *and nowhere else*' (my italics). As Jan Boetius and Edward Harding have pointed out, it is instructive to compare that doctrinaire statement with what Schmidt had conceded twenty years before: 'There seems but little reason to suppose that all specimens are spawned within a single, very limited district inside the places where the small larvae have been taken; on the contrary, the vast extent of this area seems to indicate the reverse.'

What had happened in those twenty years to obliterate the possibility that eels might also spawn outside that thrush's egg in the Sargasso Sea? To be sure, Schmidt had assembled a vast weight of evidence that spawning took place within the egg. But to that old caveat – 'it would be necessary to ascertain, not only where the youngest larvae were to be found, but also where they were not' – he had not been true. No 'comprehensive survey' had been carried out, by him or anyone else. To achieve certainty, Schmidt had deliberately abandoned the way of science. He had become a lawyer, seeking and obtaining a verdict. Such was his authority, it never occurred to anyone at the time to challenge either his conclusions or his methods. It was to be almost thirty years before an assault was mounted.

SIX

Challenge

A newspaper photograph of *Dana II*'s homecoming shows a dense crowd packed onto the quay in Copenhagen, dignitaries and local worthies to the front. Down the gang-plank and out into the June sunshine step Johannes Schmidt and his team, wearing bright cream uniforms designed by the expedition leader himself. There are handshakes and short speeches. It is a proud occasion for this little seafaring nation.

Somewhere in that crowd was a boy of twelve, already fired by a passionate curiosity about the living world around him. Currents as insistent as those of the ocean were to pull the boy and the eel together, and inspire in him a longing to explore and understand its ways. That boy, Jan Boetius, is now a tall, bowed old man well into his eighties, long retired from his career as Europe's foremost eel investigator; although his wife Inge, who was his partner in a quarter of a century of study and experiment, is still actively involved in research work and continues to attend the conferences and seminars where the experts wrestle with the remaining mysteries.

I had come to Denmark with a picture of Johannes Schmidt in my mind. It was two-dimensional, of a man of science moved by pure passion for science. I had read Schmidt's own work, and marvelled at its lucidity and energy, and I had studied the respectful notices of his colleagues and the tributes paid to him as a matter of course in the subsequent tellings of the eel story. I was hugely impressed by the epic nature of his quest, which seemed to me to show the human hunger for knowledge in its most admirable form. There seemed, too, to be a fine scrupulousness about his approach; that – having in all significant respects resolved the matter before the outbreak of the Great War – he should have refrained from claiming the crown then, waiting instead until he had collected the evidence to satisfy the high requirements of his discipline.

At the top of a staircase at the back of the Zoological Museum in Copenhagen hangs a portrait of Schmidt that is the realisation of the mental picture I had. It shows him seated, legs crossed, in a dark suit, with a cream cape draped carefully over his shoulders. At his side, illuminated by lamplight, is a table on which are arranged jars of specimens. His thick, dark hair is brushed back in neat waves from a broad brow. The demeanour is that of a leader, and man of action as well as of thought. There is no expression on his face. The painter quite fails to convey any hint of something I had also neglected: that even with men of science, the man generally comes before the science.

I found Jan and Inge Boetius's neat white-bricked bungalow in a quiet road in a quiet little town about half an hour's drive north of Copenhagen. To reach their sitting room I passed along a corridor lined to the ceiling with books and papers and journals about fish. Jan Boetius gave me a beer, and helped himself to a glass of red wine. It was half past eleven in the morning. He settled down in a chair in front of a glass-topped table on which was an array of pipes, a block of tobacco, matches and an ashtray. 'I drink and smoke all day,' he said unapologetically.

His wife joined us. She was much shorter than him, slender in black trousers and a black top, white hair cut short, spectacles, a brisk, businesslike air about her. She wanted to talk about the current state of eel research and about the work she and Jan had done together. He wanted to talk about the more distant past. At length he said: 'Now we will talk about Schmidt.' He lit his pipe and leaned back in his chair. And he did, and I listened.

But first it is necessary to go back. Schmidt's great discovery and the manner in which he presented it imposed a kind of paralysis on further work and discussion on the breeding habits of the eel. A cluster of biologists continued to be fascinated by the creature. The Italian, D'Ancona, pondered matters of gender and the workings of the digestive tract. The Frenchman, Maurice Fontaine, applied himself thoroughly to the gonads and the problems of inducing fertility.

The Dutchman, Deelder, studied the migrations to and from the great inland eel fishery, once the Zuider Zee, now enclosed and renamed the Ijsselmeer. The German, Tesch, tracked their movements in the Baltic. Winifred Frost, based at the Freshwater Biological Association on Windermere in the Lake District, analysed their diet and growth rate. The exotically named Alfonso Gandolfi Hornyold, second Duke of Gandolfi and a professor at the University of Freiburg in Switzerland, pursued them in Spain and Portugal, in the great lake of Tunis, in obscure ponds in England and the lagoons of the Camargue, producing a total of 220 papers for a host of scientific journals dealing with everything from the pigmentation of elvers to the size of the adult eel's eyeballs. In Denmark, Schmidt's pupil Willi Ege toiled for years on classifying specimens brought back by *Dana II* and delivered from every eel land in the world; finally, in 1939, publishing his epic Revision of the Genus *Anguilla*.

But no one dreamed of questioning Schmidt's work. The part of the eel's destiny that was realised in the Atlantic was untouchable. The off-limits approach was enshrined in Louis Bertin's book, the first English edition of which was published in 1956, just after its author's death. Bertin did a superb job in drawing together much of the research work of his generation, and distilling it into an erudite but accessible text. His view of his colleagues was clear-sighted, occasionally astringent (of Gandolfi Hornyold's studies, he noted: 'They constitute an inexhaustible source of information which their author, unfortunately, did not always know how to interpret').

Bertin placed Schmidt on the loftiest of pedestals. His tone, whenever Schmidt's name cropped up, was reverential.

The 'discovery of the breeding grounds' was a 'crowning achievement', the catches of thin-heads made in 1920 'brilliant confirmation' of the 'classical theory'. Bertin, who as a young man had been chosen by Schmidt to edit one of the sequence of *Dana* reports, relied exclusively on his mentor's findings for his own stylish account of the eel's oceanic travels. Schmidt's word was gospel.

Three years after Bertin's death, a carefully aimed mortar exploded without warning within this encampment of academic complacency. It had been assembled and primed by a brilliant British zoologist, Denys Tucker, who at that time – but not for much longer – was Principal Scientific Officer in the zoology department of the Natural History Museum. Tucker was born in Exeter, the son of a church brass-engraver and a shoemaker's daughter. His talents were recognised at the age of eighteen with the award by Julian Huxley of a medal from the Zoological Society. He served with the RAF during the Second World War as a flight lieutenant, and joined the Natural History Museum in 1949.

Tucker's gift for science was accompanied by a taste for controversy and a considerable flair for causing annoyance, particularly to senior colleagues at the museum. Through the 1950s he devoted himself to the study of various deep-sea fishes – notably the coelacanth – and to his revision of the family Trichiuridae. It was almost by chance that he became interested in the unseen pathways taken by the freshwater eel.

Tucker, now in his eighties, says he never had vivid curiosity about the eel as an animal. His interest, always essentially intellectual, was triggered by reading some research carried out by Schmidt's pupil, Age Vedel Tåning, into the reproduction of trout, which revealed that sudden variations in the temperature of the water in which trout eggs hatched affected the number of vertebrae in the young fish. Tucker did not trouble himself with any research of his own into the eel (he told me he had never touched one). His paper, 'A New Solution to the Eel Problem', which was published in *Nature* in February 1959, was an exercise of the mind, based entirely on published work, principally Schmidt's own. As Tucker explained it to me: 'The jigsaw had been put together by Schmidt, and it had a few pieces missing. I wanted to see if I could take it apart and reassemble it to make a different picture, still with a few pieces missing.'

There were three propositions supporting the structure of Tucker's argument, all of them, in the context of conventional wisdom, wholly heretical. The first was that European eels did not return to their birthplace in the Sargasso Sea, but perished early in what Tucker termed a 'fruitless suicide migration'. The second was that the European eel, *A. anguilla*, and the American eel, *A. rostrata*, were not separate species, as Schmidt maintained, but eco-phenotypes, or separate breeding populations of the same species. The third, the most startling and daring, was that the population of eels in both Europe and America consisted of the offspring of *A. rostrata*.

It should be made clear at once – more than forty years after Denys Tucker detonated his explosive device – that no one believes he was right. Tucker himself admitted that 'my actual theory . . . has been shot to smithereens.' Nevertheless his argument was beautifully and elegantly presented, energised by a young man's vigorous scepticism towards long-accepted convention, and touched here and there with a haughty impatience calculated to enrage. Jan Boetius said admiringly to me: 'Tucker was a very, very clever man. It was a very, very clever piece of work, and it could have been right.'

Tucker's intricately plotted case can be summed up quite briefly. He argued that the European eel was physically incapable of covering the three thousand miles to the Sargasso Sea, and that it was not sensorily equipped to negotiate its way through the complex and contradictory ocean currents to such a small and distant target. It therefore followed that it perished on the way. Thus, by elimination, the hosts of thin-heads delivered to the European coastline must have been produced by the American eel, which had a much shorter and less hazardous journey to make, and was, Tucker asserted, in much better shape to make it.

There was one immediate and overwhelming objection to Tucker's hypothesis. It had long ago been 'established' by Schmidt that eels found in America had a slightly but consistently smaller number of vertebrae than those of Europe. The average – according to the results Schmidt chose to publish – was 115 for the European and 108 for the American. On this basis Schmidt stated as fact that the species were distinct (he also used the same data to assert that all European eels came from one breeding population).

Tucker, in arguing against separate species, was confronted with the same obstacle that Schmidt had had to contend with, viewed from the other side. How was it that some thin-heads, born of one species in one area at the same time, were ready to migrate into American waters within a matter of months, while the rest were programmed for an enormous ocean odyssey lasting for up to three years? And why did the American eels have fewer vertebrae? His solution was quite as ingenious as Schmidt's, even if it was to prove rather less sustainable.

Tucker accepted that there was a single spawning area for all eels, the Sargasso Sea. But Tucker argued that it was divided latitudinally into two sectors. In the more northerly, the temperature rose gradually from eight degrees Celsius at a depth of eight hundred metres to twenty degrees at the surface; whereas in the more southerly there was an abrupt jump of four degrees between two hundred and one hundred metres, reaching twenty-five degrees at the surface. Tucker's contention – put as simply as possible, without citing his supporting evidence – drew on Tåning's experiments with trout ova. It was that newly hatched larvae rising through the water layers of the southern sector would, upon encountering that sudden rise in temperature, stop developing the muscle segments known as myomeres which become vertebrae. Those in the north, protected from such a shock, would continue to develop a fuller complement.

This scenario enabled Tucker to accept Schmidt's argument that the American thin-heads grew faster. Indeed, he offered confirmation, reasoning that the higher temperatures in his southern sector would stimulate a higher rate of metabolism, assisted by the greater availability of zooplanktonic nourishment. There was also, he stated, a handy current to take the larvae away to the west.

Denys Tucker's missile breached the walls around the Schmidtian orthodoxy without warning. Schmidt's disciples knew nothing about Tucker, except that he – unlike them –

had never dirtied his hands with eel-slime. Yet here was this upstart, without ever having done a day's fieldwork, daring to challenge their high priest. 'Biologists in Denmark were mad,' recalled Jan Boetius. 'They considered Tucker's thesis an attack on Schmidt and on Denmark itself.' What caused as much annoyance as the challenge itself was its confident, undeferential tone, and, in particular, the paragraph in which Tucker said:

> As a syllogism, the new hypothesis may at least claim parity with Schmidt's, since both theories provide an explanation for the origin of the European eel larvae and both make a single, unsubstantiated assumption. As a biological proposition, however, the probability of the assumed effect of temperature with its numerous precedents may be considered more reasonable than that of a 3,500 mile directive migration for which there is no parallel among fishes.

This was too much for the keepers of the Schmidtian canon. First out of the blocks was the veteran Italian eel watcher, Umberto D'Ancona, of Padua University. He observed – quite mildly – that 'there is no evidence to support the idea that a temperature difference of a few degrees would be enough to induce two sets of genetically homogeneous larvae to acquire such different numbers of myomeres.' Tucker responded by intimating that D'Ancona had been unwilling or unable to grasp his argument.

Next came Dr Jones of Liverpool University, who flatly contradicted Tucker's assertion that European eels were too debilitated to reach the Sargasso. On the contrary, said Dr Jones, they were 'vigorous and energetic', quite up to the task of travelling the fifty-odd miles a day necessary for them to participate in the nuptial orgy. Tucker's return of fire was venomous:

> I am not subdued by Dr Jones' experience with thousands of eels . . . The great curse of the voluminous work upon eels has been that too much of it has been mechanical and repetitive, replete with experiments unintelligently planned and mountains of data inadequately pondered, parochial alike in the range of its geographical experience and its isolation from relevant literature from alien countries and related disciplines.

Floored by this uppercut, Dr Jones temporarily retired from the fray. Into the ring hopped Holland's acknowledged champion, Cees Deelder, armed with fourteen years' experience as fisheries biologist on the Ijsselmeer. He also disputed Tucker's assessment of the physical condition of migrating eels. Tucker had backed his cause with the observation that silver eels had almost never been caught at sea by trawlers or research ships. Deelder effectively countered this by pointing out that the agility and 'cleverness' of silver eels rendered them difficult to entrap in trawls in enclosed waters, let alone the open sea. He also argued that, were large numbers of adult eels to perish annually on the Continental Shelf – as Tucker maintained – corpses would have been retrieved by deep trawlers. This had never happened.

But Tucker would not retreat, although his tone in rebutting the Dutchman's challenges was rather more placatory than that employed against the hapless Dr Jones. Clearly aware of the furore he had unleashed, Tucker said: 'I would like to correct an impression in certain quarters that my new interpretation of Schmidt's work is in any way derogatory to his memory. Dr Anton Bruun has generously exonerated me of any such charge.'

For reasons to be outlined shortly, Tucker's response to Deelder, published in *Nature* in February 1960, was his final contribution to the debate. But the battle was by no means over. The Anton Bruun referred to by Tucker had been a pupil of Schmidt, and had subsequently emerged as his successor as Denmark's pre-eminent oceanographer. He inspired devotion in a generation of Danish biologists – including Jan Boetius, who worked very closely with him – and was described by Tucker in a letter to me as 'a charming man'. Tucker added: 'I thought that Bruun might have resented me besmirching the fairest jewel in the scientific crown of Denmark.' Evidently he did not. But he was the obvious person to conduct the counter-offensive against the Englishman's heresies. This he did in a lengthy, densely argued paper eventually published in the journal *Advances in Marine Biology* in 1963. Not wishing to go any further into the abstrusities of the conflicting cases, I shall restrict myself to observing that Bruun offered a most convincing defence of Schmidt's work, countering Tucker's most questionable conclusions extremely effectively. But, in the absence of any new evidence, he was not able to manoeuvre himself into a position to deliver the knockout blow.

Bruun died more than a year before his counterblast appeared in print. Denys Tucker never responded. By then he had been overtaken by a whirlwind of events that was to leave his reputation in tatters and deprive him of his livelihood for good. In the light of his personal catastrophe, the cessation of his interest in eels is understandable.

In the summer of 1960 Tucker was summarily dismissed

from his post at the Natural History Museum for what was cited as 'long-continued vexatious, insubordinate and generally offensive conduct' towards the museum's director and other senior staff. He was also – in an unusually vindictive sanction, whatever the background to the affair – excluded for ever from the museum's collections and library. Tucker's case was taken up by his union, and generated a good deal of publicity – particularly because of the suggestion that he might have been victimised because of his declared belief in the existence of a Loch Ness monster, and his insistence on spending his holidays looking for it (Tucker himself is at pains to point out that no evidence of any such victimisation ever emerged).

The case reached Parliament. Tucker's MP, Sir Cyril Black, instigated a debate in which he said there had been a 'denial of justice'. Sir Edward Boyle, Financial Secretary to the Treasury, upheld the decision of the museum's trustees, maintaining that Tucker had had 'repeated warnings' about his conduct. Tucker fought on, to the High Court and finally – seven years after his sacking – to the Court of Appeal, where Lord Denning ruled that employees of the museum were servants of the trustees and could be dismissed at the pleasure of those trustees without reason or recourse to the principles of natural justice. It was the end of the fight for Tucker, and the end of his professional career. He was thirty-nine when he was fired, and he never obtained another scientific post. The opinion of his immediate superior at the Natural History Museum, Ethelwy Trewavas, that 'Dr Tucker is to be classed with a few of our most brilliant colleagues' counted for little against the verdict of the trustees.

Thirty-five years on, I was curious enough about the scandal to track Tucker's address down and write to him. I received in reply a letter of great length, packed with information and suggestions about my research, spiced with humorous asides concerning his erstwhile colleagues and other forgotten academics, suffused with a sense of injury but oddly free of bitterness. Eventually I telephoned him, and found him reluctant to meet me (realising that his story was slightly off the point, I did not press him). He told me that, having become accustomed during the war to decisions being taken and carried out, he had found the practices of what he termed 'the effete bureaucracy' at the museum irksome. He laughed as he recalled being summoned to meet the chairman of the trustees, the Arch-bishop of Canterbury, Geoffrey Fisher – 'a very odd bod, flew into a rage, then all smiles, pawing my knee and urging me to turn to God.'

I asked him about eels. 'I was never that interested in them. It was once suggested to me that I should join an expedition to the Sargasso Sea to help net the larvae. But that is a murderous task – heavy, repetitive manual labour. Either you have to have an intelligence so dull that you don't mind it, or be very highly motivated about obtaining a result. I was neither.'

Tucker's paper for *Nature*, as originally submitted, had ended with this thrust: 'There is no doubt that the greatest single contribution to our knowledge of the eel was made by Johannes Schmidt. Whether the greatest single contribution to the mythology of the eel was also made by Johannes Schmidt, or by Denys Tucker, must be left to posterity to decide.' This provocation was deleted at the insistence of the department head, F. C. Fraser ('timorous soul that he was,' commented Tucker).

It may have been of some comfort to Denys Tucker that his brief, dramatic invasion of the tranquil world of the eel watchers caused a salutary stirring of the waters. Although he was almost certainly wrong in his main hypothesis and several of its crucial assumptions, he had succeeded in exposing fault-lines in Schmidt's classical theory, and stimulating others – with, it must be said, a greater appetite for the necessary hard graft – into examining them. It was as if Tucker's instincts had told him there was something amiss with Schmidt's work. What was actually needed was not a new thesis, but a long, hard look at the old one.

During the 1960s occasional potshots were taken at the classical theory. A Canadian biologist, Vadim Vladykov, challenged Schmidt's assertion that both species of Atlantic eel bred in roughly the same area, arguing that – for rivers in the Caribbean to be stocked – the preferred spawning ground of *A. rostrata* must be well to the south and west. A little later a scientist with the British Fisheries Laboratory, Roy Harden-Jones, disputed Schmidt's differentiation of the species as defined by vertebrae counts. He surmised that Schmidt must have considered the possibility that the variations were determined environmentally rather than genetically, and he found it 'astonishing' that Schmidt had not reached the same conclusion as Denys Tucker.

He was getting warm. Had he – or indeed Tucker – known what was to be revealed much later about Schmidt's analysis of vertebrae counts, their challenges would have been much more serious and outspoken. The evaluation was carried out by Edward Harding of Cambridge University, and the results were published in 1985 in a special edition of the journal of the Danish Institute of Fisheries and Marine Research, *Dana*, which was devoted entirely to the freshwater eel. Harding compared the data published by Schmidt with data available to him, but not published; and, further, with vertebrae counts made by Jan Boetius of thin-heads collected by Schmidt but never, apparently, examined by him, and of elvers caught by Boetius in 1972. To the amateur, Harding's is an intimidatingly complex piece of work. But his conclusions were straightforward. He found Schmidt's claim of 'complete homogeneity' for all European populations – which was critical to the theory of a unique spawning place – overstated. Schmidt had deployed the data that most clearly supported him, neglecting that which did not. Harding found there was 'significant inhomogeneity' in the unpublished data, and speculated that 'multiple spawning grounds' might be an explanation.

In the context of scientific literature, and the chronic tendency of the academic world to qualify, understate, and obfuscate, this was powerful stuff. It is impossible to tell whether Schmidt knowingly ignored – and in effect suppressed – evidence of inhomogeneity because he did not like it; or unknowingly neglected it because he was not aware of it. Harding scrupulously refrained from drawing any inference. But his analysis did, at the very least, raise the possibility that one of Denmark's most illustrious sons had carefully selected and arranged the material most supportive of a critical aspect of the 'discovery' on which his reputation rested. And elsewhere in the same issue of the *Dana* journal

– named in honour of the ships Schmidt commanded – was another, truly monumental piece of detective work which posed even more intriguing questions about Schmidt and his methods.

The task of reviewing the whole of Schmidt's work on the Atlantic eel was undertaken by Jan Boetius – that boy who had watched Schmidt come home from his last voyage fifty years before, who had been the pupil and colleague of Schmidt's pupil and colleague Anton Bruun and who himself had succeeded Bruun as the acknowledged leader of Danish eel research. It was a daunting assignment, which meant analysing every aspect of the mission which had occupied Schmidt for twenty years, assessing every decision and conclusion, evaluating the evidence on which they were based, and comparing the evidence actually presented with that available. In effect, Boetius had taken it upon himself to determine whether his country's foremost marine biologist had a case to answer. Well aware of the nature of the labour, he asked Harding to help.

The results were clearly not intended for the general reader:

> The southernmost positive station (846) is the 4th or 5th (tie) from the south, the northernmost (866) is the 27th. Hence the latitude range is R^{lat} equals 23 or 24. The easternmost (842) is at position 7 and the westernmost (855) at position 27, giving a longtitude range of R^{long} equals 21. Therefore R^{lat} is 2.5 S.D.s less than expectation (P equals ca.0.03) and R^{long} is 2.5 S.D.s less than expectation (P equals ca.0.006). These results are significant.

The evidence is sifted with the care of a forensic

scientist searching a body for samples of DNA. But the two investigators are scrupulous in their rejection of the role of prosecuting counsel. There is no criticism of Schmidt, no attempt to read what may have been going on in his mind. It is almost as if they did not wish to grapple with any implications, and were relieved to take refuge behind the conventions of the scientific journal.

Boetius and Harding's starting point was that seemingly so scrupulous declaration in the 1922 Royal Society paper concerning the need to establish where the thin-heads were and were not to be found. As we have already seen, there was no 'comprehensive survey'. By minutely checking the movements of the various vessels under Schmidt's direction, Boetius and Harding established beyond all doubt that Schmidt deliberately dodged anything that might have compromised his hypothesis. The bias in his approach was most vividly illustrated by the legend 'NO LARVAE' printed in heavy ink below the twenty degrees latitude line on his celebrated chart. Boetius and Harding revealed that Schmidt's evidence for this was based on a handful of unproductive hauls of the nets, most of them by one commercial steamship whose methods were wholly haphazard, and all of them in November – at least seven months after the spawning season. They commented, with extreme dryness: 'Possibly, then, larvae are absent from this area in November.'

Fortunately it is not necessary for me to attempt a distillation of this remarkable enquiry. The authors did it themselves, with a series of conclusions which together amount to an indictment all the more powerful for the reticence with which it was offered. They found that:

1. The assertion that eels do not spawn in the Mediterranean was founded on very sparse data.

2. The homogeneity of the European eel population was dubious, and Schmidt's claim of uniformity was not justified by the data.

3. Schmidt's hypothetical separation between the European and the American eel lacked foundation and his argument for it was unsound.

4. The fact that larvae of forty-five millimetres were found throughout the Sargasso area at all times of the year meant that they could not fit into Schmidt's proposed growth regime, and thus could not support his claim of a very localised spawning confined to a few months of the year.

5. The intermingling of the species almost at the heart of Schmidt's main 'spawning area' did raise the possibility that larvae from there did not reach the coasts at all.

6. The closed contours in Schmidt's chart were 'to some extent an artefact of his distribution of effort', and there was no evidence of an east–west limit.

Fifteen years after the publication of this tremendous piece of analytic detective work, I found Jan Boetius apparently anxious to put living tissue around the skeleton he and Edward Harding had assembled. Although he had not known Schmidt personally, he had been friends with and worked closely with a cluster of outstanding biologists who themselves had grown up in Schmidt's shadow, having been selected by him for some subordinate assignment or other. Boetius himself was of that tradition, but sufficiently distanced from its dominant figure to feel comparatively uninhibited by it. He had also, clearly, pondered the nature of the legacy. He talked of those pupils of Schmidt: Bruun, Ege, Poul Jesperson, Tåning. He thought it significant that, though they had readily recalled their work with Schmidt, none had ever discussed his personality, or spoken of him with any personal warmth.

Behind rising clouds of pipe smoke Boetius offered his own assessment:

> He was, I think, a very, very clever scientist, but pathologically ambitious. To begin with he wanted to prove that the Italians were wrong. Then he real-ised that this would make him famous. He wanted to be like Scott or Amundsen or Peary. The Sargasso was his North and South Pole. You know, he was a chauvinist. This was for Denmark, and for him. He was always the leader, and he never wanted to give too much credit to the people who helped him, his students. He wanted to take the glory for himself. And of course no one could challenge him. He was too famous, too powerful.

I asked if he admired Schmidt:

> I do not admire him as a man. As a scientist, yes. And even as a scientist – I mean, Schmidt says the eel breeds in the Sargasso Sea and nowhere else. How could he say that? Even now it has never been proved. You see, he wanted to find the adult eels there, or at least the eggs. But how could he identify the eggs of *Anguilla anguilla* when he did not know what they looked like? No one knew, because no one had ever found them.

Like Schmidt, Boetius hoped to find the spawning eels and end the mystery. He had been on no less than four expeditions to the Sargasso Sea and, like everyone else, had found no eels, no eggs, only thin-heads. He had also, with his wife Inge, devoted more than twenty years to attempting to get eels to reproduce in captivity. Their work, which involved injecting hormones to induce sexual maturation, achieved some remarkable results – the most dramatic being movingly illustrated by a photograph taken in one of their tanks of the embrace of a female hugely distended with ripe ova and a wide-eyed male at the moment of ejaculating sperm. But, although they succeeded in producing fertilised eggs, they could not coax them into hatching out (Japanese scientists, working with *A. japonica*, have secured larvae, without ever being able to keep them alive for more than a few days).

Jan Boetius was entirely philosophical about his failures. 'Yes, we always hoped to find the adults in the Sargasso, and we always hoped to produce the larvae. And we did not, so we leave something for our children to find out.' With the satisfaction of an old man whose labours are behind him, and whose hunger for discovery has quietly faded away, Boetius quoted for my benefit a Danish aphorism: 'What we know is wonderful. What we understand is wonderful. But most wonderful of all is what we do not understand.'

The next day, in the basement of the Zoological Museum in Copenhagen, I saw hosts of the thin-heads. Thrust away onto dusty shelves were the bottles and jars, the fruits of all those voyages – of the *Thor*, the *Margrethe*, *Dana*, *Dana II*

– a thousand castings of the little nets into the grey, heaving waters of the North Atlantic and the restless Bay of Biscay, the blue Mediterranean, the bluer, pellucid Sargasso among the great clumps of floating weed. Ten thousand thin-heads floated in their tombs of formalin, some almost a hundred years old, their eyes black dots, their backbones black threads, their bodies ribbed like the sea sand. Those from European waters, as long as a small hand and as wide as two fingers, looked insubstantial enough, those from the Sargasso impossibly so. The notion of these slivers embarking on such a journey was unimaginable.

As I looked at them, I realised that I had lost sight of the point of the story. I had been hacking away for so long through the thicket of research papers, pausing every now and then to witness the replay of an old joust between men of science and to listen to the dull clash of thesis against thesis, that I had forgotten the wonder of it all. Now, as I peered at those unearthly splinters of extinguished life shifting weightlessly in the yellowing liquid, I was swept by it again: the thought of men crossing oceans to catch these scraps, the scraps crossing oceans to make new life.

Later I walked the canals in the chilly October sunshine, watching the streams of cyclists, thinking about Schmidt and what he had achieved. So, maybe he had, in small but significant ways, arranged and shaped the evidence to support his case, distorted it, misrepresented it, slanted it, call it what you will. He must have known that his classical theory, with its symmetries and certainties, was too neat. The natural world was not like that, the eel was not like that. Yet, without him, would the story have become a story? To give it dramatic coherence took someone with a vision and imagination rare in the field of scientific enquiry. Although Schmidt's personality remains an enigma, and some of his methods were questionable, he was surely a great man and a great scientist, blessed with an imagination, energy, soundness of instinct and will to succeed amounting to genius. It helps that he was right.

SEVEN

Leaving

S chmidt had filled in the greatest and most enduring gap, telling how, in his words: 'We came to see great parts of the life-history of the eel emerge from the darkness that surrounded it.' At the end of the account he published in *Nature* in 1923, he wrote: 'No other instance is known among fishes of a species requiring a quarter of the circumference of the globe to complete its life-history, and larval migrations of such extent and duration as those of the eel are altogether unique in the animal kingdom.' No one would dispute his contention that the spawning of the eel in the Sargasso Sea, and the journey of the infants back across the ocean, represent the most extraordinary episodes in this extraordinary creature's existence. But at the same time they form but one part of the overall drama.

We humans generally mate at home and have our babies in the local hospital. So it is natural for us to view with awe and astonishment the migrating instinct implanted in some animals. Our own migrations are undertaken for economic and sociological reasons, rather than biological. We like to think of them as rational, decided upon through the exercise of our free will.

The imperatives that send a creature over a vast distance in order to have sex, thereby exposing the puny and vulnerable fruits of these unions to batteries of perils and assailants are beyond our ken. Why does the leatherback turtle feel obliged to flap its way across thousands of miles of ocean to meet another turtle with which to mate? And why does the female, by laying her eggs so far from the shore, impose upon her pathetically ill-equipped babies that desperate scramble across the burning sand to reach sanctuary? Why must the lonely albatross be condemned to skim the wave-tops in an endless succession of pointless expeditions, with no more than the occasional break to make albatross eggs? Why must geese head south in the autumn, and swallows north in the spring, and the Atlantic salmon imperil its survival by insisting on giving birth in the river of its own birth and spending the rest of its time fifteen hundred miles away out at sea?

Our wonder at these immense journeys is tempered with an element of exasperation. We ask ourselves if there couldn't be a more sensible, less wasteful way. Could they not get together, those foolish turtles, and find somewhere more convenient to have sex? After all, we have learned to treat hotel rooms, beaches, fields, the back of the car, the wall behind the pub and an array of other locations as acceptable substitutes for home.

As autumn approaches, a biological command is transmitted through the domain of the eel. Through the shallow waters of the Baltic, and up the rivers that feed it, in the lakes of Scandinavia and Germany, in the loughs and lochs and meres and fens of Britain and Ireland, up the Loire and the Garonne and the rivers of Spain and Portugal, in the lagoons of the Camargue and the Italian littoral and along the coast of north Africa, in harbours and estuaries everywhere, in all the innumerable and disparate greater and lesser waters populated by the eel, the most compelling instinct of all is at work. For some, the quiet life of hunting, eating and digesting which they have pursued this past ten or fifteen years is coming to an end. They are preparing for a journey, to fulfil their destiny. Their backs and flanks darken from greenish to near black, while their bellies turn from yellow to silver. They become firmer to the touch as fat is stored in their body muscle. Their nostrils dilate and their eyes expand. They cease to eat, and their digestive tracts degenerate. The salt content in the blood diminishes. The sex organs, which run like ribbons through the bodies of males and females, swell.

The order to move is generally sensed at night, and the external circumstances that stimulate have been known for thousands of years and exploited to mankind's dietary advantage. The night is dark and stormy, and barometric pressure is low. The moon is in its last quarter, small and growing smaller. The river is high, swollen by rain, and the current is strong. The wind blows from the lake into the mouth of the river leading to the sea, the stronger the better. Although there will be a trickle of migrating eels at any time, in any conditions, between August and the end of the year, it is this concert of effects which triggers the sudden and overwhelming collective impulse to depart, the mass exodus.

The scale of this rush can be staggering. On the lagoon of Comacchio, in north-eastern Italy – which has seen continuous large-scale eel-harvesting for at least eight hundred years – the fishermen used to light bonfires beside the traps to alarm the mass of fish forcing their way in and restrain their flight. The records of the Comacchio fishery relate that on the night of 4 October 1697, the fishermen took 322,520 kilograms of eel – around three hundred tons, perhaps three quarters of a million fish, in one night's work. An eighteenth-century Cumberland cleric, the Reverend W. Richardson, witnessed the exodus at a place called Eel-stank on the River Eamont a little way down from Ullswater in the English Lake District:

> Here is an immense quantity of the silver eel. In five or six hours eight or ten horse loads have been caught, but such large quantities only on the darkest and stormiest nights . . . It is worthy of remark that they scarcely stir if the moon peeps out, or when there is lightning; the fishermen even think the light of a candle prevents their movement.

In general, these mighty harvests belong in the distant

past. But one of the fishermen I talked to on the eel traps fixed at the top of the River Bann in Northern Ireland recalled a long and taxing night in the early 1980s during which he and seven others, pulling in the nets in rotation without cease from dusk until dawn, landed six thousand stones of eel, the best part of forty tons.

While darkness, high water flowing strongly and a following wind are obviously conducive to travel, the role of the moon is something of a puzzle, as the reluctance of eels to run in the waxing phases obtains even when the planet is wholly obscured and other conditions are favourable. Some scientists believe sensitivity to lunar activity is a mechanism required and therefore bestowed from infancy; others, that the eels can detect micro-seismic motions associated with the phases of the moon.

Once they have made that surge into the river that leads to the sea, the eels become comparatively passive, surrendering themselves to the flow, conserving their strength for the mission ahead. But in order to reach their escape route, they are capable of amazing exertions. Their ability to travel considerable distances overland to reach running water presents an eerie sight to those fortunate enough to have witnessed it. The eighteenth-century surgeon and naturalist Sir Charles Hastings, who founded the British Medical Association, included this account in his *Illustrations of Natural History in Worcestershire*:

> A relative of the late Mr Perrott was out in his park with his keeper near a large piece of water on a beautiful evening, when the keeper drew his attention to a fine eel quietly ascending the bank of the pool and with an undulating motion making its

way through the long grass. On further observation he perceived a considerable number of eels quietly proceeding to a range of stews, nearly the distance of a quarter of a mile from whence they started. The stews were supplied by a rapid brook, and in all probability the instinct of the fish led them in that direction as a means of finding their way to . . . their ultimate destination, the sea.

A more prosaic description is included in Hugh Falkus and Fred Buller's classic reference book, *Freshwater Fishing*:

Between 11pm and midnight, while walking from one part of the river to another [the Petterill, near Greystoke in Cumbria] I saw a moving, shimmering mass in the moonlight. I saw it was a stream of eels, none of which was more than a foot long. They kept moving steadily forward through the long, wet meadow grass and were not halted by my walking among them; in fact several of them passed over my boots. I followed to the river and saw them dropping into the water from a steep bank about four feet high.

It is curious that this should have occurred on a moonlit night, and striking that the eels were so small, suggesting that they were males, which migrate at a much smaller size than females.

Another angling writer, Joscelyn Lane, also encountered eels on nocturnal manoeuvres. He was driving along a country lane late at night when he spotted a black band ahead. Investigating, he found that a wide column of eels was coming out of a field into a ditch running along the side of the road, then crossing the tarmac into another ditch which led off into the darkness. There was no water in either ditch. In 'Vision', one of the sequence of poems Seamus Heaney wrote about the eels and eel fishermen of Lough Neagh in Northern Ireland, the spookiness of the phenomenon is memorably captured:

> He stood at night when eels
> Moved through the grass like hatched fears
>
> Towards the water. To stand
> In one place as the field flowed
> Past, a jellied road
> To watch the eels crossing land
>
> Rewound his world's live girdle
> Phosphorescent sinewed slime
> Continued at his feet . . .

Although other fish, notably the sturgeon, can survive protracted periods out of water, the eel is uniquely versatile in its ability to function in an alien element. It can do so because its skin is able, when moist, to absorb up to ninety per cent of its oxygen requirement. The skin also plays a vital part in permitting the fish to pass without distress from freshwater to saltwater. Without going into the full range of its epidermic attributes, it is enough to say that the thickness of the skin and the mucus with which it is so lavishly coated make it unusually resistant to the process known as osmosis, in which salinity invades the body of a freshwater fish and kills it (salmon, trout, sticklebacks, shad and lampreys are similarly endowed). The gills, the blood and various internal organs also assist the eel in adapting to the sea, which remains its element until death.

Eels smell the sea. At Comacchio, the water is shallow and brackish and reaches high temperatures through the hot summer. The fishermen there worked out centuries ago that, with the coming of autumn, the eels could be stimulated into making a move towards the open sea by raising the sluices on the canal leading to the Adriatic and allowing the cooler, saltier seawater to be pushed in by onshore winds.

So they gather for the journey, the eels of Europe (and America, where the pattern is exactly the same). Some will have travelled great distances, forcing their way around, over, through and under formidable obstacles. Others, such as the eels of Comacchio, will have had an easier time of it. Some do not have to exert themselves at all, for a large proportion of the eel population eschews freshwater altogether, preferring the leisurely life in estuaries and harbours. Whatever their antecedents, they come together to answer the same call. They slip away beneath the waves, on their way.

As they disappear, so do the certainties. Instances of mature eels being accidentally caught at sea are extremely rare, for the obvious reason that they do not feed and therefore cannot be caught on bait, and are able to slip with ease through the mesh used by trawlers. The single record of an eel being found in the open Atlantic dates from 1898, when one was recovered from the stomach of a sperm whale reportedly captured near the Azores by the Prince of Monaco. But beyond indicating that the eel does traverse the ocean and that it travels, at least some of the time, in mid-water – the level at which sperm whales feed – it tells us nothing useful.

A few years earlier a female carrying ripening ova was caught in the English Channel near the Eddystone lighthouse. A dozen migrating eels netted off the Cornish coast in 1912 included a big female, almost black, with enormous eyes and distended ovaries. The movement of silver eels in the Baltic has been extensively studied, because the shallowness of the sea and the narrowness of the exit between Denmark and Sweden make it a comparatively straightforward exercise. Unfortunately the same factors render it pretty unrevealing. The eels swim at all levels and at varying speeds, in several variations on a general westerly direction, favouring the northern shore, until they find their way out of the neck of the bottle into the North Sea, whereupon they vanish.

Once the eels reach the open sea, the eel watchers are left behind, struggling somewhat. They have done their best by devising all kinds of interesting experiments to furnish information about the fish's physiology and the more accessible stages of its life cycle. (For example, Dr Teichmann, in his 1957 paper, 'Das Reichvermogen des Aales', claimed to have proved that eels could detect the scent of roses when diluted to a degree corresponding to one millilitre dissolved in a body of water fifty-eight times greater than that in Lake Constance.) They cut them up by the thousand, separate their vital organs, pore for incalculable numbers of hours over microscopic blobs of tissue, and can tell us, for instance, that the central neurohypophysis of the pituitary gland interdigitates with the adenohypophysis, which itself is divisible into the anterior pars distalis, with rostral and proximal parts, and the posterior pars intermedia.

They cannot, however, tell us how the eel reaches the Sargasso Sea. They cannot even tell us whether the Baltic eels, having emerged into the North Sea, head around the north side of the British Isles or along the Channel, or both. The obstacles to study are vividly illustrated by a paper very kindly sent to me by one of the world's foremost repositories of wisdom about our slippery friend, Professor Jim McCleave of the School of Marine Sciences at the University of Maine.

This paper is entitled 'Movements of yellow and silver phased European eels tracked in the western North Sea', and was written by Professor McCleave and his friend Dr Arnold from the Lowestoft Laboratory in Suffolk. It describes, with daunting thoroughness, what happened when eighteen captured female eels – fourteen in the process of migration and four resident – were fitted with acoustic tags and released off the coast of East Anglia. The non-migrating or yellow eels generally swam towards the shore. The migrating silver ones did not. Some eels seemed to make use of the tides to move north. Others did not. Some moved continuously up and down through the water levels. Others were markedly less energetic. Most engaged in what are described as 'periods of well-oriented directional swimming'. The authors come to no conclusions. They concede with admirable honesty that the great advantage of telemetric study – that it permits close study of individuals – is also its drawback, in that practical considerations, mainly those of cost, restrict the size of the sample so tightly. Furthermore, the necessity of using eels captured far away, holding them captive, inserting the tags, and then abandoning them somewhere they would never have chosen for themselves, means their subsequent behaviour cannot be taken as representative of their fellows in the wild.

Once the eels are on their way, hypotheses gather like clouds when the barometer is falling. How does this fish, which has spent its juvenile and adult life gliding round the dark and familiar depths of its place of residence, navigate its way across three thousand miles of ocean, through its shallows and over its abyssal depths, through its currents and counter-currents to a remote sea devoid of obvious geographical features?

Louis Bertin magisterially rejected the easy way out of this riddle. 'It is possible,' he wrote,

> to shelter behind the prodigious phenomenon of heredity. It would be simple enough to say that the eel changes to a silver individual because it is born of silver eels, and only resembles its parents. But it would be a far-fetched and lazy explanation . . . To invoke a migratory instinct is not an explanation – 'fishes and birds emigrate because they have the instinct to emigrate.' This is merely to say, with Molière's doctors, that opium lulls to sleep because it has a soporific virtue.

Having vigorously repudiated the lazy way, Bertin attempts to break down the instinct into a succession of taxes, or responses provoked by environment – among them rheotaxis or reaction to currents, thermotaxis (reaction to heat), and halotaxis (reaction to salt). He employs these convincingly to explain how the eel gets out into coastal waters. But then he is confronted by the insoluble. It is fanciful to suggest that the eel can smell the Sargasso Sea from the Bay of Biscay, or feel its warmth. Bertin gives up: 'The silver eel,' he notes resignedly, 'eludes observation once it has reached the waters around the European coast.'

Some later experts – including Jim McCleave – continue to favour the theory that smell is the guiding principle, at least in the later stages. Others conjecture that the creatures steer by the stars, by maintaining a particular angle to the earth's magnetic field, by alignment to electrical fields, or by a combination of these and other stimuli organised through some as yet unanalysed piece of machinery in the head – helpfully labelled by one eel watcher as 'an innate directional mechanism'.

Their destination is the one fact about the eel that most school students know. The chief characteristics of the strange and wondrous place known as the Sargasso Sea are, baldly stated: its great depth (as much as fifteen thousand feet), its extreme salinity, the stable warmth of its upper layers, its lack of movement, its incredible clarity, and its dearth of life. Nobody knows what it is about this marine wonderworld that is so conducive to the copulation of eels that they feel compelled to swim across such a vast expanse of ocean to reach it. It follows that we also cannot tell if the conditions sought with such pertinacity are unique to the Sargasso Sea, or whether they are duplicated elsewhere; and thus whether the eel has other as yet undiscovered breeding grounds, or whether its insistence on the Sargasso is derived from an impulse other than an inherited, common awareness of its unique suitability.

The breeding area is located in the southern sector of the Sargasso, below 29°N. There is convincing circumstantial evidence that it is confined to the north by a meandering latitudinal band in which temperature and salinity rise markedly, which the eels encounter as they travel south and recognise as a cue to get down to business. The boundaries to east, west and south are – despite Johannes Schmidt's assertions to the contrary – unknown.

Somehow they get there, somehow they know that they have got there, that it's time to stop moving and find a mate. The mystery of the migration becomes the greater mystery of the breeding. From late February, through March and April, into May and possibly June, about six hundred feet below the surface of that basin of still, warm water held in the upper levels of the sea, mass copulation takes place. No adult eel has been captured in the Sargasso Sea or anywhere near it. No eggs have ever been recovered (there have been claims to the contrary, never authenticated). From experiments carried out in captivity, we know something of how the courtship proceeds, that it is dominated by the females, their bodies distended by their swollen ovaries. It must be one of the wonders of the world. In a book called *The Story of the Stream* published in 1926, an English naturalist and journalist, Arthur Young, let his imagination rip:

> Born in one of the most glorious of all nursery gardens – the supremely beautiful gardens of the Sargassos – where the luxuriant vegetation of the seabed rivals the most beautiful blossoms of the tropic landscape; where the flash of rainbow fishes through the brilliant jade green gloom makes a ceaseless feast of coloured fire; where the living lamps of electric fish light the darker depths with a pale phosphorescent ray that serves to show the chameleon octopus where he clings motionless to his spur of coral, waiting vulture-like for his prey like the vicious murderer he is. Starry globes hang pendulous, and through this enchanted region, like lost spirits in a fairy wilderness . . .

It is ecstatic stuff, but entirely off beam. There is no coral, no seabed vegetation, no octopus, murderous or otherwise. There are very few fish and no starry globes, just vast clods of sargassum weed hanging in waveless, motionless water of the deepest blue over the black, abyssal deep; a place of utter stillness and silence.

While the frenzy of procreation continues below, the fertilised eggs of the eel, each held up by a minuscule drop of oil, rise. Within a day or two – possibly even hours – they hatch into slivers of tissue a few millimetres long, so entirely transparent that every organ and muscle segment may be seen, even the colour of the blood. The infant assumes the shape of a minute willow leaf, no thicker than a pencil line, its pinprick of a head comprising round black eyes and a pair of jaws.

Incalculable numbers of these fragments of life begin to drift in the sluggish currents of the Sargasso. At a month old they are perhaps ten millimetres long, growing quickly on their diet of microplankton, but far too puny to be capable of swimming. They must wait upon the caprice of the great eddy in which they are trapped. Many, perhaps most, will never escape. But some – enough – are eventually pushed to the periphery where the flow is more purposeful. Some filter south-west, to the Caribbean and beyond. But most emerge to the west, and are carried north by the Florida Current until they encounter the Gulf Stream off Cape Hatteras. The offspring of the American eel, being bigger and stronger, are able to move vertically through the water levels to find the intruding cross-currents by which they detach themselves into the coastal waters down the eastern seaboard of North America. The job of delivering the European thin-heads for distribution is completed by the Gulf Stream and the North Atlantic Current.

It is a comfort for scientists already stretched to account for the arrival of the adult eel in the Sargasso after a three-thousand-mile search across featureless ocean to be able to invoke the global system of currents to explain how the feeble little fruits of mating get home. In general they are happy to leave it at that; it is a neat arrangement of the very few available facts, and there is no reason to doubt its basic validity. But it does raise some tricky questions apart from the matter of the separation between American and European eels already referred to. How, for example, do countries like Venezuela, Guyana and Cuba, which are well to the south of the breeding grounds, receive their portion of thin-heads? Why are the eels of Bermuda, which geographically lies on the route home for the European larvae, exclusively American? Why does Iceland alone have a population of hybrids? How do the American thin-heads reach Greenland against the south-flowing Labrador Current?

Jim McCleave stylishly identified the flaw that impeded and distorted much of the earlier speculative work on the oceanic migration of the larvae. He pointed out that much of it – for instance Vladykov's assertion that Schmidt must be wrong about the breeding place of the American eel – depended on the assumption that the process is an efficient one, and that the survival rate must therefore be high. In fact, McCleave points out, for the species to maintain itself at a stable and healthy level, the process has only to deliver to suitable habitats enough infants to replenish stocks to the degree by which they have been depleted through migration and other losses. Given the prodigious fecundity of the female – which may carry anything from two million to twenty million eggs – a huge proportion of the thin-heads born in the Sargasso could perish (i.e. fail to migrate) without the balance and dynamism of the species as a whole suffering any adverse effect. Since we have no idea how many adults make it to the breeding grounds, or how many billions of babies are produced, we cannot begin to compute survival rates. But it is more reasonable, McCleave argued persuasively, to assume that the infants that do complete their journeys represent a minuscule proportion of the original stock, than to assert an improbable capacity for directional travel and a much higher success rate. The fact that the great majority do not make it does not diminish the wonder attached to those that do.

Before being reunited with the multitudes of thin-heads as they reach the end of their odyssey, there is another aspect of the Sargasso episode to be considered, which is the fate of the adults after mating. They do not return home, which leaves two possibilities – that they continue their existence somewhere in the depths of the sea, or that they die, their destiny fulfilled. The question moved the Frenchman, Louis Bertin, to one of the infrequent bursts of poetic eloquence in his classic treatise: 'We have to think of the Sargasso Sea as being at the same time their tomb, and the cradle of their offspring.'

EIGHT

Homecoming

It begins in late summer. By the time the adults start slipping away from the estuaries at the start of their exodus,
the influx of the infants is already well under way. They will
pass through the same water, parents-to-be and children of
past migrants moving in opposite directions. The invasion
of the thin-heads reaches Portugal first, in late summer,
then branches north towards France and south towards
the Mediterranean. The Basques are netting them in the
autumn and soon after Christmas they are pressing into the
rivers of western France: the Adour, then the Garonne, then
the Loire. By late March they penetrate the Channel and
the Irish Sea, and the elvermen of Gloucestershire whose
forefathers have dipped their wide nets along the Severn

for centuries are making ready. One stream goes up the western side of Britain, the other along the Channel to reach the North Sea by early summer. By now the momentum of dispersal is faltering and the numbers are small. The majority of those making it around Denmark into the Baltic have left infancy behind and become immature, or bootlace eels.

It takes between two and a half and three years for the European thin-heads to break free from the Sargasso Sea and reach home waters. Some time ago ripples of disagreement disturbed the world of the eel watchers after it was observed that the combined propulsion of the Gulf Stream and the North Atlantic Current should deliver the larvae within two years at the most, unless, for inscrutable reasons, they resisted it. A French biologist subsequently caused astonishment by claiming that the journey was in fact completed within months. Her assertion was based on an examination of growth rings in the thin-head's otolith – the organ at the base of the skull which enables a fish to keep its balance – and depended on the assumption that these rings (of calcium) were deposited daily, and the dubious proposition that these feeble little slivers of transparent tissue were in such a hurry that, rather than surrender themselves to the currents, they actively swam with them.

It was subsequently pointed out that, since very little was known about how much and how often the thin-heads ate on their journey, it was impossible to confirm that growth rings were deposited daily; and that if you could not be sure how frequently they appeared, using them to calculate age was, to put it mildly, a fallible procedure. Moreover, several reliable authorities, having examined the thin-head's negligible muscle structure, strongly challenged the notion that it could possibly achieve the necessary 'sustained directional swimming'.

Once the thin-heads reach the Continental Shelf of Europe, it is time for a change, time to start looking a little more like an eel and less like a leaf. Beginning at the extremities, the creature thickens into a more or less cylindrical shape. At the same time its length diminishes from about seven and a half centimetres to six, and its weight plummets by as much as nine tenths. It loses its jagged canines, and – for reasons that are probably of limited interest – its anus migrates forward. At this stage of metamorphosis the skin remains transparent, and the head appears enormous in relation to the shrunken remainder. It is known as a glass eel.

The process begins as the *leptocephali*, having traversed the great ocean depths, encounter the first rising slopes at six hundred to a thousand feet. In general, the further north they go, the bigger they are and the later they arrive. Louis Bertin proposed a neat theory, to the effect that the wider the Continental Shelf and the more gradual the shelving, the more inclined the thin-heads were to linger at sea, and therefore the larger they were when they finally made their move. It is not known if the distribution is organised mainly out in the ocean – under the influence of the North Atlantic Current and associated flows – or in inshore waters controlled by local currents; or by a fluctuating alliance of the two. Unlike the salmon, the eel has no homing instinct to direct it to a specific river. In the absence of such a straightforward organising principle, the performance of the thin-heads strikes one as extraordinarily haphazard.

The principal population flow washes against the Iberian Peninsula. Today, only in Portugal, along the Basque coast of Spain and the western coasts of France and Britain are the quantities of glass eels sufficient to sustain commercial fisheries – of which the French is by far the biggest. This suggests that the majority head north. But, historically, enough penetrated the Straits of Gibraltar into the Mediterranean to stock the rivers of Italy, Greece and north Africa, although very few got as far as the Black Sea. The fact that they were found in the Mediterranean as thin-heads rather than metamorphosed glass eels used to be adduced as evidence of a separate Mediterranean population, breeding in one of that sea's several marine abysses; and – more recently – that they must be capable of sustained directional swimming, since the flow through the Straits is westerly, against them. But Jim McCleave has argued convincingly that the larvae move vertically through the water levels to find a contrary, easterly tidal bore which comes on stream shortly after high water and carries them through; and that thereafter they pick up the predominantly easterly currents to continue on their way towards Italy, Greece and points east.

The overall shape of the dispersal is reasonably clear. But questions linger. Are the arriving thin-heads entirely at the mercy of happenstance, or are they able to exercise some obscure preference? Is it wholly a matter of luck whether they go right or left when they reach Europe? How do they know where to stop and when? What determines whether, having reached the Western Approaches of the Channel, they join the throngs forging their way up the Severn, go left towards Ireland and Scotland, push on east and ascend the rivers of Southern England, or keep going for Holland, Denmark and the Baltic?

Sooner or later the glass eels taste fresh water for the first time, setting off the next stage in metamorphosis. Initially they shy away, hugging the bottom. Little by little their respiratory systems begin to adapt to desalination. Pigmentation develops from the tail forward, and the texture of what little flesh they have becomes firmer. This period of waiting is elastic, but can last for several weeks, with the gradual rise in temperature acting as a signal to move. Migration is evidently not dictated by aversion to salt water, since many of them find everything they need in harbour, estuary or lagoon, and never bother to go any further.

Those that are minded to forge upriver exploit the flood tide to penetrate the lower reaches, and drop down to the riverbed to avoid being washed back by the ebb. With this commitment and the darkening of the skin comes a new name: elver (although commercially they continue to be known as glass eels, and the two terms tend to be used indiscriminately). In the times of plenty – times past – this invasion of the elvers was a thing of wonder throughout the enormous distribution range of the European fresh-water eel.

Part of the wonder was the incredible abundance of the little fish. In the winter of 1923–4, almost five hundred tons of glass eel – several billion individuals – were traded at the market in the Basque city of San Sebastian, to be eaten, turned into pig food, used as fertiliser and in the making of glue. As recently as the 1970s, combined catches for the commercial fisheries of western France amounted to several thousand tons in one season; and this, of course, represented only a proportion of the total numbers passing through.

The ascent of the elvers was a spectacle. The antiquarian William Camden described in the 1600 edition of his celebrated compendium of national curiosities, *Britannia*, how:

> Sometime in the spring the river [the Bristol Avon] about Cainsham is yearly covered over and coloured black with millions of little eels scarce so big as a goose quill tho' some would have them a particular species. These, with small nets, they scoop up in great numbers and, by a peculiar way of ordering them, scour off their skins. Being thus stripped and looking very white they make them up into little cakes which they fry and eat.

On the Thames the elver run was known as the eel fare. It usually began towards the end of April and was the occasion for Londoners to arm themselves with sieves and nets, take off their shoes, roll up their trousers, and help themselves. In 1832 Dr William Roots of Kingston upon Thames kept watch on a column close to the bank. It proceeded continuously for five days, and he calculated that up to 1800 elvers were passing each minute. A Scottish minister, the Reverend G. Mack, witnessed the phenomenon on the Dee:

> They direct their progress only along the edges of the river, in a line following the windings. My hand was put in to touch the line. The line became discontinued when my hand approached but it united again as soon as my hand was withdrawn. The progress with which they advanced was not less

than four miles an hour; and this continued for eight days and nights together, and there was no apparent diminution of it when I left the place.

A mid-nineteenth-century French writer described the young eels coming in from the sea in spherical masses from which 'the individuals detach themselves to form a cord, like a ball of wool unwinding . . . This kind of process lasts fifteen days without a stop.' The Loire fishermen called it the cordon. 'Sometimes,' wrote one witness,

> the cordon measures several kilometres in length, practically uninterrupted, of about one metre in width and half a metre in depth. The elvers, by millions, congregate to form it. In full daylight they separate, stop, spread out on the bottom and dig into the mud or burrow among the stones. At nightfall, once more active, they resume their course and reform the cordon in which each, straining to advance, profits by the efforts of its neighbours and the whole community.

To those who have witnessed the sight, the pertinacity of the baby eels – what the Reverend Mr Mack called their 'unremitting assiduity' – is as remarkable as their numbers. A BBC television film about the Australian freshwater eel (which, incidentally, gave the wholly false impression that adults had been filmed in the act of mating in the Pacific deeps off Vanuatu) showed the upstream migration of elvers encountering a dam on an un-named river in Victoria. The forty-foot-high expanse of concrete was moistened by a trickle of water from above, and up it the eels forced their way, so that whole face of the structure shimmered in the moonlight with the squirming hordes.

Sir Humphry Davy – who had first guessed that eels came from the depths of the sea – was present at Ballyshannon in western Ireland, when the elvers came into the River Erne:

> The mouth of the river ... was blackened with little eels, about as long as the finger, which were constantly urging their way up the moist rocks by the side of the fall. Thousands died, but their bodies – remaining moist – served as the ladder for others to make their way; and I saw some ascending even perpendicular stones, making their road through wet moss, or adhering to some eels that had died in the attempt. Such is the energy of these little animals that they continued to find their way in immense numbers to Lough Erne.

The casualty rate among the tiny travellers is tremendous. Apart from those which perish from exhaustion, huge numbers are taken as prey – by fishermen, by gulls and other birds, by water rats, otters, and mink, and by virtually every species of fish, including, in nature's cold-eyed way, adult eels. The Irish authority, Christopher Moriarty, recalled catching one of about a pound in his bare hands 'so intent on her cannibal feast that she ignored my approach'. She had fifty elvers in her stomach.

But they are dauntless. The stamina and resolve that make possible the journey of their parents to the Sargasso Sea is present to its fullest degree in their offspring. In all the battery of mechanisms and attributes with which this creature has been endowed to do what it must, this – its unquenchable determination – seems the most extraordinary. The Victorian sportsman and naturalist, Charles St

John, watched the elvers ascending the Findhorn, on the north-east coast of Scotland:

> It was some distance from the mouth, where the stream, confined by a narrow rocky channel, ran with great strength. Nevertheless these little eels persevered in swimming against the stream. When they came to a fall which they could not possibly ascend, they wriggled out of the water and gliding along the rock close to the edge where the stone was constantly wet from the splashing and spray of the fall, they made their way up till they got above the difficulty, and then again slipping into the water they continued their course ... For more than a week the same thing was to be seen every day. The perseverance they displayed was very great.

That quality enables the freshwater eel to colonise an enormous range of habitat. The dynamics of distribution are not really understood at all – what makes one eel linger in the river estuary, another to stop a mile or two upstream, another to follow the first tributary and another the second; what impels others to press on and on, through lakes, up smaller and smaller flows, until the whole river system – up to its minutest rivulet – has received its complement; which still leaves a last intrepid remnant prepared to take to the ditches and dewy meadows until they find the dark, quiet refuge of their choice.

In some subtle way, this process determines sexual differentiation. Elvers and juvenile bootlace eels are neutral in gender. Subsequently there is a general veering towards femininity, followed by a phase of hermaphroditism – when the eel is between eighteen and thirty centimetres long –

during which the male and female sides are in balance. Then, with full maturity, the eel goes one way or the other. Generally speaking, female eels are bigger (anything over forty-five centimetres is likely to be a female), less numerous, and live longer. They stick together, as do males. Some of those who have immersed themselves in matters of spermatogenesis and oogenesis are convinced that gender orientation is fixed at birth, and that the arriving elvers select an appropriate habitat – the males tending to remain in estuaries and brackish water, while the more muscular and enterprising females head upstream. Others insist that distribution is random, that the elvers are wholly asexual, that gender is shaped by the company they find themselves keeping; and even that they are able to change sex should circumstances deposit them among opposites.

The question is unresolved, and I don't suppose it troubles the eel much. It has survived the hazards of its epic journey and the lottery of the dispersal, and has found its home. It will be many years before sex rears a head even uglier than its own. Until the call comes, it has nothing more to concern it than staying alive and finding enough to eat.

In Günter Grass's great novel, *The Tin Drum*, the drummer boy Oskar, his mother, her husband Alfred Matzerath, and her lover Jan Bronski, are wandering along the seashore at the port of Danzig (now Gdansk) when they encounter a longshoreman sitting at the end of the breakwater where the River Mottlau reaches the Baltic. The old man hauls in a clothes line, clutches at something in the water, heaves it out and flings it on the breakwater: the head of a horse.

Little eels dart from it, and the screaming gulls dive to seize them. The longshoreman crams a dozen or so into his potato sack, then squeezes darker, thicker eels from within the horse's head. Prising the horse's mouth open with his club, he pulls out two from the gullet, as thick and long as an arm, whereupon Oskar's mother throws up her breakfast of egg and bread and *café au lait*, and the gulls start fighting over that. Finally the old man extracts the biggest eel of all from the horse's ear, accompanied by part of the beast's brain looking like 'a mess of white porridge'. He stuffs it into the sack, explaining to Matzerath that the eels writhe in the rock salt inside until their slime is removed and they die, leaving them ready to be rubbed in peat moss and hung over beechwood to smoke. There is some discussion of the ethics of this practice, which is banned on the grounds of cruelty, but Matzerath and the longshoreman agree it is fair, since eels eat horses' heads and human corpses when they can find them. While Matzerath talks eels, his wife walks up the shore with her hand in her lover's trouser pocket.

The comedy is appalling and savage, and authentic. Someone who did not know his eels would have made the horse's head rotten, but Grass is well aware that they shun decomposed flesh: 'It was a horse's head, a fresh and genuine horse's head, the head of a black horse with a black mane, which only yesterday or the day before had no doubt been neighing.'

The catholicity of the eel's appetite has doubtless contributed to its sinister and undeserved reputation for voracity. In the salt water of estuaries, harbours and lagoons they munch happily on small crabs, prawns, shrimps, little fish and worms. In fresh water they rely upon the great and seething larder of minute forms of life: leeches, nymphs, caddis larvae, midge larvae, louses, shrimps. They are fond of crayfish where they can find them, and have a notable relish for the enormous freshwater mussel (quite how they manage to extract the orange flesh from within the formidable shells is unclear – Christopher Moriarty believes they seize the foot with which the mollusc propels itself, and then employ their rotational skills to twist the body out). They are thoroughly opportunistic, but there is no evidence to support the charge – endlessly repeated by ignorant proprietors of trout and salmon fisheries, river keepers and some anglers – that they are destructive predators of salmon and trout eggs. These fish generally spawn during the winter and early spring, when eels are buried in mud, motionless and fasting, their metabolism merely ticking over. In common with the rest of the animal kingdom, with the notable exception of humankind, eels eat when they need to; and they are frequently caught with entirely empty stomachs, which – considering it takes them up to three days to digest a meal – suggests an abstemious attitude to the pleasures of the table.

Broadly speaking, the bigger eels grow, the more fish they eat. Favoured prey are perch, rudd, char, and little eels. Their cannibalistic proclivities were illustrated by a strikingly cold-blooded experiment conducted in the aquarium of the Jardin des Plantes in Paris in the late 1930s and described with great relish by Louis Bertin. Two biologists arranged for a thousand eight-centimetre elvers to be put into a tank of water entirely devoid of shelter. They were fed daily, but even so a year later there were only seventy-one eels left, now up to twenty-five centimetres long. Two months later – after what Bertin describes gloatingly as 'daily scenes of cannibalism' – there were twelve survivors. A month later the number was down to three. Ten days after that, on 17 October 1938, a champion was left. She had eaten one rival and killed the other, and was thirty-two centimetres long and fifty-five grammes in weight. Left in solitude, and fed on meat and worms, she grew, and by 1941 she weighed 135 grammes. Subsequently, as a result of the Nazi occupation, she was neglected and died.

It is a shame no such hard evidence exists to support the age-old belief that eels are fond of vegetables – so fond, in fact, that they forsake their home waters to search the fields for favourite varieties. Albertus Magnus, writing in the thirteenth century, was neutral on the subject: 'The eel is said sometimes by night to crawl out of the water on the fields where it finds lentils, peas and beans.' Christopher Moriarty quotes a vague reference to eels in Pomerania 'betaking themselves to the peas' and being trapped by peasants in the furrows between the rows. *The History of Scandinavian Fishes*, published in English in 1893, contains a surreal account of events on the Countess of Hamilton's estate at Hedelunde in Sweden, where the eels were said to have devoured peapods 'with a smacking sound, like that made by sucking-pigs when they are feeding . . . but only the outer soft and juicy skin covering the young pods.' Jonathan Couch, in his *History of British Fishes*, referred, without a tinge of scepticism, to the eel's reported weakness for 'newly sown peas', and to a 'reliable' report that one was found 'in a field of turnips, a quarter of a mile from a river'. Dr Couch was also informed – whether reliably or not, he does not reveal – about another wandering eel which 'has been taken on the land by means of a hook baited with a worm and set to catch a bird.'

Whether sustained by peas, turnips, lentils, or more mundane nourishment, *A. anguilla* tends to take its time about growing, at least in the wild. Long ago, eel farmers in Japan established that, given a constant water temperature of between twenty-three and thirty degrees Celsius, elvers will feed throughout the year, achieving a marketable size of two hundred grammes in less than two years. But in temperate Europe, the wild eel does not approach such growth rates. In most lakes and rivers the temperature never exceeds twenty degrees, and during the winter months is below or around the twelve-degree mark, at which eels become inclined to skulk in the mud hardly feeding at all. In favourable circumstances, females in the wild may mature and be ready to migrate after eight years. More often the span is double that. Eels thirty years old and upwards are uncommon, but far from unknown. And in unusual circumstances they can live remarkably long lives.

Thomas Boosey's 1887 compendium, *Anecdotes of Fish and Fishing*, tells the story of John Meredith, 'an officer of the excise' who, in 1781, placed a small eel in the well outside his cottage in Brecon. Long after the passing of Mr Meredith, the creature was forced by 'a recent inundation' to reveal itself, whereupon it was caught in a pail by the new tenant, Mrs Price. She described it as being 'as thick as her arm', and, according to Boosey, it was then returned 'to its former element, where it had subsisted for thirty-one years upon the *animaliculae* contained in the water.'

Such cases normally involve eels thwarted in their migrating urge. A pet female housed in what must have been a very large earthenware pot by the family of Professor Desmarest of Alfort lived from 1828 to 1865, reaching a length of five feet. An albino eel was on display at an aquarium near Cadiz between 1913 and 1946. But the undisputed champion for longevity was a Swedish eel called Putte, which achieved (and to a degree retains) celebrity status. Putte was captured as an elver near the port of Helsingborg in 1863, and kept as a pet until presented to the local aquarium in the 1930s. Putte – reputedly a male, by then in his seventies – survived the Second World War, finally passing away in 1948 at the estimated age of eighty-eight, an event which received extensive coverage in the Swedish media. His body has been preserved, and Karin Ohlsson of Helsingborg Museum told me there were plans to put it on display – although, at forty centimetres, she admitted that it was visually rather unimpressive.

The eel's hardiness, self-reliance and discreet way of life make it a suitable low-maintenance pet for those temperamentally inclined. I have promised myself that one day I shall build myself a pond and place in it specimens of our more amiable and less glamorous fish – tench, gudgeon, perhaps a perch, certainly an eel or two – which I will train to take worms from my fingers, and encourage to live in harmony with each other. The trouble with pets, though, is that it is easy to grow too fond of them. According to the seventeenth-century divine Doctor George Hakewill, the Roman orator Hortensius wept at the death of his pet lamprey 'which he had kept long and loved exceedingly'. (It seems to me much more likely that his companion was an eel, since lampreys live no more than a few years, and are disfigured with a blood-red sucker which makes them revolting to behold and surely impossible to love.) Boosey referred to the grief of a family from the village of Darvel, near Ayr, upon discovering that their pet eel, which answered to the name of Rob Roy and 'readily ate morsels from a horn spoon pushed below the surface by the children', had choked to death on a large frog.

The matter of monster eels is satisfyingly shrouded in legend and nonsense. Pliny the Elder claimed in his *Natural History* that in the Ganges they grew up to thirty feet long, which is clearly ridiculous. But there are several among the fifteen or so species of *Anguilla* in the southern hemisphere which comfortably outgrow their northern cousins. The long-finned eel of New Zealand often exceeds twenty pounds in weight and I have seen a report of a leviathan being dragged from the waters of Lake Waitapu in 1882 that weighed a hundred and thirty pounds. I would like to know more about that creature, and about a vast and rapacious Samoan eel allegedly seen pursuing rats through the fields and devouring them with a single snap of its jaws.

A fish of five pounds is a large specimen of *A. anguilla* and would be the best part of a yard long. Christopher Moriarty – who has spent half a lifetime catching and examining eels in Ireland – says he has yet to encounter a ten pounder. Given those dimensions, I'm afraid one has to be sceptical about some of the stories about monsters. This evidently occurred to Dr Couch, who recorded in his *History*: 'I have a printed note of one which weighed sixty-two pounds, but I must confess that I regard this as apocryphal.' The Reverend David Badham asserted that 'in

Prussia eels attain occasionally a length of twelve feet. In the Elbe specimens occur up to sixty pounds weight.' Badham's famous contemporary, Frank Buckland, speaks of a thirty-six-pound eel coming from the Ouse near Cambridge but confesses: 'I cannot help thinking this eel must have been a conger.' Izaak Walton refers to an eel 'caught in the Peterborough River in the year 1667 which was a yard and three quarters long.' Perhaps sensing a raising of eyebrows, he says menacingly: 'If you will not believe me, then go and see it at one of the coffee-houses in King Street in Westminster.'

Such an eel would have weighed at least twenty pounds. A reasonably trustworthy record of a fish six feet long and weighing twenty-eight pounds was noted by another nineteenth-century clerical naturalist, the Reverend Leonard Jenyns, for many years the incumbent at the parish of Swaffham Bulbeck in Cambridgeshire. This monster, and a slightly smaller companion, were captured when a dyke near Wisbech was drained. The zoologist William Yarrell – a generally reliable witness – wrote in his 1836 *History of British Fishes* that he had seen the preserved skins of the two eels, which he put at twenty-seven and twenty-three pounds.

Another story – whose tone almost compels the suspension of disbelief – is told in a delightful Irish book, *A Life on the Boyne*, by a shopkeeper in Trim, Jim Reynolds:

> One afternoon in the late Fifties, Major McVeigh came into my shop and while waiting for his order he overheard a chat between The Gael, Paddy Canty and Garda Egan about a big eel that had been caught in the traps . . . It was estimated to be in excess of seven pounds . . . Major McVeigh then told how

his workers or their families would never go near one of the two lakes on the Drewstown estate, as the old people would tell of monsters being seen in it. Once, when he was home on leave from India as a young officer, the herd at Drewstown poisoned some dogs that were worrying the sheep. As it was spring and the ewes were yeigning, he was too busy to bury them so he dumped them into the 'haunted' lake. Some time afterwards two enormous eels were found floating on the surface of the water, dead. When Major McVeigh described the size of the eels there was a lot of laughter. This grand old man, who claimed to be a friend of the great T. E. Lawrence, was so annoyed by their laughter that he asked them to meet him again the following morning. When he arrived he was armed with a photograph complete with frame and picture cord and also carrying a diary. The photograph showed the McVeigh family, the butler and all the staff gathered around looking at two eels draped down the pillars of Drewstown House. The diary said the year was 1907 and the larger eel measured just over twelve feet, had a girth of 25 inches and weighed forty-one pounds. The other one was ten feet long and had a girth of 19 inches, and weighed twenty-nine pounds.

Although I have not been able to corroborate Major McVeigh's testimony, and despite the astounding dimensions ascribed to the eels, I like this story so much that I am inclined to believe it. However the only fully authenticated monster eel story I can offer came in a somewhat prosaic form from one of Denmark's most distinguished ichthyologists, Dr Jorgen Nielsen of the Zoological Museum in Copenhagen. He told me that he had recently examined the corpse of a huge eel taken from a small pond in a rural area. It was 125 centimetres long, and weighed a little over nineteen pounds. The poor creature had been beaten to death with a shovel after being accused by the owner of the pond of attacking his ornamental waterfowl.

All these cases, however fanciful, concern eels that were, by one means or another, captured. But it is the nature of the beast that the biggest specimens will never give themselves up to be measured and classified, and therefore that the maximum dimensions must remain a matter of guesswork. If an eel such as the one inspected by Dr Nielsen could weigh almost twenty pounds for a length of just over four feet, one two feet longer could weigh forty pounds. Cameras trailed through the depths of Loch Ness have recorded fleeting glimpses of prodigious eels slithering through the darkness. And there are thousands upon thousands of refuges scattered throughout the creature's range: great lakes, nameless ponds, moats, meres, tarns, lochans, dykes, ditches. The monster of monsters could be in any dark, unconsidered pool, trapped, whatever damp route it took to get there now cut off, confined to its murky, muddy domain, growing older, thicker, heavier. There would be no reason to suspect its presence. And what if some passer-by were to glance one day at the still surface and see a creature as long as a man and as thick as his leg, a thing with a flattened head and the body of an anaconda, gliding through the green water setting slow ripples to flick against the reeds? It would be one thing for the word to get out, quite another to get the eel out. No ordinary angling tackle would prise such a brute from its lair. And who, anyway, would willingly grapple with it once it was on the bank?

NINE

Babies

The Sèvre Niortaise unwinds in an unhurried fashion out of the marshes of Poitou to reach the Atlantic to the north of La Rochelle. It comes out of a flat, wet land to merge with the sea rather than meet it. To the north and south, beyond the low banks, stretches marshland – some of it claimed for agriculture, some left to the birds and the bog. To the west, shielding the mouth, is the Ile de Ré, a colourless smudge low in the sky. Distinctions between land and water, between river and sea are blurred by the tides. The estuary – any estuary – takes some knowing. They breed a special kind of person – tough, watery, salty, comfortable with ceaseless flux, able to make sense of obscure signs, at ease with flatness.

When I looked across this estuary in daylight, I could make nothing of it. I could not tell which was the north bank, and which was the south. I could not distinguish island from mainland, nor tell where the sea was. I had arrived in the dark, after rattling through the deserted streets of the little town of Charron at three in the morning. I was with a Dane, Thomas Nielsen, whose business was with men who were accustomed to being about when the world slept and were necessarily familiar with the ways of the estuary. As a young biologist, Thomas had specialised in eels, and circumstances had bound him to the species. He was my means of obtaining a glimpse of a way of life I knew nothing about. Not that there was anything illicit about it. It is merely that any occupation conducted out on the water, at night, during the coldest, stormiest season of the year, in places no one would dream of visiting for their visual or cultural charms, is likely to proceed without attracting attention from outside.

The water of the Sèvre Niortaise gleamed and flickered in the dark. Overhead thick piles of cloud marched in from the ocean. A fleet of boats moved restlessly at anchor, their lights swaying with the movement of the water, their rigging rustling and tinkling in the breeze. A pickup truck bounced into the yard. A little man with a pug face got out, introduced himself to Thomas and me with the briskest of handshakes, pulled on waders and waterproofs, hitched up a dinghy and drove it down a wide concrete ramp into the river. He gestured to us to hop in. I had a waterproof coat on and serviceable boots, but nothing usefully impermeable between. I sat down on the narrow seat, on something damp that was not water. By the time I smelled it, the substance had seeped into the fabric of my trousers. I put my hand down, then sniffed my fingertips. For a moment the mediocre dinner Thomas and I had disposed of in the roadside restaurant a few hours before threatened to reappear. The stink – from what daylight, when it finally crept in, revealed to be a colossal deposit of seagull or cormorant shit spread across most of my backside – was awful beyond belief, and distressingly persistent, hanging around like the pub bore, trailing whiffs of putrefaction and fish and swamps.

Our host, Bruno, took us to his fishing boat, a tubby, stumpy craft called the *As de Coeur*, the Ace of Hearts. On board he darted about through the jumble of buckets, boxes and coils of rope, checking his gear, occasionally re-tying a knot or tightening a fixture. The tide was running, he explained. We would have three, maybe four hours' fishing divided either side of high water. The engine came to life with a chesty cough, and we turned downstream, against the tide. Three or four other boats slipped anchor at the same time. But most, the great majority of the eighty or so elver boats on the lower Sèvre Niortaise, remained where they were, their skippers – including Bruno's three brothers – at home. This was the last tide of the season, the last chance to make a killing and pay back some of that big bank loan raised to buy the boat. And most of the fishermen were in bed.

It had been, they said – those who bothered to turn out – a disaster. We thought last season was bad enough. But this one! My God, could there ever have been a year like it? Storms, gales, rain, rain, rain – floods everywhere, even a lazy, leisurely river like the Sèvre Niortaise transformed by the endless downpours into a big, mean flow for weeks and months on end. And you wouldn't mind all that, if the fish were there. If the fish were there! There was only one answer to that. The fish were not there. Not on the Loire, not on the Charente, not on the Gironde, not on the Adour, not on the Sèvre Niortaise.

The fish in question does not look much like a fish at all, more like an animated aquatic toothpick. These translucent threads, with their two black pinheads for eyes, are the wanderers come home. Not long ago this creature was like a big leaf, a passive slice of tissue tossed and turned according to the ocean's whim. Now it had become something else, hardly thicker than a pencil lead, no longer than one of the lines on the palm of your hand, but charged with its sense of purpose. It had journeyed from the weed forests of the Sargasso to this bleak shore, and now – at the last – it was denied. Instead of wriggling its way upstream to find a dark, peaceful place of refuge, it was wriggling nowhere; caught against mesh, a fragment of merchandise.

It takes between 3500 and 5000 of these minute creatures to make up a kilogram in weight. In 1976, on a single river, the Loire – the most productive glass-eel fishery in Europe – nearly eight hundred tons were removed, amounting to three billion or more individuals. No one questioned the scale of the slaughter. A mere quarter of a century ago confidence in the inexhaustible bounty of the sea was still unassailable.

In those days the market for glass eels was geographically limited and modest in value. Some were transported around Europe to stock existing wild eel fisheries. The rest were sold for eating, mainly in Portugal and Spain (where the classic dish, *angulas a la bilbaina*, requires that they be tossed for a moment in smoking olive oil, garlic and red chilli, served in an earthenware pot, and eaten with a wooden fork). The fishing was unorganised, haphazard and opportunistic; a local food source exploited cheaply and disposed of casually. The abundance had always varied enormously. When the glass eels turned up, the fishermen took what they could, ate what they wanted, sold what they could sell, fed the rest to the pigs or dug it into the ground as fertiliser. In years of scarcity they did not bother.

Gradually more potent market forces came to bear. Consumer demand for adult eel was buoyant, and the pioneers of fish farming began to get interested in it. They knew that while it can take ten years or more for an eel to mature in the wild, under controlled conditions – of which the most important is a consistent temperature in excess of twenty-three degrees Celsius – the process can be compressed into two years. At the same time, as Japan became the most dynamic economy on the planet, the appetite of its people for *kabayaki* expanded way beyond the capacity of its own eel farmers to satisfy it.

The science of eel farming – while perhaps not of great interest to anyone other than an eel farmer – differs from other kinds of aquaculture in one respect that is of significance to the welfare of the species as a whole. With other farmed fish, the only constraints on production are economic and – to a lesser extent – political and environmental. In the case of salmon farms for instance, the capacity of hatcheries to supply fry to be grown on into adults is almost unlimited. A salmon farm could produce a million fish a year, or ten million, according to its size and the ability of its owners to sell the fish. But with the eel, the inability of biologists and geneticists to devise a way of rearing infants artificially continues to impose an absolute dependence on supplies from the wild.

For the best part of a century the eel farms of Japan were sustained by glass eel of Japan's own species, *A. japonica*, caught in Japan's own rivers. But as demand from the *kabayaki* restaurants mushroomed, the farmers found they could not lay their hands on enough native glass eels. Initially the shortfall was covered by supplies of European glass eels flown direct to Tokyo and grown on in Japanese farms. But there were problems. The European glass eels wanted cooler water than their Japanese cousins and died if they didn't get it. Moreover they brought with them an unpleasant infection called Red Spot disease, which they could tolerate but *A. japonica* could not. After a series of major fish-kills the import of live glass eels was banned.

But the Japanese hunger for eel fillets thrice dipped in soy sauce and thrice grilled was as ravenous as ever, and fish-farmers in Continental Europe – particularly Holland and Denmark – sensed a golden opportunity. They had access to as many glass eels as they wanted close to home. All they had to do was to duplicate the Japanese pond system, feed them up to the required size for *kabayaki*, air-freight them to Tokyo and count the cash rolling in. Unfortunately for them, the same opportunity was spotted rather closer to the market. China, with a centuries-old tradition of fish culture, a vast network of small fish farms, much lower labour costs, and no scruples at all about making use of an alien species, began hunting for European glass eels.

This sudden quickening of interest had a predictable effect. Prices rose, strongly, then dizzyingly. Within a few years glass-eel fishing – traditionally a casual, seasonal, marginal activity – was electrified by the current of incoming cash. Families which for generations had dipped their nets when the elvers ran and when the mood was on them and when they had someone to buy them were fishing night and day. Intruders muscled in, and unpleasantness would break out. Middlemen descended, offering to organise the collection and distribution of the fish and negotiate prices. Men of oriental appearance with bulging pockets were encountered on riverbanks at the dead of night in the depths of winter offering incredible sums of money to anyone who would sell them glass eels.

This boom was milked most energetically on the west coast of France. The first pulses of the arriving infant eels reach Portugal in the late summer. They infiltrate the rivers of northern Spain and the Basque country in autumn. By Christmas the first influx is reported in the Adour, the chief fishery in the extreme south-west of France. Early in the New Year the fishermen of the Loire and the other major rivers of the western seaboard make ready. The season can last until the end of April. By then the northerly impetus of the immigration is faltering, although it is sufficient to deliver successive waves of elvers into the Severn estuary in south-west England, where the fishing starts with the spring tides of March and continues to the end of May.

The method employed by the baby eels is simple and pre-dictable, which makes intercepting them a straightforward business. They ride the tides, coming in on the flow, dropping down to hug the bottom as the ebb gathers force. The higher the tide, the further upstream it propels the fish and the more of them seek to come aboard. It is no coincidence that the two most productive elver rivers in Europe – the Loire in France, and the Severn, which divides England and Wales – are the two with the greatest tidal displacement.

The elvers prefer to travel by night, favouring routes close to the banks, where the power of the ebb tide is weakest and places of refuge are easily found. The time-honoured way to catch them was to take up position at a point contiguous to the route, submerge a large hand-held net every few minutes, taking fish until that pulse of incomers had spent itself; and that is still the way in Portugal and on the Severn. But French fishermen worked out that a boat equipped with fine-mesh nets could, by sweeping up from behind or bearing down from above, harvest a far greater proportion of each intake. The French technique brutally repudiates the romance of the lone elverman with his net, his lamp, his stool, dipping into the flow, a dark shape against the shifting greys and dull silvers of the current. It is also far more harmful to the fish, which suffer severe stress and damage when pressed for any length of time against a rigid mesh. But it is – or appears to be – vastly more efficient, in the corrupt sense that it makes possible the removal of a much greater share of the aggregate, thereby producing the profits needed to pay for the boats and equipment. The *As de Coeur*, Bruno told Thomas Nielsen and me, had cost him more than £100,000.

We went downstream, against the tide, a salty breeze in

our faces. It was a mild enough night, if – for me – a rather smelly one. I wondered what it must be like in bitter January, with the wind whipping like a knife out the blackness, the water thickening into grue in the mesh of the nets, ice on the decks, numbed fingers fumbling at knots. We moved in close to the northern bank. Bruno lowered one of the two nets, which were supported at either side of the boat by frames resembling rugby posts. We followed the bank. Occasionally another boat passed, a green or red light wobbling in her rigging, offering a comradely belch on her hooter as she went.

After ten minutes or so Bruno stopped the boat, detached the tail from the net and dragged it dripping onto the deck. He had placed a yellow plastic box beneath the deck light, with a flat, rectangular sieve on top, into which he tipped the contents of the net. With a stick he spread the haul across the mesh of the sieve. The baby eels, impossibly small and delicate threads of life, squirmed through the ball of green weed. As they wriggled they found their way through the holes in the sieve and dropped into the box, leaving behind the weed, some skipping shrimps and little crabs, a few infant mullet, one salmon smolt. Bruno tipped up the box so it rested on one corner, and brushed the eels together. The collection, a double handful or so, frothed as the babies writhed. He tipped it into a tank bubbling with circulating water. A hundred and fifty grams. Pathetic.

In all the nets were plied five times, with and against the running tide. Daylight seeped out of the grey sky. Dawn did not break, but crept in, like old age, bringing a fine rain with it. I stooped to enter the cabin. Bruno, who was not much more than five feet tall, said he had had the floor raised to enable him to see out of the window at the front. On the instrument panel were a radar screen, electronic charts, a depth-finder, two radios – one for the outside world, one for Bruno and his brothers alone – a computer screen and keyboard. Bruno logged on and brought up on the screen a chart of the river mouth with the *As de Coeur* creeping up it. I asked him if it would tell him where the *civelles* – the glass eels – were. He shrugged his shoulders, said something about not needing a computer for that. He clicked the mouse a few times, until suddenly the shape of the Severn estuary appeared. He asked what would happen if he took the *As de Coeur* up there. I told him the Severn elvermen were used to fighting among themselves, God knows what they would do to a Frenchman. But the fishing might be good, he hazarded. One thing was sure, it couldn't be worse than on his river.

Ten years ago it had been so different. Then Bruno could catch the glass eels on every tide, day and night. If they weren't high in the water, he could find them down below. Everyone was making money, and borrowing more money to buy better boats to make more money. No one thought about the fish except as so many francs in the shape of little eels. The notion that this wealth might be finite, that there might ever be a slackening of this flow of liquid gold, does not seem to have flickered across the collective awareness. Everyone was too busy helping themselves.

Now that notion had become a nasty fact. At first it was possible to mask the decline by working harder. But over the past three years the slump had become stark and inescapable. Bruno reached out for explanations and consolations. The river, he said, had been degraded by intensive agriculture upstream. The weather had been terrible. The scale of the runs had always fluctuated, sometimes drastically. But, almost in the next breath, he conceded that bad years had come in twos and threes, and had given way to good years. Now there were only bad years and worse years.

He thought overfishing must be a factor, maybe the main factor; that there must be a case for restricting fishing, even banning it altogether. But he got sixty per cent of his annual income from the glass eels. Without them he would be finished, as would his brothers, as would the fishing community on the lower Sèvre Niortaise. Perhaps, he mused, there would be compensation, from his government, from the EU. Then he might survive, and stay in bed of a morning.

Bruno needed to take two kilograms of fish to cover his costs. That morning, back at the collection depot, he registered 1.4 kg. Of the half dozen fishermen who had been out that morning, his was the second best catch. In the tea room heads were shaken in the haze of caporal smoke. My God, what a season!

Thomas Nielsen deals in glass eels. He moves between suppliers and buyers, smoothing, soothing, fixing, persuading, temporising, extemporising. It is an arduous occupation, requiring an unusual combination of qualities – among which a capacity for hard work and tact are probably the most important. Between November and April Nielsen is at it seven days a week, eighteen hours most days. He represents most of the eel farms in his native Denmark, as well as several in Holland, Sweden and elsewhere in Europe, and a cluster of Chinese buyers based in Hong

Kong. He has an office in his elegant, airy home, built in the Basque style a little way outside Bayonne. But during the season he is rarely there. The nature of the business does not permit him to be a disembodied fax and e-mail presence. Glass eels are precious, delicate creatures. They require tender handling, as do the feelings of those involved in their capture.

This is an extremely murky, volatile little world. At the bottom end are the glass-eel catchers, the men out on the water; above them, the bankside collectors, with the contacts, the local depot, the tanks, the pickup trucks; above them the distributors, with the truck and airline contracts, the big storage centres, the clout. And then – generally at some distance, their influence refined through the dealer – come the buyers, the energy source. Demand and prices fluctuate constantly. In the course of the 2000/2001 season the price per kilo reached over three thousand francs, and fell to less than half that. Buyers hold off, hoping for a slump. Suppliers do the same, hoping for the opposite. Deals are made by word of mouth. Most are honoured, plenty are not. Alliances are made and unmade, backs are stabbed, covered, stabbed again. Friendships become feuds, remembered slights fester into hatreds.

Officialdom hardly impinges at all. Apart from fixing the season, issuing licences, and defining permissible methods, the authorities – whether local, national or supranational – tend to keep away. In France there are supposed to be limits on the size of engines, to restrict the speed of boats and thus curb catches and the damage to the fish. But enforcement is minimal, and there are no quota restrictions on catches. The declared ones are filed away, to be considered by scientists who draw graphs and argue politely among themselves as to whether the fishery constitutes a threat to the species. The undeclared join the declared in being sold to the highest bidder. In the absence of anything resembling a system of regulation, the only dynamics are demand, supply and price.

During the two days I spent with Nielsen, his mobile phone was hardly quiet. Switching effortlessly between English, French, Danish and German, he ducked and dived and dealt and dissembled with the skill of an Olympic fencer. The season was drawing to a close, supplies were elusive and meagre, and the buyers who had waited overlong were becoming anxious. One farm in Denmark wanted a ton, one in Germany half a ton. A consignment dispatched to northern Europe had been short of the contracted eight hundred kilos, and Nielsen wanted to know why. The Chinese were agitating, ringing him at two in the morning to make impossible demands, then backing out when the arrangements were made. Four hundred kilos which he'd been promised and which he'd promised had vanished. He needed to see his chief source, to see what could be done.

Three quarters of the trade in European glass eels is controlled by half a dozen families based in a nondescript but prosperous village in the Basque country of northern Spain, a few miles from San Sebastián. Aguinaga stands on the river Oria, which is famed for the firmness and succulence of the elvers that seek its waters. Along the banks descend wooden ladders, used by generations of *anguleros*, elver catchers. There are more clues to the eelish inclinations of the place along its main street, in the shape of discreet signs decorated with serpentine drawings advertising *angulas* – elvers. There is such a sign outside the premises of Mayoz, one of the eel dynasties. On Saturdays whichever of the Mayoz brothers are in town sit down in the local bar to play cards with their rivals. The rest of the time they do battle.

Aguinaga owes its pre-eminence as much to geography as to the acumen of its eel barons. It is handily placed to take deliveries from Portugal, northern Spain and coastal France, to sort the baby eels, package them, and send them on their way. Mayoz have another facility a few miles away with tanks in which the fish can be kept alive and healthy for several weeks. Consignments for the European market are transported by truck, the glass eels in stacks of polystyrene boxes kept cool and damp by dripping ice. Those for the Far East are sent by truck to Paris, then air-freighted to Hong Kong or Shanghai. Nielsen loads the orders he is responsible for himself. If more than five per cent die in transit his commission suffers accordingly.

On the wall inside the Mayoz distribution centre in Aguinaga is a relic of the old days – a round elver net with an immensely long handle of ash. And they still talk of the old days: how, when the border with France was rigorously checked, they would send the women of the village over on foot, to return in the evening with bags of eels strapped to their waists beneath their skirts, making sure they dropped a bag or two at the frontier to keep the customs men blind to these damp, transitory pregnancies; how, in one night, they handled twenty-five tons of glass eels, and eight hundred in the season. Now, the old net is for adornment only, and the trucks are able to thunder back and forth without impediment, and the romance has departed – along with most of the eels.

Fortunately for the brothers Mayoz and the small army of sons, daughters, in-laws, nephews, nieces and cousins who work for the business, they have been thrown a lifeline which does not depend on the dynamics affecting populations of baby eels. It takes the form of a gleaming, clanking, hissing stainless steel production line, superintended by men in white uniforms, hats and gloves. In a giant vat at one end, a block of frozen, pulped pollack from the north Pacific is thawed, mixed with black squid ink, and pounded into a grey sludge. This is fed into a chamber and extruded from the other end in a blizzard of authentically pigmented ersatz elvers, lacking only the black eyes that are added in the next tunnel. At the end of the line, popping out with rhythmic regularity, come the four-hundred-gram boxes, frozen and ready for delivery to shops, supermarkets and restaurants.

Mayoz produce one and a half tons of the fake elvers a day. Marketed as 'Mayulas', they are denounced by self-proclaimed defenders of Basque cuisine. I found them distinctly fishy – even, with a little imagination, eely. I have no idea how they compare with the genuine article, and with a couple of mouthfuls of true *angulas* retailing at about fifty dollars, I had no great inclination to find out.

The production system was devised by a team of Japanese scientists, and originally installed by one of the other eel clans of Aguinaga, prescient enough to see the crisis of natural stocks coming. Their competitors mocked at first, then fell over each other in their haste to embrace the new technology. The originators sued for breach of copyright and won. Mayoz found themselves defending a court action, their lawyers arguing that the addition of the black eyes – by a means too secret to be revealed to Thomas Nielsen or myself – amounted to the creation of a new process.

Nielsen's perspective on the business that sustains his modestly affluent way of life is deeply ambivalent. He views the rampant commercialism that is its outstanding characteristic with distaste, most forcibly expressed when discussing the highly mechanised French fishery. He says contemptuously of the fishermen of the Loire – whose use of deep nets and powerful boats inflicts exceptional stress and injury to the fish – that 'they think of the eels just as merchandise, swimming money'. And he is troubled by his part in the business of exploiting a creature that continues to fascinate him. He is intensely nostalgic for the departed era, when the exploitation of this fragile resource was small-scale, harmless and uncontaminated by greed. Nielsen collects old eel spears and hangs them on his walls. A man could plunge one of these quaint implements down on the eels every day of his life and do no damage to the species, while helping to feed himself and his family and keeping alive that old, innocent way of living.

He is deeply pessimistic about the future. The total European catch of glass eels for 2000/2001 – excluding England – was no more than a hundred and fifty tons, compared with two hundred and fifty tons the previous year, which itself was reckoned a disaster. 'The eel is condemned, like the sturgeon,' he told me. He believes the spread throughout Europe's wild stocks of a parasite, *Anguillicola crassus* – which originated in Japan and attacks the swimbladder, affecting the ability to maintain swimming – is likely to complete the process initiated by gross commercial overfishing.

For some time Nielsen had been investigating and cultivating alternative sources of supply. As soon as the European season was over, he was in Maine, arranging deliveries of American elvers for his eager customers. A more embryonic possibility was revealed to me in his garage: a tank constructed by Nielsen himself in which swarmed a host of infant eels even smaller than the ones I had seen in Bruno's nets. They were, he explained, the offspring of the east African freshwater eel, *A. mossambica*. They had been caught in the rivers of Madagascar, in handnets plied by women, and brought back by one of the Mayoz nephews, who told Nielsen that they thronged the estuaries in unimaginable quantities. Now he was waiting to see how they developed, whether they would make acceptable *kabayaki*. I had a brief vision of Nielsen, cool and calm in the heavy heat of the tropical night, making deals with the elverwomen of Madagascar.

The name, the Bore, comes from the Anglo-Saxon 'barra', the wave. In Elizabethan times it was called the Hygre or Eagre, and Shakespeare's friend, Michael Drayton, celebrated this wonder of the west in hyperbolic fashion:

> . . . afar as from the main it comes with hideous cry
> And on the angry front the curling foam doth bring
> The billows 'gainst the banks when fiercely it doth fling;
> Hurls up the slimy ooze and makes the scaly brood
> Leap madding to the land affrighted from the flood;

> O'erturns the toiling barge, whose steersman
>   doth not launch
> And thrust the furrowing beak into her ireful paunch.

Although the reality falls somewhat short of Drayton's apocalyptic vision, the Severn Bore remains – in a land short of natural marvels – a remarkable and impressive phenomenon. At its height, around the spring and autumn equinoxes, it produces a tide of over thirty feet and a wall of water which charges upstream at the speed of a fresh horse at the canter. But it takes time for the Hygre to gather itself. Above Beachey, which is well upstream from the two Severn bridges, the river broadens into an irregular sausage shape, tapers at Sharpness, opens out again at Frampton, before narrowing decisively as it passes by Hock Cliff and Arlingham. It is not until the incoming tide has been subjected to this progressive squeezing that it acquires its urgency. The flood sweeps around the loop enclosing Arlingham, devours Pimlico Sands, bursting in a great whirlpool at Framilode. Onwards it rushes, with a roar that is heard a mile away. At Epney the wave is big enough to surf. At Stonebench, twelve miles further up, the wave is nine feet high. A big tide will cover the forty miles between Sharpness and Tewkesbury in two and a half hours. In exceptional circumstances the Bore has reached Worcester, sixty-six miles from the sea, on occasions bringing exotic visitors with it. William Daniel – an early nineteenth-century parson whose passion for hunting, coursing and wildfowling, in the words of the *Dictionary of National Biography*, 'shocked even his tolerant age' – recorded in his book *Rural Sports* that a man bathing near Worcester was gored to death by a swordfish.

One may have doubts about the swordfish. But there are reliable accounts of other marine oddities drawn in by the pull of the Severn's tide. In the Middle Ages Bath Abbey received – or at least was due – half a dozen Severn porpoises a year. As recently as the late 1930s a school of dolphins penetrated up to Minsterworth, but could not find their way back and perished. In 1620 John Smyth, steward at Berkeley Castle, witnessed the capture of a '22 foot young whale or Jubertas'. It was somehow manoeuvred onto a cart, which required thirty-five yoke of oxen to pull it, and 'the fish yielded an oil then saide and still believed to be very soveraigne and medicinable for aches etc.' Among the fifty-three Severn fishes listed by Smyth were such curiosities as 'the hogge, barne, Roncote, horncake, huswife, and quaver'; and – not so curious – 'a fauzon or great fat eel'.

The most celebrated Severn fish was that strange and primitive monster of fresh and saltwater, the sturgeon. The Severn was England's most notable sturgeon river, and they have been captured up to ten feet in length and two hundred and forty pounds in weight (big enough, but in sturgeon terms a pygmy – I have seen a photograph of one dragged from the mighty Dnieper in Russia which was estimated at 3,400 pounds, a ton and a half). The sturgeon was (and still would be, were any left) royal property. However, because of the difficulties in transporting them to court before decomposition set in, the kings and queens were generally content to grant the privilege of disposing of them to local worthies such as the Abbot of Gloucester or the current Lord of Berkeley.

Lampreys were another matter, for no delicacy has

aroused such passionate greed among the monarchs of England than this unsightly parasite. As we have seen, Henry I's death was popularly ascribed to guzzling lampreys (although they may have been eels). His great-grandson, John, fined the people of Gloucester twelve pounds, thirteen shillings and fourpence for failing to provide him with enough Severn lampreys. And his son, Henry III, attempted to impose a price ceiling of two shillings per lamprey, ordering his sheriff to 'bake for him all the lampreys he can get and send them by his cook. And that when he shall be nearer Severn, then send them unbaked so long as they may come sweet, for him and his Queen to eat.'

But for the fishermen of the Severn, it was first and foremost a salmon river and an eel river. The salmon were netted the length of the estuary and as far upstream as Worcester; in 1863 it was estimated that more than eleven thousand putts – fixed wicker salmon traps – were being operated along the tidal section. As a consequence, the Severn was never other than mediocre for salmon angling. And now, for reasons beyond the scope of this book, the numbers are so pitiful that hardly anyone – netsman or angler – bothers any more. Eels were netted, trapped in wicker baskets, speared, hooked out by crooks called stickers, even tweaked out of their winter quarters with eight-foot-long tongs. Unlike the salmon, the eels are still there, and a certain amount of fishing for the adults still goes on.

But the prodigy of the Severn was and is its elver run. For the baby eels drifting north from the Bay of Biscay past Brest towards Ireland, this immense funnel held out at the Irish Sea exercises an irresistible pull. Once sucked in, they find themselves being carried along on a transport system unmatched in Europe, capable of delivering them – within days – far inland on a river system that extends almost two hundred miles into the hills of Montgomeryshire. As the height of the tides increases, the trickle of nomads swells, becoming a stream within a river. From Lydney by Frampton, Newnham, Elton, Framilode, Epney, Bollow, Minsterworth, and Elmore to Gloucester, and beyond, past Maisemore and Ashleworth, to Tewkesbury, the elver fishers make ready at the vantage points used by their ancestors to dip their nets into the swimming harvest.

The Severn tide is one hour reaching its height, and eleven hours on the ebb. For the elvermen, the call to arms comes after the high point of the night tide. The Bore has raced through, with its mass of water behind. The charge ceases. For five minutes the river is as still as a duck pond, the driftwood motionless. Then there is a sort of tremor, and within five minutes full retreat is sounded. The baby eels, bereft of the force that has carried them so far, are swimming as if for their lives. If they surrender they will be carried back. Their instinct drives them on. Their puny strength is hardly sufficient to sustain progress at all. But for an hour or two they strive to advance, and the nets take their toll, until the ebb becomes too much for them and they descend to hug the bottom, seeking sanctuary. The fishing ceases, until the next night.

The first Severn elverman to emerge by name from history's shadows is one Thomas Pyrry from the village of Blaisdon, a few miles from Gloucester on the northern side. An inventory of his belongings dating from September 1587 includes 'an elver nete' as well as a 'grynston, three chrathes, and other trumphry' (accurately translated as a grindstone, three crates or panniers, and other odds and sods). Thomas was a law-breaker too, an early inheritor of a long and honourable Severn tradition. An act of 1533, signed by Henry VIII, referred sternly to 'the great hurte and dayly inconvenyance unto all the Kyng's subjectes of this Realme by the gredie appetites and insaciable desire of theym . . . by taking, kyllyng and destroying the yonge spaune, frie or brode of yeles and salmon'; and outlawed the taking of 'any frye, spaune or brode of yeles called yele fares or ell vares'.

This legislation reflected one of the guiding principles of fishery management through the ages, that to catch and eat fish in their infancy was to undermine God's purpose in putting them there. The elvermen, had they ever been called on to state their case, would probably have argued that, by providing baby eels in quantities so far in excess of the river's ability to sustain them, God must clearly have had an additional purpose in mind. Nevertheless, the prohibition was renewed in 1558, and again in 1677. A century after that it was relaxed to permit elvers to be taken, but not sold. But a century after that – as a consequence of new laws designed to curb the slaughter of salmon parr and smolts – the elvermen became outlaws again.

Not that they paid a great deal of attention. Between 1874 and 1876 thirty-six men were brought before the magistrates in Gloucester to face charges of illegal fishing. The first three had the case against them dismissed after their solicitor argued ingeniously that the legislation did not apply, because no one had ever proved that elvers were the fry of eels. For the next prosecution the authorities enlisted the help of England's greatest fish expert, Frank Buckland, who testified that elvers were indeed eel progeny. Four men were convicted and fined a shilling each. Feelings began to run high, as the elvermen protested that their ancient rights were being trampled upon. The local newspaper reported that large gangs of Gloucestershire men were out on the river at night, determined to 'set the law at defiance'. One elverman, William Worrall, was fined twenty-seven shillings, and when he refused to pay was put upon the treadmill at Gloucester Prison 'every day for fourteen days'. The fishermen found a person of education and breeding to champion their cause, John George Francillon, a retired naval commander. He petitioned Parliament, an enquiry was ordered, and its result was the Elver Act of 1876 by which a curious, picturesque and generally harmless local speciality finally achieved legitimacy.

Traditionally, elvers were eaten by Severnsiders and not many others. At Epney they liked them fried in bacon fat, then mixed with cider and made into an omelette. Otherwise they were usually fried like whitebait or flavoured with onion and herbs and pressed into cakes or cheeses. However, according to the Severn historian Brian Waters, the enthusiasm for them was geographically limited, and five miles from the river they were almost impossible to sell.

A generation after the successful conclusion of Commander Francillon's crusade, a new market appeared. In 1908 a delegation of fishmongers and fishery owners from Hamburg arrived in Gloucester. They had heard of the extraordinary scale of the Severn elver run, and wished to obtain supplies with which to supplement the stocks in German rivers and lakes which were insufficient to meet demand for eel. They were given permission to establish a depot at Epney, behind the Anchor Inn, from where the babies were shipped live back to Hamburg. It was an unusual trading link, but evidently a profitable one, for the depot was still flourishing in 1939, when the Ministry of Agriculture took possession of it and sent the Germans home on the grounds that it was no longer appropriate for British eels to feed Nazi stomachs. Three tons of elvers were dispatched that spring, the elvermen receiving a shilling a pound.

After the war the depot was sold to a consortium of Billingsgate eel merchants. Elvers were exported by land and sea to Holland and Denmark, and on at least one occasion a Russian transport plane removed several tons to Poland. The operation expanded in the 1960s after the depot was bought by an Austrian company, the principal export market being the restaurants of Spain and Portugal. The arrival of Japanese buyers in the 1970s stimulated a brief, heady period of rocketing prices, which encouraged the setting up of a rival collection centre a few miles downriver. When Japan banned imports of live elvers, prices collapsed, and the premises behind the Anchor were taken over by an Englishman, Peter Wood.

Twenty-five years later, Wood's business, UK Glass Eels, dominates the English elver trade, and has a strong presence in France. Wood pioneered the air-freight of live elvers, maintaining his own aircraft for conveying them around Europe and a long-haul contract for dispatching them to the Far East. His English distribution base is now on the outskirts of Gloucester, and the Epney station lies derelict.

Economically, Severn elver fishing has been absorbed into the global trade. With fish fetching anything from a hundred and fifty pounds a kilo to double that, the savour of elvers frying in bacon fat is rarely met these days. Commercial imperatives have made it a hard-nosed affair, unleashing fierce competition between fishermen that has on occasions spilled over into outright violence when intruders have strayed onto Severnsiders' territory. In short, the catch is a commodity attended by much the same dull and mean realities as any other. It is a relief to turn away from the trade to the river, to the catching of the fish.

The Severn runs by Jim Milne's house, and he shares in its moods and rhythms. Yet he is an outsider. He came from south-east London, between Bromley and Lewisham, not far from Catford and Penge; and after sixty years on the river his voice has nothing of Gloucestershire in it. His flat tones belong to faraway suburbia. The activity which, at eighty plus, remains his passion is elverin': three even syllables delivered uncadenced, the final consonant amputated in a Londoner's way.

Although Jim Milne could not be taken for a Severnsider born and bred, he is, through every fibre of his being, a Severn man. He was first introduced to its ways as a lad, by his cousin Anselme, whose family farmed at Water End on the south bank. From the start Jim learned to see the river as a provider rather than a playground. He learned to sweep the salmon-holding waters with the long net, and he dabbled with the art of the lave-net, in which the fisherman, with a Y-shaped handnet held before him, wades at speed across the sands in pursuit of the loom of a fleeing salmon. He learned wildfowling, sitting motionless in a punt at winter's dusk or dawn, waiting for the ducks and geese to flight, wondering if the marrow in his bones would freeze first. He learned to pat for eels, threading worms and worsted into a ball to snag the teeth of the slimy foragers of the mudbanks. But always it was the elverin' which moved Jim Milne most powerfully.

To this day the Severn elverman uses a handnet, and no other way is permitted. To the casual observer it seems a laborious and quaint method, yet there is sound sense in its anachronistic nature. For all that it has survived a three-thousand-mile journey across a vast, turbulent ocean, this little fish is easily hurt. Pressed for any length of time against a moving net – as is the case with the French trawlers – it loses its translucence and goes milky, and can easily die.

But the Severn net is benign. It is shaped like a cradle with a handle anything from five to nine feet long, fixed through a headboard at the nearer, slightly narrower end. In the old days the handle was of willow or ash, the headboard of elm, the net frame of withy, and the side strainers, which kept the cheesecloth netting taut, of briar. Those charming but perishable materials have generally been replaced by alloys and nylon, but the manner of the fishing is wholly unchanged. The elverman, encumbered with net, bucket, lamp and two sticks of peculiar design, positions himself (or herself, for there have been a few notably fierce and energetic elverwomen) at the chosen spot, known as a tump. In the old days everyone knew whose tump was whose. They were for life, and were handed down from one generation to the next, and woe betide anyone who failed to respect the unwritten code. Inevitably, the increasing commercialisation of elvering lured those who knew nothing of any code and cared less, and had to be taught – sometimes forcibly – that Severnsiders did not give up their tumps lightly.

The ideal tump is a knob of ground with the current right up against it and slack water behind. As the ebb sets in, and the elvers contend against the flow, the fisherman goes to work in earnest. At times of plenty he would dip the net every few minutes, standing and holding it. These days it is more customary to use the two sticks to fix the net at the desired angle against the stream and leave it for a while, a practice known as tealing.

All this Jim Milne learned, and a great deal more besides. After the war he and his wife Ruth moved to Cheltenham, where Jim worked as a commercial artist. His expertise with an airbrush enabled him to achieve photographic verisimilitude – he showed me an illustration of an office which he had done, and which I took to be a photograph until he disclosed with sly pleasure that he had painted in a typewriter at the request of the commissioning company. Jim was much valued for his uncanny precision, which was as well, considering the demands on his time from his other life. During the elver season, March to May, he drew and painted at his place of work by day, and fished by night, a fifteen-mile bicycle ride away. 'I didn't sleep much,' he replied when I asked how he managed.

The beauty of elverin' was that it was a paying passion. As an outsider, comparatively unburdened by the weight of convention, Jim approached it in an unusually flexible way.

It was the custom that a Severnsider always fished the same tumps, never straying far from home. But Jim was ambitious. He analysed the tides and the way the elvers used them, and realised that the influx was progressive. A twenty-foot tide brought the main body of fish up to Epney. On succeeding nights, the height increased and the tide penetrated further, driving the fish onward. At its zenith, the Bore swept over the weir at Tewkesbury, ten miles above Gloucester. Little by little, careful not to tread on toes, Jim extended his range so that he could keep up with the fish.

He became well known for his methods, and for the scale of his catches. In the 1950s, with the help of various partners, he averaged a ton of elvers a year. Sold to the depot at Epney, to the MacFisheries chain of fishmongers, and by the pint from a bath at his front door, they brought in three hundred pounds a year, no mean sum. For a time in the 1960s and 1970s he was involved in running the Epney depot, but later he returned to the fishing he loved. The Japanese came and went, and the Austrians, prices rose, fell, rose again, elvermen came and went. But Jim Milne – by now resident by the river with two good tumps at the front and the sound of the water with him waking and sleeping – carried on, like a feature of the landscape.

I talked to Jim about his life and times one April morning, with the Severn – still swollen from the rains of the wettest winter he or anyone else could recall – rolling by. He walked slowly, with some difficulty, and – while perfectly hale – looked his eighty years. Assuming thoughtlessly that he had retired and that the best I could hope for was a useful dose of ancient history, I asked him if he missed the fishing. He was puzzled for a moment, then corrected me: 'Oh no, I'm still elverin'. I was out at last night and I'll be out again tonight.' He took me to a little shed. There was a bucket on the floor, its bottom obscured by a seething mass of baby eels. 'We had 'em last night, not bad, a couple of hundred quid's worth.'

I had to come back that night, of course. I found Jim ready for action. He had a lamp fixed by elastic on the top of his head, giving him something of the air of a coal miner. His ruddy face and spectacles were framed by a blue woollen helmet. Over a thick jersey he wore a short coat, its stains strongly evocative of its hunting history. He was pacing around in his gumboots, impatient to be at it, but we had to wait for the tide to start ebbing, and for the arrival of Jim's partner, a retired army officer called Peter Kavanagh. At length he turned up, exuding military briskness, and revealed himself to be in the grip of an elver obsession quite as potent as his venerable partner's. 'My daughters call me the Severn Bore,' Kavanagh confessed. 'My wife says I used to be good company, but she complains that, as a result of too much of this, I have become silent and lacking in conversation.'

We ate cake and drank tea in the warm, cluttered kitchen, while outside the river prepared to go back on itself. Then we left the lights of the house behind us. The river was a broad band, gleaming dully under a broken sky, the surface darkened where the cloud was dark, with black blotches of drifting wood. The water sucked quietly at the stems of the reed mace along the bank. From the far bank came a sound like that of a distant waterfall. It was the water draining back into the river from the low fields that the tide had covered an hour before. Peter Kavanagh's tump came into view first. He laid his net facing downstream. When he lifted it the beam from his lamp picked out the pale threads squirming against the mesh.

It was time for Jim Milne to start fishing. I went with him down to his tump, a classic bulge of reedy turf with a little eddy behind. He moved as slowly as a tortoise, placing each boot with great deliberation on the downward-sloping slick of mud. He told me that, not long before when fishing alone, he had been unable to get back up the bank. Ruth was asleep, unable to hear his cries, and there was no one else about, so he had sat quietly until daybreak, watching the water pass.

At last he was ready, secure on his stool, net at hand, bucket and tealing sticks within reach. I asked him why, at his age, he preferred to be here rather than in bed. It was a foolish question, but he answered it thoughtfully. He said that he could not imagine not doing it, that he wanted to show – himself, mostly, I guessed – that he could still do it. The money was a factor, the fact that he was earning. He said that three years before they had made twenty thousand pounds in the season. He lifted the net with an easy swing, tilting it towards the bucket. He had placed a sieve over the bucket with a mesh just big enough to allow the elvers through, while denying entry to weed, other little fish and river rubbish. The catch was meagre, but he was careful that nothing should escape. 'Look, there's two there, they're worth five pee each,' he said as he shook the reluctant loiterers out. And this from a man who'd once taken three hundredweight in a single night, fifty pounds of them – not far off one hundred thousand fish – with one dip of the net.

Tonight there was no more than a trickle coming through. Jim was convinced that the main pulse had gone up past Gloucester. Normally he would have gone after them, to fish from a couple of good tumps he rented from farmers between Gloucester and Tewkesbury. But the foot-and-mouth epidemic was on the land, and most of the best spots were out of bounds. He was fortunate to be able to fish from his front garden – although perhaps fortunate is not the word, as with Jim Milne and his elverin', matters were as finely calculated as the strokes from his celebrated airbrush.

I left him by the water, hunched and still. This was something far removed from sport, this uneventful vigil punctuated by regular and repetitive lifting and lowering of a net. It was something more elemental, beyond my understanding. For sixty years this old man had done this, whatever the weather. Nature delivered, he accepted: that was the contract. In the simplicity of that arrangement, considerations of comfort, physical weakness, the convention that our species rests at night, were irrelevant. For Jim Milne, the nights of spring – when the cycle of the year brought the baby eels in from the sea, and the cycle of the moon and its magnetic pull sent them up his river – were not meant for rest. They were meant for elverin', and would be while those old legs could still carry him down to his tump.

TEN

Sweet Thames

It is hard to imagine anyone going to Erith on a whim. The guidebooks of a hundred years ago allow it a touch of Kentish rusticity, derived from a strip of market gardens and orchards to the south. But to the visitor of today, whatever charms it may once have possessed have been submerged without trace in the sprawl of flats and shopping centres and car parks and supermarkets and hideous yellow-brick and stained concrete civic amenities stretching along the south side of the Thames estuary from Dartford up to Plumstead, Woolwich and beyond. The cheerless character of this smear of suburban sameness is magnified by the river that bounds it.

Words such as dismal, desolate, and bleak do not begin

to do justice to the river scene which greeted me on a Saturday morning towards the end of October. A bitter little wind blew towards the sea, carrying a mist of chilly droplets. The view was framed to the east by the curve of the Dartford Bridge, with the bulk of Littlebrook power station puffing threateningly at its side. On the far side of the river a dome was being created, Erith's version of the notorious symbol of national pride (or shame) gleaming like a huge silver jellyfish up at Greenwich. 'That's Europe's biggest rubbish tip,' said the man I had come to see, with ironic satisfaction. Lorries ground up and down it like worker ants, disturbing multitudes of squabbling, screeching gulls.

A little way upstream from Europe's biggest rubbish tip was one of Europe's biggest plants for processing oil seed rape, kept company by another monster, spewing forth Uncle Ben's Rice. Were anyone minded to continue an excursion inland along the northern bank, they would come next to an industrial complex extending away as far as the eye can see – Ford's Dagenham assembly plant, a strife-torn and doomed kingdom of the motor car whose partial closure was announced a month or so later. Facing it across the water was a brutal agglomeration of concrete in which human excrement was being treated with fire and turned into fertiliser, which is surely better than dumping it in the river as in times past, but is not a picturesque activity. At the base of the shit-burning plant foamed a hot water outlet, over which flapped another flock of gulls, dipping their beaks at something on the surface.

Everywhere, littered along both banks, were the relics of the estuary's maritime past: black greasy wharves looming high, with rusting ladders and slimy staircases leading to the water and metal pustules on top to take the hawsers and ropes; little piers on weedy wooden frames poking out over the mud; wooden barges tilting at defeated angles, keels deep in the ooze, sides gaping with timbers sprung like broken ribs; derelict tugs and steamers, streaked and spotted with rust. The scene seemed frozen, seized by a silent paralysis. It was like a theatre set suddenly abandoned. The audiences had stopped coming, the money had run out, the cast had dispersed, and the creditors had decided it was not even worth collecting the props.

As instructed, I found a pub called The Running Horses, and parked my car beside one of those gardens beloved of local authorities, cluttered with hard benches and patches of scrawny grass and dabs of bark decorated with depressing evergreen shrubs bearing blotchy berries. On the river side of the road extended a long wall, with a 'walkway' beyond it, and more hard benches, on which one might sit and survey Europe's largest rubbish tip and other attractions. Along the foot of the wall was a broad band of grey mud, furrowed by little channels, pitted with mysterious holes, a resting place for supermarket trolleys, road cones, steering wheels and the odd hubcap; from which issued forth strange sucking noises, distinctly audible over the distant noise of traffic. The Erith Causeway extended across the mud to the distant water. There was a sign on it warning users – perhaps superfluously – of the dangers of falling off the side. The chances of anyone witnessing such a mischance – let alone effecting a rescue – seemed remote. The place seemed as lively as the moon.

But then I detected movement at the end of the causeway. There was a boat which, unlike most of the visible craft, was afloat. In it, bending to his business, was a man in yellow chest waders. This was Dave Pearce. The boat – the *Ada*, eighteen feet of severely utilitarian fibreglass built around a thumping diesel engine – was his, and this godforsaken riverworld was his, too.

Pearce is a fisherman, which in his case means rather more than that he catches and sells fish. The water of the estuary is as much part of his being as the blood in his veins. And it is more his element than the land at its edge. For as long as he can remember he has fished, and he is as familiar with the dynamics of life beneath the surface as a skilled surgeon with a patient's physiology.

He lives in Gravesend, keeps a trawler at Southend, and occasionally accompanies his uncle out of Ramsgate, so is pretty well acquainted with the waters hereabouts. He makes a living, just about, helped by a regular slot sitting underneath the skeleton of a new bridge over the river, watching for suicides (so far, Pearce told me, he'd rescued two hats and a pair of goggles). He catches anything that swims and can be sold – sole, bass, mullet, cod, whiting, sprats. But he likes eels best.

Generations back, Pearce's family fished out of Erith. They were driven away by the transformation of the Thames from river to sewer. Between 1800 and 1880 London's population rose from fewer than a million to almost five million. The city's waste was simply poured untreated into the Thames – not just sewage, but all the filth from slaughterhouses, tanneries, breweries, gas-works and a thousand and one other dirty businesses. Although pipes were laid in the mid-nineteenth century to take some of the muck downriver to outflows at Beckton and Crossness, it was still untreated, and huge rafts of suspended faeces were regularly pushed back up the river by the tides, wafting a fearsome stench across the city and on one famous occasion compelling Parliament to suspend a sitting.

Life in the river was extinguished by lack of oxygen. First the runs of salmon ceased. The smelt, lamprey and whitebait fisheries were wiped out. The water ran black, scummy and smelly. A survey in 1914 found very few fish of any kind between Chelsea and Gravesend. By 1950 twenty-five miles of the tidal Thames was entirely devoid of oxygen in the summer months, and biologically defunct.

Although the seaward migration of silver eels and the elver run were obliterated, resident populations of eels did survive away from the worst of the poison. In the 1960s a major programme of sewage treatment was implemented, so thoroughly and successfully that by the early 1970s yellow eels were once again plentiful in the estuary and through London up to Wandsworth. In 1980 the Thames Water Authority and the Port of London began to issue permits for the commercial fishing of eels, with Tower Bridge as the upper limit. For a time catches notified to the licensing authorities totalled ten or eleven tons a year. They are now less than half that, a decline more attributable to waning fishing effort than any scarcity of stocks. A mere handful of licences are now issued, and Dave Pearce maintains he is the only regular eel catcher left.

I hopped aboard the *Ada* and we chugged off in the direction of Europe's biggest rubbish tip. A little way offshore, well out of the main current, Pearce put the engine into neutral and lobbed a grappling hook into the soupy water. Up it came, rope around its prongs, and he began to drag in his line of fyke nets. I was astounded by the catch Pearce heaved aboard. There were eels, though not many, for it was late in the season and they were beginning to lose their appetites and bed down for winter. There were whiting, little cod, little bass, smelt, dabs, flounders, and the odd fat-lipped mullet. There were also prawns, and a scuttling host of crabs, among which the small, dark English specimens were greatly outnumbered by the much bigger mitten crabs, so-called because of the furry down on their claws. These originated in Chinese waters, and having casually hitched a ride aboard a London-bound vessel, dropped off to find matters in the Thames Estuary very much to their liking. They set about eating the puny resident crabs, digging burrows in the bank, and multiplying at a terrific rate.

Pearce sorted the catch, throwing back the undersized stuff. 'My mates say I'm fucking mad, touched,' he said as his powerful hands plucked the mittened pincers from his nets. 'I don't care. It's all I ever wanted to do, go out fishing. I'll tell you a rhyme about eels: "When the daffodils are out, the eels are about." I like 'em because they're always here. It's just a matter of finding them.'

We went upstream, the only boat abroad on the water. I asked him if he wanted for company. 'Nah, I like being on me own. I did have a bloke with me, but I had to get rid of him, we just wasn't making enough. I used to be married, not any more, never again, mate.'

The smell of oilseed blew over us. The Dagenham car works came into view, and Pearce tracked across towards the warm water outflow near the shit-burning plant, where the gulls were scooping up fry. He set his nets close by, in the shadow of an old, gaunt pier. They liked the cover during the day, he said, and then would creep out at night. It was a good place. Mind, they were all good places. There were eels everywhere; you just had to be careful not to fish one place too hard. Pearce told me he had been doing some survey work for the Environment Agency, who'd wanted to know about eel populations higher up. 'So I put the nets down just up from Tower Bridge. Bloody stiff with them they were, I could hardly get the nets out of the water for eels. Fuckin' amazin'. I brought my uncle Billy up here one day. When he was a lad there was no eels here, no fish at all, and the water was black. He couldn't bloody well believe what I was catching.'

We came back downstream, past the deserted wharves and a score of derelict barges. It was sad to think of the life departed from what had been, for the best part of a thousand years, the busiest waterway in the world. Pearce pointed out Dartford salt marsh, a dreary expanse of scrubby grass between the mouth of the River Darent and the power station, cherished by students of prehistory on account of its display of five-thousand-year-old tree stumps, which stood out on the shore like blackened teeth. We stopped close to an assembly of water craft of all types, shapes and sizes, in all conditions between spanking new and terminal decay – a place which combined the roles of marina and maritime burial ground, in the middle of which, resting on a muddy eminence well away from the water, was a gaily painted wooden boat with a banner identifying her as the headquarters of the Erith Yachting Club. Visions of men in blazers and white flannels, sipping cocktails and discussing the merits of their sloops and catamarans, sat uneasily with this scene of disorder. Pearce keeps the *Ada* moored here, and periodically works in the yard, building new boats. I asked about the yacht club. 'Yeah, well it's not Cowes. They're a bunch of scallywags.'

He lifted the last fleet of nets, sorting the eels big enough to sell into a dustbin, throwing everything else back, most of it alive. When he first began fishing for eels, ten years back, he'd got £2.50 a pound for them. Now the price was down to £1.50 and the competition had withered away, along with the market. Pearce had a regular buyer, who took a hundred pounds a week for jellying. Any more than that, and he had the aggravation of trying to sell them at Billingsgate; an exercise which, given the notorious blunt-speaking of the merchants there, Pearce regarded as being more trouble than it was worth.

The eels slithered audibly in the dustbin, generating a thick froth. Their backs were greenish, like onyx, their flanks buttery, their stomachs pearly. Dave Pearce says his eels are much handsomer than the blacker ones found upriver, or the still darker ones occasionally washed out of the marshes and down the Darent. He left the catch – about thirty-five pounds of good-looking estuary eels – in a sunken, perforated tank, ready for transport in a few days, and deposited me back on the causeway. After four hours out on the water I was shaking with the cold. I wondered what would make a man choose a life like that. Pearce had said to me: 'When your hobby's your job, you've got it made.' That was as close to an answer as I was going to get.

Dave Pearce is the latest, perhaps the last, in a long line. One of his predecessors is depicted in a splendid print dating from around 1800, called *Eel Bobbing at Battersea*. An old woman is sitting in a boat held in position a yard or two from the bank of the Thames by a pole driven into the mud. Beyond her, on the far side, standing out against a pale coral sky, rise the spire of a church and a windmill. She has a pipe jammed into her mouth, a round hat on her head, a blanket over her knees, a barrel in the stern. She is grasping a sturdy piece of timber in her horny hands, from the end of which, descending into the calm, oily water is a line. Somewhere beneath is the ball of worsted and worms, and once she feels teeth in it, up it will come, and there will be pie for supper, or perhaps eel in jelly.

Eels have been harvested in the Thames for aeons, probably since our heavy-browed Neanderthal ancestors first shambled down to its banks a hundred thousand years ago. The first documented reference to the fishery is in the Chronicle of Abingdon Abbey, dating from the middle of the eleventh century AD, recording the payment of a hundred eels a year by the people of Oxford in return for leave to dig a navigation channel on church land. The *Domesday Book* listed a total of twenty-two eel fisheries on the Thames, which – calculated for taxation purposes – produced 14,500 eels a year. The eels were speared, netted, bobbed for, caught in baited traps, and intercepted in the V-shaped weirs known as kiddles. According to *Domesday*, Walter of St Valéry paid the State five shillings a year for the right to net the Thames at Hampton. The eel fishery at Taynton – far away up the Windrush – was assessed to be worth sixty-two shillings and sixpence a year. Two hundred years later the accounts prepared by the bailiff on the Cookham estate near Maidenhead show an income of thirty shillings from the sale of eighty 'stikkes' of eels, a stikke being reckoned at twenty-six fish. That conscientious functionary also noted an expenditure of eightpence on willow rods used to make a fish trap, which itself engendered a profit of three and sixpence.

During the Middle Ages many of these lucrative fisheries fell into the hands of the religious houses. An examination of the lavatories used by the Benedictine monks at Westminster Abbey revealed how fond the brothers were of their eels – virtually every sample analysed contained eel bones. The records of Syon Abbey, a few miles upriver, show that in time of Henry VII the nuns derived a substantial part of their income from eel fishing. By the time the old lady of Battersea was pictured at her bobbing, the tradition of small-scale eel fishing had been long established all the way up the river. Hers was one method. Another, also designed with the resident yellow eels in mind, involved the use of baited traps made of wicker, and known on the Thames as grig-wheels ('weel' was an Anglo-Saxon word for trap, and 'grig' a term for eel). The traps were designed with a narrow funnel at one end, in the words of C. J. Cornish – in a sweet little book called *A Naturalist on the Thames* – 'to make the entrance of the eels agreeable and their exit impossible.'

Cornish advised obtaining them from 'that old river hand, Mr Bambridge, at Eton, weighted, stoppered, and ready for use for seven-and-sixpence each.' He quoted the advice of that noted expert: '"For bait nothing can beat about a dozen and a half of small or medium live gudgeon . . . offal I have tried but found useless."'

One of the most charming accounts of the fun the Victorians had from their river is called *The Delightful Life of Pleasure on the Thames*, by James Englefield, a contributor to *The Field* for many years under the pseudonym Red Quill. Between 1864 and 1866 he leased the rights to catch eels from the Maidenhead Corporation, and also secured permission from Sir Roger Palmer at Dorney Court. Englefield would lay his baskets of an evening and raise them early the next morning. 'It was,' he wrote, 'an extra inducement to rise betimes and meet the blushing dawn face to face; indeed I often bathed first, at the White Bucks or Boulter's weirpool, and took the baskets up as I punted back afterwards, and at once emptied the contents into the capacious well of my punt.'

During those three seasons Englefield caught more than four hundred eels. His purpose was to supply his own table – 'they were esteemed a delicacy by my home people' – and his friends. Being a meticulous fellow, he calculated his costs exactly, and found that his eels cost him fifteen and a half pence a pound, whereas he could have bought them at tenpence. He was most particular about his traps, which were made of 'dry, slender withy rods worked into the form of an elongated narrow basket', fifty-six inches long. 'The arched end,' he noted, 'may be described as the entrance hall, the centre as the reception room, and the large body of the basket as the dining room, where the anguillidae meet at supper, quite unconscious that it is the last meal of prisoners doomed to death on the morrow.'

The autumn migration of the silver eels down the Thames presented obvious commercial possibilities. To exploit them, many of the wealthier owners installed formidable and picturesque fixed engines known as eel bucks. These were barrages comprising six or seven wicker baskets, each about ten feet long, with a wide open end facing upstream, and a small chamber to the side of the tapered downstream end, into which the running eels found their way. The bucks were fixed to a wooden stage, the open ends held in grooves so they could be kept raised above the flow, except when the run was on. The eel bucks survived long enough for their charm to be captured in some of Taunt's celebrated Thames photographs, but not by much. In 1902 Cornish reported that 'few perfect sets now remain'. By the time Patrick Chalmers published his celebration of Thames fishing, *At the Tail of the Weir*, in 1932, the only ones left were on Lord Boston's estate at Hedsor near Maidenhead.

Less conspicuous than the bucks were the simple grids similar to that operated today by Roger Castle on the Stour and by eel catchers on the Test, Itchen and other rivers. These were generally found incorporated into mills on tributaries of the Thames rather than on the main river. Cornish visited one on the Thame at Dorchester, where the miller broke off from grinding barley-meal to show the contents of his holding box in the foaming water by the wheel-house. 'Seizing a long pole with prongs like walrus teeth, the miller felt below the water . . . And by a dextrous haul scooped up a monster eel to the floor . . . he had more, some of five pounds weight, which had come down with the floods – an easy and profitable fishery.'

The eel bucks and traps fell into disuse and disrepair for the simple reason that the eels were no longer present in sufficient numbers to make it worth anybody's time and trouble to maintain them. Well before the end of the nineteenth century, the days of the Thames as a significant producer of eels lay in the distant past. As early as the 1860s, the fishermen operating the bucks at Taplow were complaining that catches 'had failed very much in the last thirty or forty years'. Twenty years later the *Dictionary of the Thames* compiled by Charles Dickens' eldest son, also called Charles, reported that 'eels have greatly fallen off in individual size and collective numbers in late years.'

The cause of the decline is not difficult to find. For centuries the start of the annual elver run, or eel-fare, had been the signal for Londoners to roll up their trouser legs and wade forth with muslin nets, sieves and buckets. Edward Jesse had tracked 'one regular and undeviating column, about five inches in breadth and as thick together as it is possible for them to be' as high as Chertsey, thirty miles from Tower Bridge. James Englefield recalled witnessing the eel-fare in Reading when he was at school there in the 1840s. Yet by 1878 Houghton, in his *British Freshwater Fishes*, recorded that 'the eel-fare, once a striking and remarkable sight on the Thames, no longer exists, on account of the filthy water around London.'

The transformation of the Thames, in so short a span of time, from a living river to a conduit for sewage and toxic industrial waste was a biological catastrophe. Apart from its impact on local fishermen, it also signalled the eventual demise of a long, remarkable and now forgotten chapter in the trading history of London.

Holland might have been designed with the eel in mind: Fenland writ large, a land in which water and earth were held in unstable balance, an ideal home. From the time of the earliest settlements, the eel was a dietary staple, and the fish played a central part in the watery way of life that evolved on that immense inland sea, the Zuider Zee. But the Dutch were much more than a race of hardy fisherfolk. They were mariners, too; their seafaring driven more by their shrewd aptitude for trade than by any hunger for the glory of conquest. By the early Middle Ages they were already combining their expertise with eels and their eye for a marketing opportunity to profitable purpose. Using partially sunken canal craft, they transported eels alive back and forth along the North Sea and from the Baltic states to Holland. They had discovered that, when carefully looked after, the fish would tolerate long journeys and prolonged confinement in holding ponds. The eel's nutritious flesh and unique endurance made it ideal for selling in Europe's fastest-growing city, just across the North Sea.

Although the English caught and ate the eel, trading in it was small-scale and, in general, localised. According to Frank Buckland, the supply of live eels to the one great central fish market – at Billingsgate in London – was already largely controlled by the Dutch well before 1412, when the Lord Mayor decreed they should be sold by weight only. The vessels used for transporting and storing them were known as *schuyts*. Bulging with their perforated eel prisons, they became a familiar sight in London, as the companies owning them had been granted the right to anchor off Billingsgate for ease of access. In the late seventeenth century the official concession to supply eels to the market was bestowed by royal decree, partly in acknowledgement of the part played by the masters and crews of the *schuyts* in fighting the Great Fire of 1666 and providing food and shelter for the homeless victims. The main condition of the concession was that there should be at least one ship filled with eels in position at all times.

Yarrell's 1836 *History of British Fishes* records that the business was then in the hands of two Dutch firms, each with five *schuyts*, each vessel able to hold ten tons of eels at a time. Billingsgate records show that in 1861 eight hundred tons of Dutch eels were sold through the market. The combined British and Irish contribution was a mere fifty tons.

A handsome volume called *The Thames from Source to Sea*, published in 1891, contained a colourful description of the *schuyts* written by a journalist and teacher, James Runciman:

> Strange in build, startling in colour, outlandish in rig, their bulging bows are like the breasts of some Titanic women. The low sweep of their bulwark makes it astonishing that they can ever go to sea . . . You hear the sound of wallowing, and when you look into the gulf of the hold you see a strange, weltering mass of snaky-brown things of which the aspect makes an unaccustomed man shudder. Tons of eels welter in these watery caverns, and the landsman sees with astonishment that the sides of the vessel are perforated to allow in the rush of the water, and that each ship is neither more or less than a huge floating sieve.

Much earlier in the nineteenth century, the growing filthiness of the river had forced the *schuyts* downstream from their age-old moorings off Billingsgate – first to Erith, then to Greenhithe, then to Gravesend, where Runciman found them. Soon Gravesend became intolerable too, and Holehaven became the base for Dutch operations. But even here the mortality rate was high, as were the costs of transporting the fish to distant Billingsgate. A trade which had kept Londoners supplied with their favourite fish for six hundred years was on the verge of disappearance because of what Londoners had made of their river.

But one of the eel companies, H. J. Kuijeten, based near Haarlem in the heart of Dutch eel country, was loath to bid farewell to what was still a profitable business. Kuijetens specialised in shifting live fish – carp and tench, as well as eels – throughout western and northern Europe, using a fleet of canal barges. After the Great War, Johan Kuijeten began to concentrate on Baltic eels, landed in Germany and Denmark, and carried by boat and by railway trucks fitted with oxygenated tanks. He still had his eye on England, and was searching for a new distribution centre within easy reach of London.

The full story of Kuijeten and Sons in the Heybridge Basin at Maldon on the Essex coast has been told in a little book called the *History of Maldon and the Tidal Blackwater* by a local historian, Clarrie Devall. The attraction of Heybridge lay in its closeness to London, and in its access to comparatively unpolluted freshwater and seawater. This made its waters thoroughly congenial to eels, enabling them to be kept for weeks on end. Johan Kuijeten began operations there in 1928, using two storage vessels with a combined capacity of forty tons. A little later timber storage barges were brought over from Holland, freeing the other ships to transport supplies.

After the Second World War, Johan's son, Hans, took charge of Heybridge, with day-to-day management in the hands of George Clark, a member of one of the old fishing families known as the Heybridge Basiners. For a time they continued to use the existing storage barges. But with business booming, these proved inadequate, and were replaced by purpose-built steel-plate barges over a hundred feet long, each able to hold thirty-six tons of fish. In normal conditions, by shifting the barges from freshwater to saltwater and back, and using a sophisticated aeration system, it was possible to keep the eels alive for up to five months. This was crucial – it enabled Kuijeten to maintain supplies throughout the winter, when his competitors were generally fishless and prices were at their highest.

His difficulty was not keeping the eels, nor selling them, but getting enough of them. Traditionally, the majority came from Scandinavia and from Holland, where production on the Ijsselmeer – as the Zuider Zee had been renamed after its enclosure in 1932 – had soared in the immediate post-war years. But Kuijeten took eels from anywhere. He had them shipped from Poland, Tunisia and Italy. For a time he tried Greek eels, but most of them died when the ships inadvertently sailed over hot springs. Sources were located in Canada and the United States, although the rigours of the eight-day crossing of the Atlantic were often too much for the cargo. On occasions Kuijeten even resorted to flying in eels from New Zealand and Australia.

His most significant coup – of which more later – was the purchase in the late 1950s of the eel fishery at Toome, where Northern Ireland's biggest river, the Bann, leaves the biggest lake in the British Isles, Lough Neagh. This secured the yellow eels caught on the lough in the summer, and the migrating silver eels taken in traps on the river in autumn – a total of up to eight hundred tons a year. But by the mid 1960s Kuijetens were in trouble. Overfishing of the Ijsselmeer and in Denmark had caused catches to plunge. The Lough Neagh enterprise was dogged by fierce local resistance to foreign control. It had become increasingly difficult to secure casual labour in Maldon, as the old fishermen aged and retired. The devaluation of the pound in 1967 made imports cripplingly expensive. Moreover, as costs rose, demand slumped. A new generation of consumers, seduced by frozen and packaged food, found the slithery eel disagreeable. There was no place within the supermarket ethos for a creature so defective in cosmetic attractions. Many of the old pie 'n' mash shops of London were disappearing, and the appetite for jellied eels contracted as the cockney became a threatened species.

In 1968 a Dutch eel-bearing *schuyt* sailed into the mouth of the Blackwater for the last time. Later that year Kuijeten closed the Heybridge Basin depot, leaving the barges as mute, rusting testimonials to a taste and a way of life that had run their course.

By the time the Dutch connection was severed, the Thames was well on the way to being rehabilitated to the condition of two centuries before, when the *schuyts* bobbed at anchor off Billingsgate with their restless eels within. But the elver run that had so delighted Edward Jesse, and brought the urchins out crying 'eel-fare time', has never been restored to its former glory. It may well be that the species' collective awareness of safe sanctuary up the Thames system was extinguished by the barrier of London's filth, and that the arriving infants were content with the habitat offered by the tidal sections. A study of Thames eel stocks carried out by Iain Naismith in the late 1980s indicated that the new blood penetrating upstream from the capital was nowhere near sufficient to maintain a dynamic population.

Broadly speaking, Naismith found that eels were abundant in the estuary, and that the numbers diminished, and the age and size of individuals increased, in proportion to the distance from the sea. They were plentiful in the lowest tributaries – the Darent, the Wandle, the Colne, the lower reaches of the Mole and the Wey, and present in reasonable numbers in the Lodden, which enters the Thames at Wargrave in Berkshire. But they were very scarce in the Kennet – once famed for the exceptionally delicate flavour of its eels – and in the Thame, the Evenlode and the Windrush. Interestingly, Naismith was told that there had been a plentiful stock in the upper Thames and its tributaries during the 1950s and 1960s – when London was too polluted to permit any significant elver run – and a drastic decline thereafter. He attributed this to the fact that, after the enforced departure of the Germans from the elver depot at Epney on the Severn just before the outbreak of war, the Ministry of Agriculture had transported several million Severn elvers and put them in the nearest convenient part of the Thames. By the time Naismith surveyed the area, the temporary resurgence had ended as the eels reached the end of their natural span.

The bringing of the Thames back to life has been a notable, but generally unsung achievement. Its innocence has gone for ever, of course – the ceaseless churning of gross cruisers, and the roar of motor traffic over every bridge have annihilated the tranquillity treasured by the likes of James Englefield (although a touch of it may still be obtained at dawn and dusk). On the other hand, in the heart of London it is clean, which it never was in his day. And it is once again, along its whole length, a fine river for angling, which is the surest measure of well-being. Big barbel hug the gravel at the tails of the weirs. Portly chub lie by the weeds. Pike lurk in the shadows, and perch chase minnows through the shallows. Big carp are regularly caught by dedicated carp men in quiet reaches kept very secret. And, as the publicity people at the Environment Agency and Thames Water will leap to tell you, the salmon is back.

Myself, I would wish that it wasn't, and that the great efforts and many millions of pounds devoted to the project of restoring it had been expended on a worthier cause. The result of thirty years of costly labour is that a few hundred salmon pass upstream each year in a doomed attempt to reproduce themselves. Even after the construction of fish passes up to Reading, and a good way up the Kennet, almost no viable spawning territory has been made available. Nor will it be until access to the gravelly reaches of the upper Kennet and streams like the Colne and the Windrush is established. A long time ago Patrick Chalmers – a passionate salmon fisherman but even more passionate Thames man – wrote: 'With regard to the Thames salmon I say that I, and all thoughtful Thames residents, prefer his room to his company.' The essence of Chalmers's argument is as valid today as it was seventy years ago – that the departure of the salmon had enabled the river to become an incomparable source of pleasure for a multitude of ordinary anglers; and that any significant reinstatement would provoke, in Chalmers's words, 'such a looking up of title-deeds and parchments as never was since *Doomsday Book* was made,' and would result in the banishment of the many to enrich a handful of riparian owners.

Fortunately, it will not happen. It is beyond the power of a few well-meaning and dedicated fisheries officers and volunteers – even with considerable financial resources at their disposal – to resurrect a breeding capacity so comprehensively destroyed. No one who has witnessed the decline of the species on other rivers of southern England – where, within living memory, they still thrived – believes the Thames will ever sustain a viable stock of salmon again. The project continues, not because it can succeed, but because the image-makers found in the familiar, photogenic, bright and beautiful silver salmon the sexy symbol they needed for the river's rebirth.

Needless to say, the humble, wholly unsexy eel was not considered for this role. However, by a pleasing twist, interest in the welfare of this mud-hugging recluse has been stirring – not for itself, needless to say, but on behalf of one of its keenest consumers. After decades on the run, the most adored of our wild animals, the otter, is staging a vigorous comeback, recolonising parts of the Thames Valley it abandoned generations ago. Being a creature of discrimination, it values the eel above any other fish. And the feeling is gaining ground among the fisheries officers that serious regard needs to be given to ensuring that the otter – an even more alluring icon than the salmon – gets what it wants.

ELEVEN

Queen of the lagoon

We drove towards the realm of the eel along a flat, wet road beneath a flat, wet sky the colour of dirty linen. On one side stretched away the sodden plain, fields corrugated with furrows of dark earth, orchards of leafless peach and apricot trees drawn in thin, regimented lines. On the other side rose a bank of earth covered in rough grass, at the top of which appeared at intervals curious contraptions demanding investigation. We stopped amid the puddles and scrambled up the bank.

The top, twenty feet or so above the road, enclosed a broad canal that led east towards the sea and west towards Ferrara, now hidden in rain clouds behind us. Beyond and below the canal were more orchards and fields, and more puddles. The curious contraption was a four-cornered net that was suspended beneath a metal arm extended over the greenish-brown water. Where it met the bank there was a windlass that was being turned by a white-haired old fellow in ancient oilskins. The net dropped into the water leaving a square of bubbles at the surface. The old man waited a couple of minutes, then wound energetically. The net reappeared, was inspected and found to be empty, and returned whence it had come. We watched this for a time, and were rewarded with the capture of a little zander, a fish which has something in its appearance of the pike and the perch, but is nowhere near as handsome as either, although it is much esteemed across Continental Europe for the dainty flavour of its white flesh.

The old man added this prize to the collection of similarly stunted zander and mullet slowly expiring in the tiny keepnet suspended at his feet. His fishing machine was known as a *bilancione*, and followed a design employed for centuries in many parts of the world. Here the tradition was in much the same condition as the fish in the old man's net. He explained that hardly anyone bothered any more, as stocks had become so depleted. He blamed this state of affairs on the invasion of the canal by alien catfish, a flat-headed, wide-mouthed, mottled, slimy predator even uglier than the ugliest eel, with gross appetites alleged to encompass water-fowl, infant humans, and corpses. I remembered reading that somewhere on the Po, which flowed a little way to the north, a shepherd had watched helplessly as his dog was seized by the head as it was drinking, and dragged beneath the water to be devoured at leisure. I wondered what such a monster would make of the fragile-looking *bilancione* and its elderly operator. It began to rain again, and we wished him good fishing.

We reached the eel town of Comacchio, which stands on the edge of the great lagoon. Here, on the seaward side, was a line of much bigger *bilancioni*, almost all of them idle, the nets suspended high in the air as if in hope of catching something to be dropped from the grey sky. One was being operated by a couple in oilskins. The woman tended to the rusty diesel engine that raised and lowered the net, while the man scooped out the catch, of tiny silver fish hardly bigger than whitebait.

The town has a very distinctive aroma, not at all unpleasant or oppressive: of fish and weed and mud and marsh, with a touch of drains. Even now that its geographical isolation is long over, the element of water still shapes its character. It is divided and subdivided by its canals, which weave between terraces of brightly painted old fishermen's cottages. There are punts peeping out from under the low, brick bridges and tied up at the quays; rowing boats propped up at back doors and in gardens, even dumped by the road. It almost feels as if it were afloat, an urban raft tethered on the edge of the lagoon.

Our hotel was a couple of punt pole pushes from Comacchio's most celebrated monument, the Trepponti – or Three Bridges – an ingenious and charming arrangement of stone and brick staircases over a junction of canals. The Albergo Trepponti made not even the most cursory gesture towards smartness. Its carpets were threadbare, its basins stained, its bath had long ago been stripped of its last vestiges of enamel. The dining room was just that, a room for eating, its menu an unadorned statement of what the kitchen could produce. For us, there could only be one appropriate dish.

It came roasted on a large plate, without any decoration or garnish, save half a lemon – two glistening, sizzling strips, black against the pallor of the china, steaming fishily. Inside the crisped skin, the flesh was as white as the plate, and fell easily from the backbone in neat fillets. It was sweet and rich and delicate, and would, I feel sure, have had old Izaak Walton murmuring in godly delight.

From the earliest times until two generations ago Comacchio lay, not on the periphery of the lagoon, but enclosed within it. The lagoon itself was framed to the north by a branch of the Po, to the south by the river Reno, to the west by the lowlands leading to Ferrara, and to the east by an attenuated strip of sand separating it from the sea. An eighteenth-century map shows the 'Città di Comacchio' rising from the waves, its encircling walls interrupted at intervals by sharp angles, each protected by pallisades to keep the waters at bay. Its highway, linking it with the sea, was itself water, the Canale Pallotto, from whose turreted mouth – as depicted by that cartographer of old – issued forth a stream of ships under sail, heading into the city. Another map, dating from 1899, underlines Comacchio's isolation – marooned on its thirteen islets, the only approach from the west being an arthritic finger of land extending from the settlement of Ostellato and tapering to an end many miles short of the town.

Founded some time in the Dark Ages by Roman fugitives from the barbarian invasions, Comacchio was for several centuries a minor possession of the noble house of Este, whose name is immortalised by the famous villa at Tivoli and the exquisite musical portrait of its fountains and soaring cypresses composed there by Franz Liszt. That ecstatic outpouring conjures delicacy and purity. But at the time of the Renaissance the name of Este was synonymous with pride, ambition and wealth on an epic scale. They were lords of Ferrara, Ancona, Modena, Reggio and a great deal around and in between; incidental patrons of literature and other arts while devoting themselves to satisfying their gnawing appetite for power-broking and intrigue. One Duke Alfonso married Lucrezia Borgia, quarrelled with two popes and had his *latifundia* restored to him by that eel-loving emperor, Charles V. Another spurned the greatest poet of the age, Torquato Tasso, and had him locked up in the madhouse. Rivalled only by the Medicis, the Estes bowed to no one. Their great moated castle that frowns over Ferrara still gives a flavour of the power they wielded, and the fear and hatred they inspired.

No Este ever went to Comacchio. Why would anyone expose themselves to the innumerable discomforts attending a journey to that dreary and impossibly inaccessible outpost unless they were under orders to collect taxes, fish, or salt – the only commodities it was deemed worthy to provide? Economically, Comacchio remained crushed under the Este boot. But its people were left to their own devices, to develop – for the benefit of the tax collectors – the wealth of their watery sphere. The Vatican viewed the income from the Comacchio fishery enviously, and in 1598 Clement VIII took advantage of the death of Duke Alfonso II to dispossess the Estes. The history books say the Pope came in person to the lagoon, to tell the Comacchiesi of their good fortune and to enjoy a dish or two of the local speciality. The same books assert that the papal rule of the subsequent two centuries was – certainly compared with the tyrannical indifference preceding it – benevolent. The Trepponti dates from the early seventeenth century, and other public buildings followed it, most notably the austere, grey cathedral and the colonnaded fish market.

But no amount of papal good intentions could do much to mitigate the hardship of life. This was God-given, through geography and climate. Sun-blasted through the summer, storm-blasted through the winter, cut off at all times of the year, the fishermen of Comacchio could only endure, and pursue their own survival strategy, which was founded on the eel. That environment, so inimical to human settlers, might have been custom-built to suit this fish: a vast paradise of warm, murky water, carpeted in soft mud, teeming with an incalculable multitude of nourishing, bite-sized crabs, juicy prawns and a host of other staples on the eel's menu of favourites, with the sea – route to the ancestral breeding grounds – a mere half-night's energetic wriggle away.

The technique for catching eels devised by the fishermen of Comacchio was dictated by the character of the lagoon, and was (and is) unique to it. No one knows when it was developed; the town's most distinguished chronicler, Arturo Bellini, believed it had been in use long before its first documented mention in a ducal edict of 1494. Certainly by the time Clement VIII came, Comacchio was already established as Europe's major producer of eels. This reputation was founded on the efficiency of the ingenious *lavoriero*, or fish-trap.

The lagoon was divided into sections, known as *valli*. These were separated from each other by embankments of mud and sand – some formed from natural spits of land and chains of islets, others laboriously constructed. Each of the *valli* – around two score of them altogether – was organised as a unit, with its own buildings for housing the fishermen and their gear, and its own trap. Although some fishing for the resident eels went on, using nets and spears, the communal effort was concentrated on the migration of the silver eels from the lagoon down to the Adriatic.

Each trap was fixed in the canal or natural channel leading from the seaward side of the *valle* towards saltwater. It consisted of a succession of Vs made of reed screens supported on timber posts driven into the mud, all pointing at the sea, each with a chamber at its apex. The sides of the first two chambers were constructed to detain the bass and mullet which also migrated, but to allow the eels to force their way through, until they reached the last chamber of all, the *otela di testa*. This was built of reed walls eight inches thick, the vertical piles strengthened by horizontal timber baulks. From it there was no escape.

Fishing normally began in September and continued until Christmas, the degree of effort being governed by the weather and the cycles of the moon. The fishing stations were far out on the lagoon, many of them a day's journey from the town. For the fishermen there was no return to a warm house and hearth at the end of a long night spent lifting eels. They lived out on the islands, sleeping and eating in dank and draughty structures of reed and straw known as *casoni*, as many as forty or fifty of them together for a month at a time. Their living conditions were unimaginably harsh – as bad, I would guess, as in the dungeons of the Medici or the Este. There was no relief from the elements: the bitter, blasting winds, the marrow-freezing fogs, the pounding downpours. They slept in their damp clothes on mud floors, fed on eel heads and those unappetising slabs of baked maize flour called polenta, their provisions strung up from the beams to keep them from the rats which scuttled among them as they lay.

The bulk of the work was done at night. And the darker, the fouler the night, the more desperate was the urge of the eels to get to the sea, and the harder the fishermen worked. Sometimes the press of fish was so immense and insistent as to threaten the walls of the trap, and the men would light bonfires to calm the frenzy.

Once the trap was full, the eels were lifted by net and tipped into giant wickerwork baskets called *bolaghe*, which were sunken up to their necks in the water. The fishing would continue, night after night, until the moon began to wax again and the runs slackened. Then these bulbous aquatic storage vessels had to be laboriously towed back to Comacchio and delivered to the processing centre. Here the biggest and the best of the eels were transferred to sunken barges resembling sharp-ended coffins, with perforated sides, in which they could survive for weeks while being hauled along the coast to various markets, of which Naples – on the far side of the mainland – was much the most lucrative. The rest were chopped up, grilled on spits against roaring fires, then salted and pressed into kegs, to be sent up the Po to Ferrara, Cremona, Pavia and beyond, or north to Venice, or by mule and packhorse along the ancient trade route to Augsburg and the heart of Europe.

This life bred a hardy race. The migration of the eels was triggered by an infusion of cool water from the sea into the lagoon, driven in by the wind from the east, the stronger and more prolonged the better. The Comacchiesi would gather in their cathedral to pray for stormy weather. It was a prayer for survival, and when it was answered with weather systems of suitable violence, they and their priests gave thanks and offerings. When it was not, there was misery and lamentation.

One of Comacchio's historians, Giovanni Bonaveri, put the matter succinctly in the middle of the eighteenth century: 'Excesses of heat and cold are the enemies of happiness in the lagoon.' The summer of 1718 was one of peculiar wretchedness. The heat – always oppressive – was insupportable and pitiless. The waters of the lagoon shrank with the evaporation. The embankments, islets and reed beds were caked and crusted with salt, and the walls of the town glistened white, as if diseased. The eels died, their upturned bellies turning the surface pale as they floated under the sun. According to Bonaveri, 'the inhabitants watched as their hopes of a copious harvest were extinguished. They rushed out to eat the dead fish, even though they were rotting, and then they fell ill.'

The late winter of 1747 saw an even greater catastrophe. The weather in February was unusually balmy, stirring the normally somnolent eels to leave their refuges and feed. Then, in March, a frost of unprecedented savagery gripped the lagoon, whipped on by a wind like a filleting knife. The water froze and the eels with it, and the people starved.

*　　*　　*

For centuries the lives, deaths and habits of the people of Comacchio remained matters for themselves, their discomforts and sufferings being no different in degree than those of anyone else. The only attribute of this obscure settlement hidden in the reedy wastes that interested the outside world was its capacity to provide eels. Nowhere else in Europe was this fish harvested in such quantities, in so organised a manner. The records show that between 1781 and 1826 the average annual catch was nine hundred tons, around three million eels. The fishery sustained a population of ten thousand, and the name of the town became almost synonymous with Europe's favourite fish. At length people became curious about Comacchio.

The illustrious Spallanzani came to investigate the biology of the eel, which he evidently found much more interesting than the lives of those who hunted it. Even when he did spare the people a glance, it was with his physician's eye: 'Although the inhabitants eat only fish and live in a marsh,' Spallanzani wrote, 'they are well-nourished, of good colour, robust and cheerful and live no less long than the inhabitants of the surrounding dry land. It is an ancient adage that if some man is debilitated, unhealthy or consumptive, he is sent to fish in the marshes to restore him to health.'

Bonaveri, who visited Comacchio earlier in the eighteenth century, did not share Spallanzani's interest in such matters as the location of the eel's ovaries. He was more intrigued by the fish's amazing curative properties. He recorded the case of a blind German woman said to have recovered her sight as a result of eating eel liver. According to Bonaveri, the application of eel grease to the relevant parts of the body promoted the growth of hair, alleviated deafness, and eased the pain from haemorrhoids. The skin, dried and powdered and mixed with wine, caused one grateful patient to 'liberate a prodigious quantity of urine mixed with little stones', and was recommended – applied via a funnel – as a remedy against 'descent and slackening of the vagina'.

A nineteenth-century French traveller, Jean-Jacques Coste, was struck by the epic quality of the landscape and by the condition of its people. In his *Voyage d'Exploration sur le Littoral de la France et de l'Italie*, he described Comacchio and its lagoon as 'une campagne plate, sablonneuse, désolée, où règnent le silence et la misère.' He remarked on the bleak tension as the people waited for the storms that would herald the start of fishing, and for the order to lift the sluice gates on the Canale Pallotto and let the sea water in. 'That day is, for the town of Comacchio, the most important event of their lives. It decides whether they will have abundance or misery.'

The catching of the eels was man's work, but the women of Comacchio played their part in the roasting house where the catch was processed. The scene within made a powerful impression on a German biologist, Leopold Jacoby, who visited Comacchio in the 1870s:

> You have before you a picture of hell, where the damned suffer all the torments that the pious imaginations of medieval painters could conceive. A huge door opens to let in the full flood of daylight. A rower guides his boat, mouthing execrations. He brings with him the souls of the damned, the eels, which lie in writhing heaps before being scooped into tubs.

In front of each tub sits a fiend armed with a sharp hatchet (the eels are chopped up). There is another diabolical duty to perform ... that of spitting on huge skewers, up to two yards long, the pieces and the live eels in coils. The skewers are taken to the fire, eight or nine large furnaces. In each furnace hang seven or eight of these spits. They are kept turning by women who, in face, age, and figure, harmonise well with their infernal surroundings. Each gang of workers chants its song, the flames roar, the smell of burning fat rises from the victims, and the picture of hell is almost complete.

Forty or so years later an American anthropologist, James Hornell, came to Comacchio as part of a global enquiry into fisheries and fishing methods which took him to China, Japan, India, Ceylon, through the islands of the south Pacific and along the coast of west Africa, to Italy and the Bay of Biscay (the result, *Fishing in Many Waters*, was published in 1951, a year after Hornell's death, and is an absorbing testament to the ingenuity and pertinacity of our species in the matter of hunting fish). Having reached Ferrara by train, he took a steam-tram to Ostellato on the western edge of the lagoon, and then a horse-drawn cart along the earthen embankment to Comacchio itself.

Hornell reached the town as 'the great bell of the gaunt grey cathedral boomed out the hour of seven'. He found a place built on water, surrounded by water, with streets of water, and a people living a largely amphibious existence – 'a life detached from the bustle and anxieties of the outside world, it is comparable to a great passenger ship anchored far out from land, visited from time to time by bumboats bringing what supplies are not available from the sea itself.'

He took a more sanguine view of that life than earlier observers. Certainly it was hard, but Hornell judged the people to be 'passively content', with living standards better than those of 'many classes of workers in Britain'. He left a detailed account of how the eel fishing was organised in the thirty-seven *valli* still maintained at that time. 'Never shall I forget,' Hornell enthused, 'the scene during the emptying of the traps. Standing on the summit of reed palisade, lusty fishermen, stripped to the waist, their bodies glistening with sweat, lunged and twisted great dip-nets among the eels imprisoned in the final traps.'

This heartening picture of a workforce in harmony with nature, at home in a harsh but essentially beneficent environment, simple people living simple, satisfied lives uncorrupted by the cheap, empty amusements of city dwellers, was also the moral of a film about Comacchio made in the late 1930s – one of a series commissioned by Mussolini to illustrate the contentment and sense of shared purpose that his leadership had brought his wayward people. It opens in tranquillity: little children scampering over the Trepponti, clogs clattering on the flagstones, men in caps and berets and tweed jackets poling slender skiffs along the canals, stooping beneath the bridges. The sky darkens, clouds scud in from the east. The music grows more urgent. Rain rattles against the windows, the wind howls. The fishermen pull on their oilskins, launch the boats and drive them through the gathering tempest to the *lavorieri*. Nets are grasped and dipped, the orchestra surges to a throbbing climax as the twisting, serpentine harvest is lifted and tipped into the chutes leading to the sunken baskets. Then we are back in the town, as the eels are delivered to the factory. A drumbeat of falling choppers leaves bins full of heads to be distributed to the poor. The bodies are doubled over, spitted, then roasted against the line of roaring fires, the handles turned by beefy wives and mothers with faces lit by flames as the eel fat runs across the floor. At length the blackened, headless corpses are gathered up and packed into barrels and kegs, before spiced vinegar is poured over them. The barrels are stacked, ready to be shipped out. The people relax and smile, smoke and chat, their job for the moment done, their contribution to the national effort made.

It survived, this watery, fishy, self-contained outpost, into the 1950s, when the architects of modern Italy took a look at it, and found it to be offensive. They decided that what modern Italy needed was, not eels, but more fruit and vegetables; not vast, undisciplined wastes of brackish water, reed beds and sand, but fields, properly regulated. A great project to drain the lagoon was begun, and the nature of the propaganda about its condemned way of life changed. Simple became primitive, hardship suffering, hard work exploited labour, living close to nature an exile among rats. The relationship between the Comacchiesi and their world was rebranded as an affront to a nation pursuing progress and a better future for all.

Film-makers played their part in shaping perceptions. In the late 1940s the young Antonioni made a documentary about the fishermen of the Po in which he deployed the untamed beauty of the delta as a backdrop to the backwardness and poverty of its people. A few years later an impossibly lovely Sophia Loren attempted, in *La Donna del Fiume*, to impersonate a worker in the Comacchio eel factory, the victim in an appropriately grim and tragic tale of passion and privation. (It is a sign of the times that the most recent celluloid homage to Comacchio's heritage should have been a sex romp entitled *L'Anguilla*, starring one of Italy's best-loved television personalities, the voluptuous blonde Valeria Marini, whose lascivious antics – both with and without eels – provoked derision from critics and indifference at the box office.)

The original plan was to drain the whole of the lagoon, getting rid of the watery enclave altogether and claiming all of that rich, dark silt for agriculture. In the event, the cost and practical difficulties limited the scale of human intervention. The extent of the lagoon was reduced to about thirty thousand acres – a quarter of its original size – and the town of Comacchio found itself, for the first time, permanently attached to the rest of the province of Emilia-Romagna. Inevitably, much of its singularity was destroyed. But that centuries-old isolation would not have survived much longer anyway. With or without the engineers, its people would have been claimed by modern society's irresistible need for conformity and uniformity, and the draining of the lagoon was as much an acknowledgement of that force as the agent of destruction. Something endures, of course, a taste of the past, enough to intrigue the visitor. The remainder belongs in the history books, the museums, the archives, where – in the meticulous, scholarly way so characteristic of Italian civic pride – those traditions are recorded, analysed, and to a degree celebrated; but also wondered at. How could anyone, in our own times, have lived like that? How could there have been a life so different from our own?

We treasure the past, but are fearful of it – fearful that

it possessed some secret, priceless ingredient that we have lost. We try to control and rationalise it, by collecting its leftovers in our museums and other repositories, while we disown the forces that kept it alive and functioning. The official guidebook issued by the Commune of Comacchio speaks of the region 'emerging today from the old drama of hunger and misery . . . there is finally reason to be optimistic that the path for a truly civil human condition is now being followed.' This is another way of saying that the town no longer has to depend on the eel for survival – which is just as well, considering how its realm has been despoiled – and that its people have been liberated by being able to eat the same food, watch the same television programmes and films, drive the same cars and scooters, share the same preoccupations and frustrations as Italians everywhere else.

In the morning my brother and I presented ourselves at Comacchio's only *palazzo*, named in honour of the historian and pisciculturologist, Arturo Bellini. It housed the offices of the commune, and we were welcomed by one of its officials, Massimo Cavaliere, a gently spoken man with a close-cropped beard and a slightly melancholic air about him, given – when not on duty – to bicycling around town in a green and grey shell suit. He introduced us to the librarian, who laid out for us the dusty chronicles of Spallanzani, Bonaveri, Coste, Bellini and the rest.

We spent some hours in the archives, assembling useful eel facts and trying to comprehend from the books and faded photographs something of that old way of life, whose every rhythm was dictated by the seasons, the water embracing the town, and the fish. Afterwards we drove east, to the strip of land separating the shrunken lagoon from the sea. Until less than half a century ago, no one had bothered much with this salty, windswept ribbon of sand and scrubby grass. Now, inevitably, it had been annexed in the cause of pleasure, to become another link in the chain of beach developments extending the length of Italy's Adriatic coast, each indistinguishable from the next. You could be in Lido degli Estensi, or Lido di Nazioni, or Lido di Spina (as we were), or Lido di Pomposa, or indeed anywhere from the Po delta down to Rimini, Pesaro, Ancona, Pescara and beyond, and the sprawl of hotels, blocks of holiday flats, restaurants, pizzerias, bars, discos, clubs and souvenir shops would be the same.

Out of season the holiday animation surrenders to an overwhelming sense of abandonment. Under that grey sky, with a chilly breeze coming off the grey sea, the place was as desolate as it must have been a century before – maybe more so. We parked and walked between the shuttered restaurants and bars across the wastes of flat, damp sand and looked out over the water. To the north, apparently floating in the air, was a white cluster of towers (belonging we discovered later to a monstrous power station built by latter-day barbarians at the mouth of the Po). Far out we could see a couple of fishing boats. But along the beach – which a month or so before had been an unbroken band of oiled brown bodies, sun loungers, umbrellas, a cacophony of pop music and yelling children, overhung with the smell of suntan oil and grilling fish – there was no life, almost no sound, apart from the anaemic lapping of wavelets.

We returned to Comacchio, picked up Cavaliere and

drove around the northern edge of the lagoon to what had once been one of the chief fishing stations, and was now doing duty as the Museum of the Valli. We were met there by General Antonio Bosco, head of the agency responsible for the lagoon: a short, powerfully built, silver-haired man in his sixties, exuding restless energy, and given to swift, decisive movements and gestures accompanied by bursts of fractured English delivered in a rasping, gravelly voice. The force of his personality immediately elbowed the languid Cavaliere to the margins, though there was evidently a close and affectionate relationship between them.

The general has a difficult job. He has to sustain what is left of Comacchio's fishing industry, now employing no more than fifty men, while developing other sources of economic nourishment – which, in effect, means tourism. Thirty thousand visitors come to the Museum of the Valli each year, most of them on coach excursions that preclude all but the briefest look at the area's other features. The problem with the lagoon is that, although its scale is still impressive, it lacks obvious charms. Bird-watchers cherish it for the herons, egrets, ducks, geese, waders and rails which live here in huge numbers. But it is deficient in picturesque diversity. Immense expanses of water the colour of pea, lentil or oxtail soup, fringed by beds of khaki marsh reeds, broken by low banks of mud topped by pale, flowerless saltwort, a complete absence of trees, elevations, or landmarks of any kind, the whole compressed by a wide, wide sky into a plate-like flatness in which water and land are indistinguishable from each other, and indeed seem to form one dreary composite element – all this, combined with the fact that there is nothing to do but look, adds up to a formidable marketing challenge.

The general acted as our tour guide in a courteous but somewhat perfunctory manner, as if distracted by other preoccupations. He showed us one of the V-shaped eel traps used today, made of steel and concrete and requiring almost no maintenance. In the old days it took all summer to check and repair the reed and timber barriers. Now the place was silent and deserted. The general explained that they were still waiting to start fishing. The high temperature of the water in the lagoon, and the non-appearance of the easterly gales needed to drive the sea water in, meant the eels were not ready to run. 'It is the only place,' he rasped, 'where we pray for bad weather.'

We hopped into a fibreglass motorboat, and he took us down to the fishing station at Serilla. The guidebook contained a picture of the old reed-screen trap there, looking very charming. But it had become sadly dilapidated, and the general admitted that he did not have the funds to pay for its upkeep. On the other side of the rotting trap stood the pink *casone*, nicely restored and containing a clutter of nets, pots, pans, chairs, baskets and other relics. While the general spoke of the times of hardship endured here, I looked out of the window at where sky, lagoon and land merged. I stepped outside to inspect the thick green water, and for a moment I felt very insignificant, a speck in that emptiness and silence.

We crossed open water, following lines of palings thrust into the mud to guide wildfowlers through the fogs that in winter hang over the lagoon for days on end. Black cormorants were perched on some of the poles, as still as carvings in ebony. Others flapped across the surface, hunting prey. Back at the museum a coach was discharging a squad of camera-waving visitors. Of fishermen there was no sign.

That night a storm burst over Comacchio with operatic violence. Lightning lit the sky and the walls of the Albergo Trepponti shook with the thunder. My dreams seethed with slimy horrors, slithering everywhere. In the morning the rain was falling in sheets, and the water in the canals was the colour of mashed chickpeas and flowing with perceptible urgency. On the front page of the newspaper was a photograph of a demonstration in Belgrade, mouths under a sea of umbrellas shouting for Milosevic to go. '*Che brutto giorno*,' protested the little lady who worked in the kitchen as she entered, trailing puddles.

I had hoped to talk to one or two of the old fishermen, who supplemented their pensions poling tourists around the canals. But the vileness of the day kept them indoors, and my brother and I spent the morning driving around the Po delta until we agreed we had had enough of flatness and wetness. I was becoming slightly concerned that I had yet to encounter a living specimen of the fish that had brought us here. In the hope of correcting this omission, we went to the fishing port of Porto Garibaldi, which stands where the canal from the lagoon reaches the sea, and where Cavaliere had told us there was a market that afternoon.

For centuries the place had been known as Magnavacca, an important seaport in its own right as well as being Comacchio's lifeline to the Adriatic. It had earned its right to a new name as a result of a single dramatic and tragic encounter between the hero of Italian independence and the lagoon.

It happened in the late summer of 1849. Garibaldi, fleeing from the Austrians after his heroic, doomed defence of Rome, had taken to a fleet of small boats, accompanied by three hundred of his followers and his wife Anita, who was pregnant and dying. He was trying to reach sanctuary in Venice, while the Austrians were bent on capturing and executing him. Off the delta of the Po, Garibaldi's flotilla was ambushed by a much superior force, and he was forced to put ashore on the beach to the north of Magnavacca. At dawn Gioacchino Bonnet, a Garibaldi loyalist from Comacchio who had been roused with news of the engagement, came upon three of the boats aground. A man was wading ashore with a woman in his arms. Bonnet recognised them as his leader, and the wife he had eloped with when serving as a guerrilla leader in Brazil.

Bonnet urged them into his gig, and they rattled off. He took them first to an isolated farmhouse on the northern shore of the lagoon. Over the next few days they were hidden in a succession of refuges, with hundreds of Austrian troops on their heels. At one point the crew of a boat hired to take them into the southern sector of the lagoon recognised Garibaldi, and abandoned the fugitive and his rapidly weakening wife on an island. Another boatman was found, who rowed them to a house deep in the marshes. It was clear that Anita could go no further, and she urged Garibaldi to make his escape. He left her, and within a few hours she was dead. He eluded the closing circle of his pursuers, slipping from the lagoon's southern fringers downriver to the pine forests around Ravenna, and away.

His saviour, Bonnet, was arrested, but his life was spared. The Austrians were not so merciful to Garibaldi's friend and spiritual support, Father Ugo Bassi, who was seized in Comacchio itself, taken in a cart to Bologna for a show trial, and shot.

The quay at Porto Garibaldi was lined with stubby little boats, their decks silvery with scales and slick with slime, crammed with nets, winches, pots, buckets and mounds of blood-stained polystyrene boxes of fish. More boxes were piled up on the cobbles: sardines, anchovies, gurnard, black bream, mullet, bass, mackerel, pitifully undersized tuna, pale pink crustacea called *cannocchie* with big, black spots on their tails. Overhead a strident mob of gulls wheeled and dived. Mangy cats wandered around digging with their paws at sardines that had been squashed into the crevices between the cobbles and munching at them. In the fishmonger's on the other side of the quay, the merchandise was displayed in a more conventionally pleasing fashion, and in the corner I found a big tank, with a dozen fat eels visible through the bubbles raised by a falling stream of fresh water. The sardines were three thousand lire a kilogram, the anchovies four thousand, the turbot eighteen thousand, the eels twenty-five thousand.

That evening, wandering along the canals of Comacchio for the last time, we came upon an unkempt, toothless pensioner wielding his *bilancione* just below the sluice gate which separated the small town canal from the big canal going off to Porto Garibaldi. Each time he raised the net, it revealed a smattering of small prawns, a few little fish called *acquadelle*, and a multitude of crabs the size of bath plugs. The old man sorted through the crabs, retaining the females – distinguished by their rounded undersides – and throwing the rest away. He told my brother there was not enough flesh on the males to make it worth the trouble of cracking them open. He had a big bucket beside him, two feet deep in crabs. He was careless where the males landed, and I watched several scuttle across the path and plop back into the water.

I crossed the road skirting the town, and walked a little way up the big canal. I scanned the turbid water, idly wondering where I would fish if I wanted to catch an eel. I came upon an angler crouched in the rushes. He had about him that familiar air of stoicism and resolve, of someone in silent communion with something. He had caught one small eel, which was dead in a bucket, pale belly up. I enquired about the fishing. It was bad. Just today, or always? Always. He smiled and shrugged, and went back to studying the end of his rod, willing it to quiver with the nibble of a fish. It began to rain again.

During the night I was awoken from eelish dreams by a rushing sound, as if a gigantic celestial bathtub was being emptied over the Albergo Trepponti. I listened to the pounding of the rain for some time, thinking of eels. It was still dark when we left next morning, after paying a startlingly modest bill scribbled on what looked like a scrap of wrapping paper. The rain had stopped, and a half-light seeped from the lowering sky as we drove out of the eel town. My brother was going back to his home in Rome, and I was going back to mine in England. He dropped me off at the railway station in the little town of Codigoro, which stands on the branch of the Po that once formed the northern limit of the lagoon. As the train clattered towards Ferrara, I looked out over the flat, dark deserted fields. The ditches and furrows were filled with water, and great pools gleamed. It was almost as if the lagoon were creeping back, intent on reclaiming its former glory.

TWELVE

Racks and pots

It was Tuesday September 25th, exactly two weeks after the attacks on the World Trade Center in Manhattan. Everyone said that, for America, everything had changed, for ever. But away from the ravaged city, and its collective mood of defiant rage and devouring, astonished self-doubt, the appearance of things was as before. The leaves were turning, scarlet maple flaring next to golden aspen amid the frowning green of the oaks; although it would be at least another fortnight before the woods of New England would achieve the full burnish of their fall glory. And through the woods, secure in the path it had followed long before humankind had turned up to make trouble, flowed the river: broad, muscular, attending to its own business in its own quiet way.

When the time came, I had not wanted to go. The first response to the horror of the twin towers and the chasm of fear and doubt it had exposed was to stay at home – to keep your head down, to fix one eye on those you loved and the other on those who wished you ill, whoever they were. But the urge to restate a belief in normality is also strong. I spoke to those I wanted to see in America and they were back doing what they did. To take an aeroplane seemed the least I could do on behalf of life as it had been on September 10th. The Air India flight was two thirds full, mainly with families originating from the region of the world where – so we were told – that apocalyptic strike against American values had been hatched. Their behaviour was reassuringly consistent with the standard for international air travel. They were greedy, restless, heedless of others, untidy, demanding and gave no sign of being worried about anything other than when the food trolley would arrive. A handsome, smilingly tyrannical stewardess urged beer and more beer on me. 'Go, take some more, you will need it, otherwise you will dehydrate. Go on, have some wine with your dinner.' On the screen *Bridget Jones's Diary* gave way to some ornate and innocent Bollywood epic as the jet hummed peacefully through the skies and people slept.

I came into the city from the east and left it next morning to the west. I saw nothing of the havoc in between, though I heard plenty, as no one could talk of anything else. The air in New York was heavy and warm, and a grey haze hung over Manhattan like a hospital sheet laid carefully over some traumatic injury. I was glad to leave that shared anguish behind, as all I could do when faced with it was to nod and mouth consolatory platitudes. I was quite unable to imagine what it would be like to lose those you loved, friends, colleagues, in such a way; to have your city thus violated, your way of life thus assaulted, to have such hatred visited on your doorstep. So, in spite of myself, my heart lifted as I headed out.

As my previous experience of America had been restricted to three days' sightseeing in New York City with my daughter, I had no idea what to expect upstate. I was amazed by how swiftly the city and its leafy suburbs were left behind; how soon and how completely the landscape was annexed by thick woodland which afforded no more than glimpses of clapboard houses concealed up drives guarded by mailboxes looking like mouths on poles. Where I come from – the Home Counties of southern England – cities and towns give way to countryside with the utmost reluctance, and, indeed, mostly refuse to do so at all. Here, on Route 23, crossing the Pesquahannock, passing by Newfoundland, Stockholm, Hamburg, Sussex and other exotic locations, I was excited by the thoroughness with which the city had been erased.

At Port Jervis I exchanged New Jersey for New York State, and spotted the blue ribbon which, on the map, divides Pennsylvania from its easterly neighbours. This was the Delaware, the river I had come all this way to see. Heading north, I picked up Route 97, which keeps generally close company with the valley for the seventy-five miles between Port Jervis and Hancock.

I had actually made the river's acquaintance before, from afar, although I didn't realise this until I reached a sign which said 'Lackawaxen'. Memory stirred, sluggishly at first, then more actively. Then I saw another sign, for the Zane Grey Museum, and I knew exactly where I was. I crossed the river on the stone and wood suspension bridge built in the 1840s by John A. Roebling to take the Delaware and Hudson canal. A little way upstream, standing on the junction between the Delaware River and Lackawaxen Creek was the expanded version of the farmhouse where the failed dentist, Pearl Zane Grey, settled with his wife Dolly to begin his struggle to be a writer; and where he had eventually triumphed to the extent of becoming the most famous, the biggest-selling, the highest-paid producer of popular fiction in the world. I knew this place, not because I had immersed myself in Grey's mythic West, but because I am a fisherman, and Grey was a fisherman, and because he wrote about his fishing with a passion and verbal intensity that had fired me long ago. The first piece he ever had published was 'A Day On The Delaware', an account of the hooking and losing of a big pike. It formed the first chapter of his *Tales of Fresh-water Fishing*, my favourite among his books. Now I remembered that the Delaware was his home river: 'I know every rapid, every eddy, almost – I might say – every stone from Callicoon to Port Jervis,' he boasted in characteristic style. And this was his home stream: 'Winding among the blue hills of Pennsylvania there is a swift, amber stream that the Indians named Lack-a-wax-en.'

The museum was shut up and no one answered the bell. In the car park a youth practised skateboarding with extreme fervour. I walked down to the smooth shallow glide where the Lackawaxen meets the Delaware, and wondered how far upstream was the stony cavern from which a giant bass – the 'Lord of Lackawaxen Creek' – had burst one day to seize Zane Grey's catfish bait, returning to it and defeating all his efforts to prise him loose. Nothing disturbed the quiet of either creek or river. The canoeists and rafters who swarm up and down these waters in the summer had departed, and the campsites were shut. Grey cloud pressed down on the wooded hills, and the melancholy of autumn was in the air.

I recrossed the river and drove on, temporarily losing the company of the water as it hurls itself through a succession of rapids between Lackawaxen and Narrowsburg. We were reunited just beyond Narrowsburg, and a couple of miles up Route 97 I came upon the Campfield residence, standing by the road with the broad waters of the Delaware gleaming through the trees below. A man with a prominent belly and a well weathered face built around a small, bristly moustache clumped heavily down the veranda steps to meet me. Floyd Campfield – former state trooper and current champion eel catcher of the Delaware – wrapped his rough hand around mine and complimented me on my timing. The fishing was good, and lunch was on the table. Inside, a long, hairy man unwound himself from the sofa. 'Hi, I'm Lurch,' he drawled, his eyes guarded as if he were challenging me to say otherwise. 'He's actually called Floyd, like his father,' Mrs Campfield commented wearily. 'For some reason he likes to call himself Lurch.'

She was called Jakoba, Cobie for short. She had grey hair, carefully styled, good skin, a quiet, friendly, I-will-take-no-nonsense-in-my-house air about her. As she distributed salads, meat and slices of apple cake around her table, Lurch confided through his immensely long beard that he had neither shaved nor had his hair cut since the last day of 1999. After a few mouthfuls he grimaced in pain and returned to the sofa. His mother explained that he was recovering from major surgery on his back. She said he was a good boy really, but didn't find it easy to settle to things. She pressed more apple cake on me.

Several slices later I rose from the table and went outside. Floyd's pickup smelled distinctly of fish, and there was the corpse of an eel on the floor at the back. We bounced down a track towards the river. A man was mowing the grass outside a large and handsome riverside residence. 'That guy is always mowing his lawn,' Floyd said in a puzzled tone. 'I mean, always. What's the point?' We stopped on a patch of rough grass separating the trees from the water. Floyd pointed out into the stream. 'There she is,' he said proudly. 'That's my eel rack. You won't see one like it anywhere else on the Delaware.' Nor anywhere else, I thought.

Fall on the Delaware means more than just the alchemy that turns the woods to gold, and the approach of the hunting season. Come September and the waning of the moon and the first dark, stormy nights, a movement is born in the water as unseen as the metamorphosis of the trees is eye-catching. Answering the same instinctive summons being felt at the same time across the rivers and lakes of two continents, eels of the Delaware cease the secret, uneventful life they have pursued these ten or twenty years and head for the sea. And someone waits for them.

They have been making the journey since the dawn of time, and the waiting for them has been going on for at least a thousand years, and probably a great deal longer than that. The character of the river – alternating between long, smooth pools and urgent riffles – is perfectly suited to the age-old Native American technique of the V-shaped stone weir with a net at its apex. By the middle of the eighteenth century European settlers had dislodged the Native American peoples from the upper Delaware. But, while they had no time for Indians, they were happy to exploit their know-how. The eel weir that Floyd Campfield displayed to me with such pride was very clearly in a direct line from that distant era.

The main difference was the means of apprehending the wanderers at the point of the V. Where the two walls of stone, each over a hundred yards long, met in the middle of the stream was a device resembling an eccentric staircase facing downstream and heading for the sky. The stairs, or falls, are about eight feet wide and five feet long, and are made of slats of tulipwood, an eighth of an inch apart, fixed at a rising angle of thirty degrees. The flow is funnelled down the V via a throat of stone into the bottom of the staircase, which is anchored to the bed of the river by the weight of boulders. Just as the water level rises and falls, so does the number of stairs exposed above the surface diminish and increase. But, from the perspective of the eels swept into the rack, there is always one stair too far, wholly out of the water and impassable. As they tumble over the lip, they fall back to the base of the ramp, from where tunnels convey them to partially submerged holding boxes at the side of the rack.

That, as simply described as I can manage, is the Delaware eel rack. But words cannot begin to do justice to Floyd Campfield's construction. He had learned the art long ago, from watching the local Narrowsburg legend, Red Knecht

– the Eel King, they called him – at work. Floyd built his first rack in 1963, and served a lengthy apprenticeship before eventually being acknowledged as Knecht's successor as the river's premier eelman. Each season he accrued a little more wisdom, for each summer the stone walls have to be rebuilt by hand so that the breaches made by the winter floods are filled; and the rack itself has to be installed again, patched and restored where necessary. Nor is it merely a matter of maintaining the trap in top condition. Its placement in relation to the flow of the river is crucial. The walls must be balanced against the dynamic of the water so that the maximum flow is channelled evenly into the throat and thus into the rack itself. One man, lifting and placing boulders by hand, does this, and it is no easy thing.

Until his retirement in 1985, Floyd had combined eel fishing with his duties as a law enforcer. He had, he told me, never sought promotion as it would have taken him away from the rack at the times he needed to be on it. Conversely, it had been difficult to realise the full potential of the rack because of the necessity of dealing with drunks, wife-beaters, demented gun-toters, poachers, arsonists, the odd murderer and rapist, and other assorted malefactors. His release from the police service had made it possible for the eel rack to assume first place in Floyd's working priorities, and his ambitions had swelled. I was shown a magazine article dating from the early 1950s illustrated by a photograph of Red Knecht's rack at Narrowsburg. It had four falls, and none of the racks illustrated had more than six. Floyd Campfield's 2001 rack – the thirty-ninth of his career – had twelve, rising to a height far above any level the river could reach while remaining negotiable in his punt. He had built it that way, not to catch more eels, but because it made him feel good.

I got into the punt and he waded out to his masterpiece, towing me behind. He lifted the lid on one of the holding boxes. Inside the eels swayed and undulated, noses against the current flowing between the planks. In the two previous weeks he had taken five thousand, but now, with the moon waxing, catches were falling off again. Nevertheless it had been a good season, and the eels seemed as plentiful as ever.

There is a straightforward reason for this. Alone among the major rivers of the eastern United States, the Delaware has largely escaped the curse of the dam builders. There are reservoirs, but they are high up on the headwaters and have little impact on migratory fish. It was a close call, for it was only after a long and bitter campaign that the US Army Corps of Engineers was forced, in the mid 1970s, to abandon its plan to construct a hundred-and-sixty-foot-high earth and rock dam at Tocks Island, which would have turned the famed Delaware Water Gap downstream from Stroudsburg into a lake forty miles long. The result is that on the Delaware – in contrast to formerly prolific eel rivers such as the Susquehanna and the Mohawk – passage to the sea is still comparatively unimpeded. Distant Delaware Bay continues to support a buoyant eel fishery, while upstream the tiny handful of fishermen who can be bothered to maintain the racks reap a reasonable return for their labours.

Floyd was cagey about the economics of his retirement trade. For many years he and Cobie smoked most of the catch in the rudimentary smokehouse at the bottom of his orchard, and sold them on the premises. They were particularly appreciated by the many German-speakers who had immigrated hereabouts, who would gather to sniff at the hickory and birch savour of Floyd's eels, then to separate the moist, sweet flesh from the backbone and savour it, muttering nostalgically about the old days and good German eels and German beer. Then the Germans had died out, and the health officials had arrived, to declare Floyd's smokehouse defective with regard to sanitary regulations. So he had shut it down, and these days he sold almost all his eels to the owner of a Korean restaurant at Swan Lake, towards Liberty.

We went back to the house for dinner. Lurch had disappeared, to be replaced by a younger brother who filled a chair rather than the sofa. This was Tom, who also had a black beard, nothing like as long as his brother's but still striking in a bushy, frontiersman's sort of way. He said very little, and what words he did utter emerged from the beard in so muted and mangled a form as to be unintelligible to me. He did, however, surprise me later that evening by telling me twice, quite distinctly, that the previous Sunday he had eaten twenty smoked eels.

Tom's wife and their two small children arrived to share the meal. The three generations were sharing the house, and there was a palpable tension in the air as the children wailed and squealed and Floyd and Cobie spoke longingly about their forthcoming departure to their apartment in Miami, where they would be spending the winter and spring far away from the frost-bound Delaware. They depicted the southern state as a paradise of warmth and peace, giving an impression which grew more powerful the longer dinner went on that their seasonal abandonment of home territory could not come soon enough.

At length Floyd stomped off, and after a final slice of apple pie, I joined him. We went back to the rack, where he visibly relaxed. The heavy cloud that had hung over the valley all day had lifted, to leave a pale blue sky with a paper quarter moon rising up it. It was a most lovely evening, but a bad one for eels, which view moons and clear skies with deep-rooted aversion. The warm air above the water pulsed with insect life – clouds of white caenis and squads of zigzagging caddis. A bald eagle came overhead, then a blue heron, low enough for the thud of its wing-beat to be audible over the noise made by the water as it bubbled over and through the stone walls of the weir. We sat side by side on one of the boxes, while Floyd talked about the strange ways of eels, about the river that had been so much a part of his life, about the otters and muskrat and the white-tailed deer he loved to shoot. He castigated the canoeists and rafters who pitched up, uninvited and unwanted, on his weir, leaving their rubbish and asking their stupid questions. He spoke of his own father, an alcoholic, and Cobie's Dutch father, another of the same inclination, how he had married her as soon as she was seventeen to get her out of a life of domestic slavery. He spoke, lovingly and resentfully, about their children, wondering why they would not or could not subscribe to his own simple ethic of hard work and self-sufficiency.

Suddenly, as the light was beginning to fade, an eel came over into the top ramp, its silver belly flashing in the foam.

Floyd jumped up and gave it a poke with his rake to dispatch it to its box. The moon behind us strengthened, casting a silver path down the river, and the stars began to sparkle. A few more eels came in, but the pace was slow. In the darkness wisps of mist curled across the water. Soon the wisps became clouds, and Floyd said it was time to go. He shone his torch into the water. 'It's cloudin' up,' he said. 'Gettin' foggy. It's been raining heavy upstream, and it's gettin' here. The eels will come in, but later.'

And he was right. By morning the Delaware had risen by a foot or more, and was covering six of the ramps in the rack, compared with three the night before. The water was brown, and the current too strong for Floyd to take me out. I watched from the bank as he paddled across to check the boxes. He looked pleased when he came back. He reckoned that at least seven hundred had been taken captive while we were tucked up in bed.

He could not contain his pride and pleasure. As I was about to leave, and was thanking Cobie for their kindness, he charged up and burst forth: 'Oh Cobie, honey, that is the most beautiful thing you have ever seen. That eel rack is just working perfectly.' She smiled indulgently at this tough, vulnerable, emotional man. He had told me that he wanted to see out one more season, build one more rack. That would make forty. No one had ever come near that, not even Red Knecht. But it occurred to me, as I drove away, that he might not find it easy to give up; and that when he did, how much he would miss the sound of the river at night, and the thrashing of the eels across the wet slats of his rack.

*   *   *

The range of the American eel extends from Labrador and the bottom tip of Greenland in the north to Venezuela, Guyana and Trinidad in the south; that is to say, between latitudes 60°N and 10°N. Most *A. rostrata* thin-heads are carried north of the Bahamas and pushed on by the Florida Current past Cape Hatteras in North Carolina, where the Gulf Stream comes into play. A proportion – dimensions wholly unknown – are carried south-west through the West Indies into the Caribbean, and via the Yucatan Channel into the Gulf of Mexico. Records of adult eels on the South American mainland are annoyingly imprecise and fragmentary, although there is no reason to think them false. Two early American ichthyologists, David Starr Jordan and Barton Warren Evermann, said in their *American Food and Game Fishes*, published in 1902, that the eel was 'abundant among the islands of the West Indies', although if they knew any more than that, they kept it to themselves. A scientific paper published more than twenty years ago referred in passing to a considerable elver fishery in Holguin province in eastern Cuba, while tantalising statistics from the United Nations' FAO agency suggest that baby eels are also caught in considerable quantities in the Dominican Republic and Mexico – although by whom, and to what end is not revealed.

There certainly are, or were, eels in the Rio Grande, which divides Texas from Mexico. Charles Frederic Girard's *Ichthyology of the US/Mexican Boundary*, published in 1859 at the instigation of the Department of the Interior, contains a handsome plate of one, classified in the wayward fashion of the time as *Anguilla tyrannus*; and refers to specimens being caught by Major Emory at the river's mouth, and by Lieutenant Couch a little way upstream at Matamoros. An equally obscure paper about the Cochiti people, printed in 1919, mentions eels being caught in the Rio Grande and their skins being used to make moccasins. Further around the Gulf of Mexico is the delta of the Mississippi, a river theoretically capable of spreading migrating eels through the interior of the country almost as far north as the Canadian border. The German expert, Tesch, states that 'of course streams from the Lower Mississippi complex are well populated by eels'. If that were so, one would have expected to be able to find records of their exploitation, which I have been unable to do. Tesch has some figures for catches in the early part of the twentieth century high up on the Mississippi system, in Illinois, Wisconsin and Minnesota, but they are too fragmentary to do anything more than confirm that eels do – or did – penetrate the river.

In 1818 an investigation of sorts into the fish life of the Mississippi's mighty tributary, the Ohio, was carried out by one of history's more obscure and ill-fated seekers after knowledge. The results of Constantine Samuel Rafinesque's exertions were published under the title *Ichthyologia Ohiensis*, a slim volume, and so rare that less than a hundred years after its issue a mere eight copies remained extant. Rafinesque's origins were as exotic as his name. He was born near Constantinople in 1783, the son of a French merchant from Marseilles and a Greek woman of German parentage, and first came to America at the age of nineteen with his father, who perished of yellow fever in Philadelphia. Returning to Europe, the young man spent the next ten years in Sicily, where he wrote a number of scholarly studies of flora and fauna. According to his biographer – one Richard Ellsworth Cass – an unhappy love affair precipitated his decision to 'woo the coy goddess men call Fortune' back in America. Having survived shipwreck in Long Island Sound, he managed to secure a position as professor at the University of Transylvania in Lexington, where he toiled on a succession of works on botany and natural history. Rafinesque's overtures to the coy goddess were evidently rebuffed, for in 1840 he 'surrendered to his last visitor, Death. Life closed in a lonely garret, amid filth and poverty, in Philadelphia.'

Among the many humiliations suffered by this exotic and pathetic figure, one of the most public was inflicted by John James Audubon. While investigating the Ohio River's scaly tribes, Rafinesque visited the great ornithologist at his home in Henderson. He was delighted to find Audubon apparently almost as well informed about fish as he was about birds, and anxious to help. Behaving in a 'cruel and reprehensible fashion', Audubon painted for his visitor several fictitious species – among them *Perca nigropunctata* and *Catastomus megastomus* – which the wretched Rafinesque attempted to classify in his book, thereby provoking considerable ridicule.

The scientific value of Rafinesque's report – 'a book redolent of the sweetness of Nature rather than of the dust of libraries' – was limited, even by the haphazard standards of its times. He did, however, find the American eel present in the Ohio in sufficient numbers for him to identify four species: *A. lutea*, the yellow eel, 'very good to eat'; *A. laticauda*, the broadtail eel, 'one individual . . . poisoned a whole family, causing violent colicks, which was ascribed to its having been taken in the vitriolic slate rocks of Silver Creek'; *A. aterinna*, the black eel, 'very good to eat'; and *A. xanthomelas*, the yellow-bellied eel.

In fairness to Rafinesque, he was not the only one deceived by the variations in the eel's appearance into deducing a multiplicity of species. A similar confusion prevailed in Europe, while David Humphreys Storer's sober and comprehensive *Synopsis of the Fishes of North America*, published in 1846, listed five species of freshwater eel – the common, beaked, silver, snake and bull-head. Among them was *A. rostrata* – *rostratus* meaning beaked or curved – which eventually won the day, although as late as 1902, Jordan and Evermann were still referring to it as *A. chrysypa*. This pair of experts, having poured scorn on Aristotle's 'absurd views' on the birth of eels and asserted that 'all essential and important facts in the life history of the eel are now well understood', proceeded with an account incorrect in almost every particular; stating that it spawns 'off the mouths of rivers, on mudbanks'; that young eels developed 'two or three months after hatching'; that 'the development of the reproductive organs takes place very rapidly' after migration; that they die as a consequence of 'this very unusual rapid development'; that 'they are chiefly scavengers . . . preferring dead fish or other animal matter'.

In a later book, Jordan painted a sinister picture of the eel's voracious eating habits:

> They devour dead flesh and will attack any fish small enough to bite . . . On their hunting excursions they overturn huge stones . . . working for hours if necessary, beneath which they find species of shrimp

and crayfish, of which they are exceedingly fond. Their noses are poked into every imaginable hole in their search for food, to the terror of innumerable small fishes.

Although populations of eels undoubtedly existed throughout the southern states with river access to the Gulf of Mexico, they were generally not abundant enough to warrant serious attention as a food resource; the one significant exception being Florida, where – as recently as the 1970s – the long-established commercial fishery on the St John's River was still recording annual catches of up to a hundred tons. At the same time, the stone and brushwood weirs maintained by the Native Americans on the rivers and estuaries would have been perfectly capable of intercepting the migrating eels that did run through, even though the main emphasis would have been on other migratory species such as shad.

It is the sweep of the Gulf Stream past Cape Hatteras that brings the eel into its own. Just north of the cape is the island of Roanoke, where England's first – and disastrous – New World colony was established in 1587. Those dismally ill-prepared pioneers rapidly found that they had to depend for survival on the generosity of the natives they had been sent (by Sir Walter Raleigh) to displace, for whom fishing was the primary source of food. An impression of how it was done was provided by an illustration in an edition of Thomas Harriot's *Brief and True Report of the New-found Land of Virginia* published in Frankfurt in 1590. Harriot's panegyric on the joys and ease of the life to be had in the American paradise was – while certainly brief – not at all true. But the drawing – probably executed by one of the colonists, John White –

seems authentic enough. It shows two reed or brushwood fish traps, and a collection of men armed with nets, rakes and spears, hunting through the shallows on foot, and in boats. Beneath one of the boats is pictured a selection of crabs, turtles and fish – one of them an unmistakable eel.

Just to the north of Roanoke are Chesapeake Bay and Delaware Bay, both offering hospitable sanctuary to the questing thin-heads, both prolific eel habitats. Stone weirs for catching migrating eels have been identified on a host of greater and lesser rivers – among them the Susquehanna, the Potomac, the Rappahannock, and the James, all of which flow into Chesapeake Bay. Traces of fixed traps have been uncovered all the way up the eastern seaboard – the most extensive of them under the streets of Boston, Massachusetts. But although the eel was a staple for the Native Americans, and for the white settlers who drove the Indians out, the fish was not a significant trading commodity in the United States, nor – until comparatively recently – did it command anything more than passing interest among scientists.

It was a very different matter north of the border, in Canada, where – since time immemorial – the mighty St Lawrence river system, and its source, Lake Ontario, had pulled in and expelled a living stream of eels on a scarcely imaginable scale. From the waters of Ontario down to the mouth of the river and the Gulf of St Lawrence beyond, the eel was speared, netted and trapped, providing food and livelihoods for generations of fishermen. Father Bressani's 'Kingdom of water and fish' must have seemed eternal to those who lived from it. Like the Newfoundland cod fishery, it was regarded as an inexhaustible resource.

In 1968 a scientist called Geoffrey Eales, of the University of New Brunswick's Biology Department, published a lengthy paper entitled 'The Eel Fisheries of Eastern Canada' in which he reported that in 1933 the total Canadian catch had been around twelve hundred and fifty tons, in 1948 about four hundred, and in 1965 not far short of a thousand tons. According to Eales, eight hundred fishermen were engaged in catching eels between Lake Ontario and Cap-Chat on the southern side of the estuary – a distance of six hundred miles. One of the oldest and most prolific fisheries was on the Richelieu River, which drains Champlain Lake into the St Lawrence between Montreal and Trois-Rivières. One weir, which had been operated by five successive generations of the same family, yielded between thirty and forty tons of eel a year. A photograph was included of an estuarine weir located at St Vallier which accounted for up to fifteen tons a year. Eales's report made clear that the St Lawrence eel fishery was still making a vital contribution to life along the great river, just as it had when the Jesuits first sailed up the estuary to Quebec more than three centuries before. Nor did his exhaustive and conscientious analysis even hint that it might be facing anything other than a viable future. Yet by the time it appeared, the seeds of its destruction had already been sown.

In 1986 catches of eel on the Richelieu River as a whole were just under fifty tons. In 1996 the total was two tons. On the upper St Lawrence – including Lake Ontario – the decline has been even more precipitous; further down the river less so, but still steep enough to cause serious alarm. The total catch of Canadian eels in 1999 was 487 tons, less than half that of ten years before.

Although fishermen, fisheries officers and scientists differ as to how to evaluate the seriousness of the situation – the diagnosis varies between critical and terminal – no one who knows anything about the eels of the St Lawrence has any doubt that they are in desperate trouble. The causes of this biological disaster are several, and the scientists who have studied it have found it extremely difficult to assess their comparative impact. The start of the process can be attributed to the urbanisation of the shores of the Great Lakes, and the transformation of the hinterland from wilderness to agribusiness, which turned these wonders of the world into sinks of poison. Contamination by a host of toxins – including mercury, pesticides such as mirex and dieldrin, and polychlorinated biphenyls (PCBs) – led to bans and restrictions on the consumption and sale of all Great Lakes fish species (the modest US fishery for eels on Lake Ontario was closed in 1982). Although chemical pollution even on such a scale as that unleashed on the Great Lakes does not kill eels, scientists believe that the build-up of contaminants over many years – Lake Ontario eels spend anything up to twenty years in freshwater before migrating – may well have damaged the eel's ability to get to the Sargasso, its reproductive capability when its gets there, and the survival rate of its offspring. Even though pollution levels have fallen markedly since 1988, many, probably most, of the females attempting to migrate over the past decade would have been exposed to the previous toxicity regime.

In the late 1950s the upper St Lawrence was impounded by the Moses-Saunders dam, constructed at Cornwall. The project coincided with the development of the St Lawrence Seaway, and together amounted to a massive disruption to the route taken by migrating eels through the ages. That disruption was compounded by the subsequent construction of an even bigger hydroelectric dam fifty miles downstream from Cornwall, at Beauharnois. At the time no one seems to have given any thought as to how adult and infant eels, heading in opposite directions, were supposed to bypass these enormous barriers. The resident population in Lake Ontario was sufficient to sustain the commercial fishery, and a steady trickle of determined recruits did manage to find its way through the locks and channels used by the ships and boats. But in the early 1970s large numbers of mature eels were spotted milling around on one side of the Moses-Saunders dam, clearly frustrated in their desire to head for the sea; and it became clear that the upstream migration of young eels during the summer must be similarly obstructed. A wooden ladder was installed in 1974, which was replaced six years later by an aluminium structure. After 1974 the numbers of juveniles ascending the ladder were monitored visually, until 1987, when an electronic counter was put in place.

In the early days there was every reason for confidence that the installation of the ladder had done the trick. It was estimated that at the height of the 1982 and 1983 migrations more than twenty-six thousand eels were making their way up and over the ladder each day. But in the mid 1980s the upstream movement of juveniles suddenly faltered. In 1986 the counter registered a maximum daily migration of five thousand. By 1990 this was down to three thousand, and by 1993 it had collapsed to a pitiful trickle of barely two hundred. Although these figures could not be treated as a measure of the full migration – there were too many variables in the monitoring regime and too many ways around the ladder for that – they were regarded by scientists as a reliable index, which pointed only one way. By the end of the millennium those involved in collating and interpreting the readings concluded that the recruitment of juvenile eels to the upper St Lawrence and Lake Ontario had virtually ceased.

But why? It was not that the barrier was too much for them – the ladder had been shown to work. They were simply not there to make the attempt. There had been a species failure further down the river. Could it be overfishing? On the face of it, this seemed unlikely. If it is assumed, for the sake of argument, that half of the 1982 national catch of 1350 tons were migrating silver eels, this obviously represents the loss of at least half a million potential spawners which failed to make it to the Sargasso Sea. On the other hand, a cursory examination of eel fishing methods reveals how 'inefficient' (i.e. benign) they are, compared with, say, the rapacious harvesting of marine species such as cod and tuna. There is no real evidence that the long-established trawling and trapping of eels on Lake Ontario and the upper St Lawrence had anything more than a marginal impact on stocks. The decline, when it came, was sudden and drastic. On the St Lawrence and its tributaries there has never been an elver fishery; and, while the weirs on rivers like the Richelieu and the Ottawa would clearly have accounted for a proportion of migrants, the nature of the fisheries – seasonal, haphazard, low-intensity – suggests it would not have been great. The traditional fishing stations along the estuary were – given their scattered locations and the vast extent of water available for the travellers – even less punitive.

Historically, then, the nature of the fishery permitted a healthy surplus of spawners to escape to the ocean. But that balance depended on an overall abundance of stocks. Were other factors – pollution, or high mortality rates among migrating silver eels minced up as they tried to get through the Moses-Saunders and Beauharnois dams – to have set off a significant fall in population levels, sustained fishing effort would swiftly compound it. Fishermen dependent on a seasonal catch for their livelihoods tend – for obvious reasons – to fish harder and longer when stocks become scarcer. The figures show that – while catches did fall significantly during the 1990s – the downward graph was nowhere near as steep as for the recruitment of juveniles.

The likeliest explanation is that a complex interaction of these and other malign forces – possibly including a failure of elver delivery due to weakening ocean currents – was invisibly at work for many years. The result is that the single most important habitat for *A. rostrata* has been and is being degraded to the point of annihilation. That does not signify globally, or even nationally. But ask the fishermen who once made their living anywhere between Cap-Chat and Lake Ontario if they miss the eel.

The condition of the species in the United States is harder to pin down because until recently concern for its welfare was for a variety of historical reasons minimal, and those who wished to catch eels were allowed to do so pretty much free of interference or constraint. But in the past few years, the Atlantic States Marine Fisheries Commission (ASMFC), which endeavours to organise conservation measures and harmonise controls on fisheries from Maine down to Florida, has given serious attention to the eel, and has made a concerted attempt to shine some light into a murky place.

This stirring of activity may be attributable, at least in part, to the burst of attention given to one aspect of eel exploitation during the 1990s. It came to the notice of the authorities, and one or two alert journalists, that incidents of lawlessness and occasional violence were taking place on remote creeks and rivers in the hours of darkness in spring and early summer. Reports that glass-eel buyers from the Far East were prepared to pay up to three hundred dollars a pound for elvers sparked off something of a frenzy on tidal waters with a reputation for sustaining a run of these insignificant creatures. Itinerant hunters with dip-nets and exaggerated notions of the fortunes to be made swarmed into quiet coastal backwaters like men fired with gold fever, searching for vantage points from which they could help themselves to the flow of liquid cash. Behind them came dealers, their pockets stuffed with notes, and trucks sloshing water from their tanks. And behind them – some time later – came the officers from the various fish, game and wildlife divisions, alerted by the howls of protest from residents, environmentalists and authentic fishermen, and stung by the increasingly colourful media coverage.

Controversy was at its hottest in New Jersey. Before 1997 the state had no regulations at all governing elver fishing. As demand and prices rocketed, the north side of one of the richest eel grounds in North America, Delaware

Bay, became a fighting ground. Traditional baymen found themselves being elbowed aside by freebooting outsiders. Some creeks were fished with small-mesh fyke nets, and stories circulated of men making sixty thousand dollars in the two months of the elver run. Punch-ups were common, and there were several cases of shots being exchanged between competing parties. The state responded, first by restricting the fishery to dip-nets; and when this failed to restrain the mayhem, by banning elver fishing altogether. This measure was greeted with fury by baymen already struggling with restrictions on other seasonal fisheries, such as the horseshoe crab. It also left state conservation officers with the task of enforcement – no minor matter, with a hundred miles of creek, river mouth and marshland from Barnegat Bay to the Delaware River to be policed, at night.

In 1992 the value of live elver shipments from major north-eastern airports was four million dollars. Three years later it was eleven million, prompting a biologist with the Fisheries Commission to observe: 'It's about as lucrative as drugs and a lot safer.' But by 1998 the majority of Atlantic states had joined New Jersey in outlawing elver fishing altogether. Of the states that do still permit it, Maine is the most significant, with around fifteen hundred licensed elver fishermen, each paying two hundred dollars for their permits. Catches reached a peak in 1995 of seven and a half tons.

Fisheries for resident yellow eels and migrating silver eels exist all the way from the rivers of Maine to the St John's River in Florida. Although official catch returns are available, they reveal little other than that a small number of people still find it worth their while to fish for eels. Reported catches peaked at 1645 tons in 1979, subsequently declining to less than 500 tons in 1997 and 1998. While the size of the harvest is affected by stock levels, it is also determined by fishing effort – which itself is dictated by the market. Since no one knows how many fishermen are involved, and how hard they are trying, the figures cannot be taken as a guide to how the eel is doing. There has, for instance, been an explosion in demand for eel as a bait for catching striped bass, a fierce marine fighter which, as a result of bans on commercial fishing, has rebounded from critical scarcity to become the most sought-after sporting fish in the eastern States. Stripers love eels, little eels, between six inches and ten. No one has a clue how many are being hoovered up in pots and fyke nets to keep the skippers of the striped bass boats supplied, since catches are lumped together into the overall total, measured by weight. But in view of the massive growth in the striped bass sport fishery, and the fact that anglers can get through several dozen baits in a day, the numbers must be huge.

These immature eels are caught before their gender has been determined. But, in view of the fact that fishing for them is concentrated in coastal waters, it is highly likely that nearly all of them would have become males, which greatly outnumber females in the overall balance of the species, and whose preferred habitat is estuarial or tidal. Upriver, where the female of the breed is wont to wander, she has been under long-running and unrelenting attack.

Rivers in the northern United States have been fought over by conflicting interests for a long time. With the overthrow of British rule in 1783, those charged with shaping the new nation were well aware of the importance of the only supply route into the interior: from Albany on the Hudson River, up the Mohawk River, through Lake Oneida, to Oswego on the shores of Lake Ontario. The journey was exceedingly laborious. The Great Cohoes Falls on the lower Mohawk required a sixteen-mile overland hike to be circumvented. At Schenectady travellers transferred to flat-bottomed, pole-driven craft known as *bateaux*. To reach the head of the river at Fort Stanwix (now Rome), these boats had to clear almost a hundred rapids. Once there, they and any cargo had to be carried two miles through the forest to Wood Creek, which flowed into Lake Oneida. From there it was a comparatively easy run down the Oswego River to Oswego itself, generally reached ten days after leaving Albany.

The first major improvements were the cutting of the Little Falls Canal, which bypassed the worst of the rapids on the Mohawk, below Herkimer, and of the Rome canal that connected the upper Mohawk with Wood Creek. To surmount the lesser rapids, the boatmen made use of the many V-shaped fishing weirs maintained by Native Americans for centuries, since the apex of the V had the incidental effect of deepening the water sufficiently to allow the *bateaux* to be poled through. Although the boating companies were doubtless appreciative at the time, it was inevitable that – as the work of subjugating the rivers to the white man's commercial imperatives continued – the interests of the fishermen would take a distant second place. In the early part of the nineteenth century many parts of the Mohawk were deepened, and so-called 'wing dams' were installed to assist the passage of boats – often in the place of fishing weirs. In 1825 the Erie Canal was completed, opening up a slackwater route for much bigger boats right into the interior, and thereby consigning the *bateaux* and their grander successors, the Durhams, to redundancy. By then the Mohawk had already been much reduced as a fishery, and the construction in 1917 of a new canal, from Rome to Lake Ontario, completed the process of turning it from the wild, white-water torrent of old to the deep, placid flow of today – now entirely without eels.

The consolidation of white settlements along the eastern seaboard of Canada and the United States, and their expansion westward, brought a concerted assault on migratory species of fish. Wholesale logging degraded the habitat, and the innumerable sawmills divided salmon from their spawning grounds and blocked the migrations of adult and juvenile eels. Much later, the exploitation of river energy was crucial to the growth of industrial society, and hydroelectric power remains indispensable in keeping the city lights burning and the air-conditioning units thrumming. Without it America would glow less brightly and sweat much more freely – a two-pronged nightmare viewed by people and politicians alike as unthinkable.

Figures from the Atlantic States Marine Fisheries Commission show that from Maine down to Florida there are more than 15,500 dams preventing or hindering access on rivers, and that eighty-four per cent of potential eel habitat is thus affected. Of these dams, fewer than ten per cent are hydroelectric. But because of the turbines – which can be likened to giant mincing machines encased in concrete – the hydroelectric installations are actively destructive, rather than merely obstructive. Studies suggest that mortality rates among silver eels sucked into them vary from five to ninety per cent. The influence of other kinds of dam on eel stocks varies enormously, and is impossible to quantify. But there is no doubt that inland eels are very much scarcer than they used to be, and that this has been the case for a very long time (Erhard Rostlund, in his ground-breaking study *Freshwater Fish and Fishing in Native North America*, published in 1953, spoke of the eel population having been 'drastically reduced' by the proliferation of dams over the previous century). Only a very few rivers – among which the Delaware, where Floyd Campfield operates, is the most notable – still sustain an eel population worth exploiting.

But in the great estuaries – particularly Chesapeake Bay and Delaware Bay – the eel appears to be under no immediate threat. And there is another east coast haven, where times – at least for the eel – are still good.

After leaving the Campfield homestead, I spent that night with some friends who live to the west of New York City. We ate two eels from Floyd's smokehouse, and – while I'm fairly sure I could not have managed twenty – I could understand why the Germans of the upper Delaware had grown so fond of them. I presented the head of one to my friends' five-year-old son. He looked at the dark brown, shrivelled object with solemn curiosity, without shrinking from it. His mother put it in a cellophane envelope so he could astound and mystify his classmates with it.

Next morning I took a train from the station at Short Hills, so spick and span as to be almost unnerving, into Penn Station; and another one out to distinctly un-spick-and-span

Lynbrook, on the Long Island Rail Road. Larry Seaman arrived in his Chevvy pickup, an urban version of Floyd Campfield's, with the same faint but insistent fishiness about it. We took a rough potholed road off the highway. I saw a sign: 'Bait for sale'. 'That's my brother's place,' Larry said. He turned into a yard opposite. It was piled high with stacks of eel pots and mounds of netting, and strewn with buoys, oars, petrol cans, plastic boxes and metal drums, rusting anchors. The air was split by the roar of an American Airlines jet, so low that its belly seemed almost to brush the top of Larry's house. 'The runway's just over there,' he said after the decibel level had come down, grinning and gesturing to the west. 'You get used to it.'

They are incongruous neighbours, the concrete and tarmac of JFK airport, and the wide, wild expanses of Jamaica Bay. If, coming in from the north-east, just before touchdown, you were to look down to the left, you would see the bay, protected from the ocean by the long finger of Rockaway Point to the south. It is a maze of islands of mud and sand: Jo Jo Marsh, Rulers Bar Hassock, Silver Hole March, Ruffle Bar split by water: Big Fishkill Channel, Big Mucks Creeks, Pumpkin Patch Channel. The islands are low, fringed by reeds and covered with rough grass tipped in mustard yellow. Big tides sweep through the channels, and when they recede a supplementary, transitory landscape is revealed, of bare mudbanks and sandbars. On every side the city impinges: airport, highways, subway trains, industrial sites, bridges, apartment blocks and housing developments. But they are held back by the uncompromising nature of the bay. The cacophony around heightens its emptiness and loneliness, the way in which it holds its secrets. You would not wish to be out in that shifting, unpredictable place unless you were with someone who knew it at least as well as the back of his hand. Which Larry Seaman does.

Larry's home backs onto a dark, arthritic, little finger of water leading off the head of the bay, called Hook Creek. It looks dark because the bottom is of black mud. But the water is clear, and you can see the little fish against the white of the clam shells. Larry's landing stage sparkled with desiccated fish scales, and his boat was spotted with dried blood and stomach juices and other unappetising stains. The craft had a large and powerful engine capable of propelling her at thirty-five knots, a winch, and a couple of upended boxes to sit on. There were no other facilities, no comforts, no attempt to disguise or mitigate the sole function of this mould of fibreglass, which was to receive fish.

It soon became clear to me how deeply rooted the Seaman clan were in this watery outpost of the great city. Larry took me in the boat past the Five Towers Motor Inn, under the highway, past the school where he graduated. 'I used to die in that classroom,' he said. 'Shit, I couldn't wait to get out of that prison, to be out on the water. The teacher would be going on 'bout sump'n or other, and I'd be wondering if the tide was turning, how my pots were, just wantin' to get out there and fish.' We passed an overgrown, silty ditch. 'That's where I was born, up there.' We went under a derelict footbridge. 'That's where my wife Lois came from,' he said, pointing into the reeds. 'My dad said to me, "So you're marrying a girl from the back of the swamp."' Later he showed me a photograph of himself leading Lois, in full wedding regalia, along a boardwalk through the reeds, on their way to church. She had died three years before and Larry mourned her with an open, smiling tenderness.

We edged out into the bay, stopping close to a huge, rusty barge moored next to a depot where sand was being noisily crushed to make asphalt. Another 747 screamed over our heads as Larry lobbed out a grappling hook. He dragged up a rope, fixed it to the winch, and set it running. An eel pot broke the surface, and through the wire mesh I could see a dozen shapes twisting. Larry tipped them out. They were good, fat eels, up to two pounds or so, and handsome for the species, with mahogany backs and bellies the colour of olive oil and pearl. He consigned them to a plastic barrel and set about rebaiting the pot. As far as Larry was concerned, there was only one possible bait good enough for the eels of Jamaica Bay: the horseshoe crab, a creature the size of a large dinner plate, whose fearsome appearance – a thick black carapace on top of a mass of legs and pincers, sloping at the front down to an appendage like a lance – is irresistibly suggestive of a monster in a *Star Wars* movie. The reality is that the horseshoe is a rather helpless and defenceless creature, its lance fragile, its pincers soft and feeble. Larry crunches them in half with a kind of home-made guillotine fixed to his landing stage, using one portion in each chamber of the eel pot. When the eels are about, the shells come back hollow, stripped of every vestige of the gelatinous flesh.

Larry lifted and emptied the second pot, which was also well filled. Then he laid them again, using the control tower of JFK and some object on the near bank to line them up, so he would know where to sling his hook next time. We swept out into more open water. I could see the jumbos parked beside the terminal. To the left of the control tower, the outline of Manhattan was framed against a soft, blue, early autumn sky. The Empire State Building appeared like a delicate stem of coral. To its left was the empty space where the twin towers should have been. It was still difficult to believe in this brutal diminution of the most famous skyline in the world. Larry had been out fishing that morning. He didn't see or hear anything, only he thought it odd that he couldn't get a signal from his mobile. Then he got home, heard the news, started watching TV like everyone else; like everyone else, not really believing it then, not really comprehending it now.

The sun glittered on the water as we passed Motts Point. There were boys fishing with rods from the walls, and others wading in the water, dragging nets – Puerto Ricans, Larry said, fishing to feed themselves. He cut the engine and we drifted as he talked of the past.

Once he would have had company out here from an assortment of local baymen. There had been a couple of Swedish fishing families who had built themselves houses in the reeds, on stilts, with holes in the floor to take their waste away. There was old Mary Gooch, in straw hat, boots and stained pinafore dress, the champion bait catcher. When the anglers came out at the weekends after striped bass, the queue to Mary's boat reached half-way round the block. They were like a family themselves, the bay fishermen, looking out for each other, always ready to stop and pass the time, talking fish, smoking, watching the planes. Now Larry was the last full-timer left, though his brother Bob and son Larry Junior helped out.

Back in the 1970s, that was the time: a different city, a different era. There had been fish markets all over the Bronx, serving Italian customers with a keen appreciation of eels. The warm, shallow waters of the bay teemed with the fish, so the pots would come up bulging, bursting with them. Larry had ventured further afield, around into New York Harbor, and found the waters off Manhattan even more productive than Jamaica Bay. He caught so many eels off the Statue of Liberty and the tip of Manhattan Island that he couldn't get them back home in his boat and had rented a derelict pier on the Brooklyn shore at a dollar a day to unload them. Some days he'd lifted almost two tons, and at fifteen to thirty cents a pound, that was serious money. Lois organised the deliveries while her man did the fishing. One day she was short of a driver, and Larry was around, so he took the truck. Then he'd met a friend, stopped for a couple of beers and screwed up Lois's schedule. 'When I got back, she was so furious she fired me,' he said laughing, shaking his head and running his hands through his white hair.

Times changed. The Italians dispersed from the Bronx, and the markets shut down. Lois had gone, too, and now Larry's daughter delivered the smaller eels to the bait shops where they were prized by the striped bass devotees. The bigger ones were collected by a wholesaler based in Maine, though Larry kept back the best for Christmas, when long-standing Italian customers, moved to extravagance by the thought of *capitone arrostito*, would pay premium prices for the choicest specimens.

There were other anxieties for New York's last eelman. The previous year officials from the conservation department – 'the green meanies', Larry called them – had applied to have his licence to fish Jamaica Bay revoked, on the grounds that he was creating a disturbance in a nature reserve. 'They know nuthin', those guys from the constipation department,' he said with genial contempt. 'Look over there.' He pointed at a wooden platform sticking up on the shore. 'They put that so's they could observe the osprey nest. Only the ospreys don't nest there, but about three miles away, over there.' He pointed up the bay. 'They said I was causing a disturbance. Shit, what about them coming out here snoopin' on people. Jesus!' Larry went to the newspapers and after something of a public outcry the meanies backed off. But they were squeezing him, he said, and he was damn sure that after he was gone, no one else would get a licence to fish on their precious reserve.

This year there was a different problem. The attacks of 11 September had resulted in New York Harbor being completely shut off, keeping Larry away from his most productive eel grounds. 'I went round once, and they stopped me. I said, "Hey, do I look like a terrorist? I just want to go fishin'." But they wouldn't listen.'

Larry Seaman had never known any other life, nor wanted any other. But I sensed that the appetite to keep going was waning. He and Lois had bought themselves a house on Chesapeake Bay, Virginia. Even without her, he liked it down there. It was warmer, quieter, there were eels and no hassle. He was getting a new boat there, and he had a woman friend who would cook him dinner and provide a little companionship. This fishing, out here on the bay, was doomed anyway. Quite apart from the sniping from officialdom, today's pampered generation shied away from the hardness of the life: up before dawn seven days a week, battered by storms and numbed by the cold, forever manhandling the eel pots in, discharging the slippery cargo, re-baiting, laying pots, casting nets and hauling them in, bending and straightening for hours on end; the labour that had given Larry Seaman his nutcracker hands and sinews like hawsers. Larry Junior said he wanted to be an eelman like his dad. But the father had noticed a distinct reluctance on the part of the boy to lever himself out of bed on dark mornings when the wind was whistling around the eaves. Bad sign.

The boat rocked gently on the ripples. In front of us I could see the aircraft in the shadow of the control tower, like chicks under the wing of the mother hen. Behind us a subway train rattled along Rockaway Beach. From all sides rose the muted din of road traffic, as insistent as insect noise in the jungle. A snow-white crane picked its way on twig-like legs along the bank, ducking its slender head to poke its beak among the clusters of black mussels fastened to the mud. Cormorants whizzed across the water. There were herons, and plovers and multitudes of gulls and terns. 'Sometimes I'm out here,' Larry said, 'and I see one of them ospreys in the sky up there, and then it dives, hits the water – whumph! – comes out with a fish in its talons. And I see those guys over there,' – he gestured at the highway, clogged with its streams of vehicles – 'blowin' their horns and getting all impatient, and I think they don't know nuthin' about what happens out here. And I think, this is the place to be.'

Suddenly a tremor seemed to pass through the water. The surface was disturbed from below, as if it were simmering. Larry stood, pointing. 'That's a big fuckin' school of baitfish, a big one. Look, they're everywhere.' There were explosions as the little fish burst into the sunlight, and ominous swirls at the edge of the shoal. Striped bass and bluefish, sleek predators in from the ocean, were working in packs to herd their prey for the slaughter. Again and again the surface was fractured as the victims sought to escape from the snapping jaws. It was a tremendous spectacle, breath-catching in its violence, theatrical in its setting, and it set the seal on one of the two or three most delightful and memorable encounters with fishermen I have ever had.

Early in the evening Larry dropped me at JFK for my flight back to London. The security procedures were wearisome in the extreme, and it had been dark for a couple of hours by the time we took off. I could not tell in which direction we ascended, where we were in relation to Jamaica Bay. But it was pleasant to think that somewhere down there in the blackness, the tide was now on the ebb, and the eels were questing over the mud for clams and crabs, and maybe their nostrils were twitching at the scent of half a juicy horseshoe crab waiting for them in Larry's pots; that in a few hours time, when the sky was paling over the ocean, before the meanies were about, New York's last eelman would be out there plying his trade.

THIRTEEN

Fishermen of Neagh

They speak the Queen's English here; at least that is what some of them would call it. But the way they speak it is very different, as are the look and feel of this outpost of the Queen of England's dominion. The countryside to the north of the lough was deep green, a patchwork of small fields enclosed within unkempt hedges, dotted with small white farmhouses, decrepit sheds, and barns with sagging roofs. Everything was very quiet, except the crows that flapped and cawed around the empty lanes as if summoned for some great and potentially contentious congress of the birds.

I angled north-west from Randalstown towards the River Bann, pursued by black clouds charging up from the south.

I crossed the river at Portglenone, coming to the bridge down a wide main street lined with old-fashioned traders' shops – butchers, bakers, victuallers. Outside, their backs turned against the raw wind, people clustered in twos and threes, talking among themselves, keeping themselves to themselves. The high walls of the police station were topped with coils of barbed wire. It looked more like a fortress than a safe place with a blue light over the door, where one might seek help. Unionist flags flapped over the bridge. An exhortation to the IRA to keep up the struggle was fading on the metalwork beside the road.

On the west side of the river I took to the lanes, seeking the water. Near Newferry I had to pull over to make way for a mud-streaked hearse splashing through the puddles. I glimpsed mourners around a corner, a knot of dark coats and suits. This was the only sign of life I encountered on my way to the deserted car park at Newferry, beyond which the Bann flowed quietly, minding itself. I turned back, skirting Bellaghy, the birthplace of Seamus Heaney, who had known the business that had brought me here. At length, after skirting the bog land next to Lough Beg, I hit the main Derry–Belfast highway and came into Toome. I stopped, while the trucks roared through heading for all points east and west.

It's easy to pass through Toome. There is a police station with towering, sightless walls, a hotel in sickly ochre, a timber yard, a straggle of shops giving way to a straggle of houses and bungalows, a school, a church, and the main road, overpowering everything with its din. Then you're on the other side of it, back in the grassy green countryside. Whatever capacity Toome has to detain is due, not to its visual attractions, but to its position, guarding the place where Lough Neagh, in Heaney's words, 'sluices towards the sea'.

On the map Lough Neagh looks like a ragged stamp stuck on the island of Ireland. Its seventy-seven miles of shore are shared between five of the six counties of Northern Ireland, but there is no great clamour from any of them to claim it, or to do anything much with it. Despite its size, it is unspectacular: a wide sheet of open water, surrounded by flat, featureless scrubland, with nothing much along those many miles of rocks and rocky bays apart from the occasional ruined church, and one or two boat clubs and marinas to cater for the sailing folk. And even its size – nineteen miles long, ten miles wide – is somehow disappointing, because the setting makes it impossible to grasp. Neagh is devoid of conventional grandeur or romantic beauty – quite unlike Erne, or Corrib, or Mask, the great lakes of the west.

So, if you stopped in Toome, it would be because you had particular business there, as Father Kennedy had almost forty years ago, when he was sent to minister to souls there. But the main business of Toome is eels, which is why I had come and stopped. Lough Neagh is the greatest wild eel fishery in the world, and noisy, untidy Toome – because it sits where the adult eels must go and the baby eels must come – is its heart and lungs.

The lough is what Comacchio once was, a place of perfection for *A. anguilla*. It has that vital artery to the sea. Its profile, that of a shallow basin sunk in soft earth, ensures rich feeding. Across its largely muddy and sandy bottom hatches a limitless abundance of midge larvae and other tiny nymphs, which sustain the smaller eels, as well as the vast shoals of perch and roach fry and little pollan (a species akin to freshwater herrings) that make for more substantial eels. This wealth of bottom feeding, incidentally, is the reason for the lough's low reputation among anglers. There are trout, many trout, but they are reluctant to pay attention to artificial flies or lures when their snouts are permanently engaged with the good things wriggling at the bottom.

The anglers do not bother, so the lough is left to the fishermen. Here, around its shores, survives a way of life as unusual and distinct as that now extinguished on the lagoon of Comacchio. On the face of it, the fishing community of Lough Neagh is an anachronism in a modern consumer society, wresting its means to live from the water in a manner not essentially different from that of two hundred or two thousand years ago. For those prepared to endure its rigours the lough and its eels sustain a level of prosperity that would have seemed an impossible dream to their oppressed and impoverished forbears. Even so, fewer and fewer are prepared to endure. It's a wonder the community can exist still; and you wonder how long it has got.

For John Quinn, the better times came a little late, but better late than never. I had the devil's own job tracking the old fisherman down in the maze of lanes criss-crossing the bulge of land on the lough's northern shore. Three different people sent me down three different tracks, all of them in good faith, for there were Quinns down each. Eventually I accosted a farmer Quinn who sent me after the fisherman Quinn, who was sitting in an armchair in the neat living room of his neat little bungalow. It was nicely placed, with the lough like a shining sheet beyond the crumbled ruins of the old church of Cranfield, the pub at the crossroads, and Quinns all around. 'Ah, there's that many Quinns,' the man said with a smile, slowly shaking his big head with its enormous ears, running his hard hands over a sparse bristle of white hair. And with twelve surviving children – though but one fisherman among them – there's plenty more to come.

This concentration of surnames in particular locations, which can make finding an individual a trying experience, is a feature of the lough people. It is the result of the centuries-old custom of living and marrying among themselves, allied to a fecundity that may well be attributable to the quantities of eel flesh they consume. Similar clusters may be found in all the traditional fishing places: of Conlons, Dowds, Hagans, Johnstons, McGarrys, Devlins, McNeills and so on. Indeed, while there is one colony of Quinns in and around Cranfield on the northern shore, there is another, much older one on the western side, at Moortown. The census of 1861 found that in one division of that parish, Cluntiquin, forty per cent of householders were called Quinn (in Moortown as a whole, almost a quarter of the inhabitants were called Devlin).

My John Quinn was now eighty, in the first year of his retirement, the season just ending being the first since he was fifteen when he had lain in bed of a morning rather than being up with the birds to bring in the long lines. As a boy he had begun, as they all did, with his father and his father's brothers. They were truly hard times, so hard as to be difficult to imagine now. The fishing was controlled by outsiders and the fishermen were kept under the heel. Any who dared dispute the bosses' right to organise matters to their advantage risked unemployment, even arrest. Bitter little clashes exploded across the lough as illegal nets and lines were seized and destroyed, and unlicensed boats were impounded.

Many gave up the struggle and sought new lives in America or England. John Quinn could have been among them. 'Many a hundred times I thought of it,' he said. 'But I never had enough money to get anywhere.' I asked where his money had gone. 'To the stout-house, that's where it went,' he replied with a short laugh at his shortcomings. It earned him a sharp look from Mrs Quinn, a little, kindly old lady, who – unasked – had brought me sandwiches as well as tea, as if she knew by instinct when a man was hungry. I wondered what her hopes might have been.

He had taken work where he could get it – labouring in the quarries, helping build the aerodrome – but always going back to the fishing because the fish were always there. Then John Quinn had had a stroke of luck. In 1970 an uncle had left him the house at Cranfield. It was nearer the water, there were fewer boats, and there was what he called a 'cleaner lift' for the lines and nets. By now a more enlightened age had dawned. The fishermen, so long harried and exploited, now, in a manner of speaking, ran the show. Prices were good, the money came in – and went out again, in the direction of the stout-house.

Four or five years ago John Quinn had begun to tire of the fishing. It was not so much the laborious and repetitive business of setting the lines and hauling them up, which he could do almost in his sleep; but the matter of sleep itself, and its fracture by the shrill of the alarm clock, day in, day out. He hated getting up before dawn, and went on hating it, the tyranny of a schedule which demanded that the lines be lifted and the eels back and ready for collection at a normal person's breakfast time, by which time he had been on the go for five hours. He was slowing up too, and the boat work was not getting any easier. So he had retired, and now slept in of a morning and pottered about during the day tending his potatoes, looking out over the water that had been his hunting ground for so long, shuffling down to the pub to add one or two to the incalculable number of pints of stout poured in his name over six decades and more, hearing the news from other Quinns and fishermen, swapping stories.

Did he miss the fishing? 'Surely to God I miss the money. That's for sure. I was content enough, I suppose. Mebbe I could have done something else. But I was never well learned, you know, to get other jobs. And, you see, I was born to the fishing. But no, I wouldn't say that I missed it. I would say that I don't miss it.'

His brother came in, a smaller version of the Quinn model, with a rounder head and less impressive ears, a good few years younger than John and still at the fishing game. I wanted to talk to him about it, but he said almost nothing, smiled a lot, then abruptly left after five minutes without having given any obvious clue as to why he had come. A while later a car drew up and decanted a granddaughter who came every school day for her tea. Every Sunday the Quinns gather at the bungalow for lunch. 'It's standing room only,' said the old fisherman proudly. 'There's more things in life than money in the bank.'

*   *   *

Around the shore towards Toome, Kevin Johnston had finished for the season and was looking for his winter job. Until the coming of BSE, he had combined the fishing with small-scale beef farming. But now the cattle sheds were empty, the meadows shaggy and ungrazed, and with bills to be paid, he would be off soon, taking any job on offer.

Johnston does not seem to resent the hardships and uncertainties of the fishing life. He is proud of his boat, twenty-six feet of solid, functional fibreglass equipped with big diesel engine, cabin, radar and fish-finder – a far cry from the handsome old wood and clinker craft powered by heavy oars fixed on thole pins and sails of calico. The rest of it – the baiting of the thousands of hooks with laboriously dug worms, the setting of the lines, the pre-dawn call and the lifting of the lines, the lugging of the barrel of eels to the back of the house to await collection – he accepts as necessities. But he clearly resents authority, being told by someone else how many eels he can catch, and when, and how. The rules state that there is no fishing between midday on Saturday and 4 a.m. on Monday, which, since the long lines are set in the evening, means a five-day week, the weekly quota being around forty stone.

Asked if the rules are obeyed, Johnston smiles a secret little smile. Everyone knows they are not, and that it's a matter of what you can get away with. Fyke nets, for instance, were banned in the 1970s on the grounds that they made catching eels too easy, tempting fishermen to exceed their quotas and spirit the excess away through unofficial channels. But the possession of them could not be outlawed, and since the lough is very big, and the nets very difficult to spot, many fishermen still resort to them on the quiet. If they are caught, they do not complain too vociferously when the offending items are impounded or destroyed, knowing that any serious upset might imperil their bonuses and even their licences. As Kevin Johnston puts it: 'They've got us by the nuts.'

He is but one of many fearful for the fishery's future. He believes the eels are scarcer, and he has to work harder to keep up to his quota. His costs, particularly for bait and diesel, rise like any other, yet the price he gets for his eels, around £1.20 or £1.30 a pound, is not much different from ten years ago. There are other, more insidious pressures. With the cessation of violence in the province has come a precarious sense of security. Investment has grown, established businesses have prospered and recruited, new businesses have sprung up. For all that the fishermen have their bungalows, their cars, their satellite TVs, an ease in their lives unthinkable a generation ago, theirs is still – by the standards of today – a conspicuously taxing, uncertain and unglamorous livelihood. It has its compensations: autonomy, self-reliance, space and solitude, the pearly dawns and crimson sunsets. Kevin Johnston would not gladly renounce it, even if that lottery win they all dream about came his way. But he doubts strongly that his son, Dualtach, who helps him in the boat, will ever be more than a part-timer.

Johnston is edging towards fifty, and has been fishing since he was a lad. Many of the others are older, and for most this is the only life they have known. But who, he asks, would choose it over a salaried, pensioned job, with car, bonuses, perks? Unless, that is, the bad times come again. The lough and its eels have always been there. That permanence provides a reassurance lodged deep in the collective memory. There have been bad times, plenty of them, when the lough fed its people. Were the bubble to burst, and all the hopes of a brighter future to disappear in the familiar plumes of smoke, the lough would still be there to go back to.

Kevin Johnston's maternal ancestors, the O'Dowds, came to the lough three hundred and fifty years ago from the west. They were part of the displacement set in motion by the Plantation – that deceivingly bland term for the process by which Catholic Ireland's Protestant conquerors sought to cement their rule and perpetuate the destruction of the old Gaelic order. By decree of James I of England and VI of Scotland, the best of Ulster's land was taken from the Irish and presented to incoming English and Scottish settlers, so that by the end of the 1630s almost ninety per cent of property in the Six Counties was in Protestant hands.

The natives were left to make the best they could of the land deemed too impoverished or inaccessible to be worth the trouble of grabbing. If they could not live on it, they either starved or moved elsewhere. Some settled on the patches of firm ground to the east of Lough Neagh. A substantial number migrated to the uplands of Sperrin, south-east of Derry, and to the bogs and scrubby woodland along the lough's western shore. Those that stopped by the water perforce learned to fish.

The population movements that gave birth to the fishing community have been recorded in great detail in Daniel J. Donnelly's book, *On Lough Neagh's Shores*. Among the earlier arrivals were the Devlins, the Quinns, the McKennas, the Conlons, the Croziers and the Campbells. The Conlons, for instance, reached the lough from the south. As they sailed down the river Blackwater, they passed the ford where, in 1598, the old Irish order had staged one of its final acts of defiance, the army of The O'Neill – Hugh O'Neill, Earl of Tyrone – and his son-in-law Red Hugh O'Donnell, annihilating a force sent by Queen Elizabeth and commanded by one of the slain on that bloody day, Sir Henry Bagenal, whose sister had been one of O'Neill's numerous wives. Some of the Conlons stopped at Maghery, on the lough's south-western shore. Others continued along the western side until they reached Anateemore, where they settled.

Another of those savage traumas of Irish history, the famine of the mid-nineteenth century, provided a further injection to the population. The potato blight struck with appalling severity in areas such as The Sperrins, driving starving families towards the lough. At around this time the first Johnston came to Toome from Coleraine, and became a boat builder. A grandson, Richard Johnston, married into one of the original fishing families, the Pogues, and built a wooden house on an island close to the shore. One Johnston girl married into the McNeills, a fishing family of Scottish origin, and another into the McErleans. One of the Pogue girls married an incomer, Billy McElroy. Now, a century and a half later, about half the northern shore fishermen are called Johnston, Pogue, McElroy, McNeill or McErlean. They are all related, as are many of them to other fishing families around the lough, forming a network of kinship so enormous and complex that even its members cannot unravel it with any degree of confidence.

*　　*　　*

That, told selectively and as simply as possible, is the story of how the fishing families of Lough Neagh came to be there. But they were only the inheritors of a tradition stretching back several thousand years. And even in the Christian era, a thousand years before those Conlons put in at Maghery, the monks there were catching eels and sending them to their brothers at the Abbey of St Peter and St Paul at Armagh. Within a century of St Patrick claiming Ireland in the name of Christ in AD 432, monastic settlements had sprung up at several sites along the Bann and beside Lough Neagh. One of the most important was founded in the sixth century at Ardboe, on the western shore, by Saint Colman (a different Colman from the one who was Bishop of Lindisfarne). According to ancient tradition, the saint himself fished for eels, using their fat to make lamp oil. The place is marked today by Old Ardboe Cross, and, according to Daniel Donnelly, the fishermen who launch their boats nearby still offer thanks to the memory and beneficent influence of that piscatory missionary.

Four hundred years after the coming of Patrick ushered in a golden age of Irish scholarship and culture, less welcome visitors sailed up the Bann into the lough. Viking invaders appeared in 838 to plunder the riches of the monasteries, and again towards the end of the century, and again in 945 when they were repelled by Domnal, first of the O'Neills. The quiet life of the monks was ended, and most of the monastic sites were abandoned. But the fishing continued, by spear and trap for the salmon and eels on the river, by net on the lough. In time, the O'Neills made themselves rulers of Ulster, and for the next six hundred years it was dominated by various factions within the clan, and left pretty much to its own devices – even though nominally claimed as a possession by the English Crown. Over that period, the reputation of its inhabitants and their chieftains for barbarism, treachery and cruelty gained the status of an absolute truth across the water. That shady Welsh cleric, Giraldus Cambrensis, was sent to Ireland towards the end of the twelfth century, and in his *Expugnatio Hibernica* undertook with relish the task of blackening the name of Ireland, relating – among many other real and fictitious horrors – how the banished King of Leinster, Diarmid Mac Murchada, when presented with the heads of two hundred of his enemies by order of his English ally, Richard Strongbow, took one he recognised and 'gnawed at the nose and cheeks, a cruel and most inhuman act'. Of the fishermen of Lough Neagh, Giraldus recorded, most improbably, that 'they make more frequent complaint about the quantity of fish in their nets and breaking them, than of the want of fish.'

Henry VIII had declared himself 'King of this land of Ireland' in 1542. But it was to be a further half-century and more before England's rulers decided it was time to bring the unruly province to heel. After Hugh O'Neill's defeat of Bagenal, the aging Queen Elizabeth dispatched the Earl of Essex to deal with the Irish, only for her favourite to disgrace himself by treatying with O'Neill. He was followed by Charles Blount, Lord Mountjoy, who was made of sterner stuff. Blount's secretary wrote of the land that it was 'uneven, soft, mountainous, watery, woody and open to wind and rain, and so fenned that it hath bogs on the very tops of mountains bearing neither man nor beast.' Nonetheless, Blount did the necessary. In 1601 Hugh O'Neill and Hugh O'Donnell, Lords of Tyrone and Tyrconnel, yielded to England's army at Kinsale, and the old order was smashed. The earls fled into exile, and their lands – including Lough Neagh and the Bann – were forfeited to the Crown.

These waters were recognised as the richest treasure of Ulster. The story of their exploitation, and of the oppression and defrauding of the people who depended on them, is extraordinarily tangled and murky. But it is also illustrative of the manner in which the conquerors of the island tended to treat their new possessions; and thus helps explain, as much as the conquering itself, the attitudes towards the conqueror that colour the relationship to this day.

The major part of that story was told in a book published in 1913, meaningfully entitled *Stolen Waters*. It was written by Timothy Healy, a man well known in Irish politics between 1880 and his death in 1928. Healy mixed his principles in a way that – a century later – seems wholly paradoxical. He was a fervent Irish Catholic nationalist and a fervent Royalist, who served for almost forty years as an MP at Westminster, where he was feared and admired in equal measure for his witty, wounding tongue. He helped instigate the downfall of Parnell, and eventually became the first Governor-General of the new Free State. Healy was also a barrister, and it was in that capacity that he enlisted in the protracted and ultimately unsuccessful legal struggle by the Lough Neagh fishermen to win their freedom. His book is a desperately hard read, consisting as it largely does of a mass of ancient documentation presented without editing, much as it would have been in court. But the case it presents is wholly compelling.

Before 1605, Healy wrote,

> the nets of the clusters of fisherfolk all around its
> [Lough Neagh's] banks in five counties swept it
> at pleasure. The Bann once formed the boundary
> between Con O'Neill and Hugh O'Neill's territory;
> in winter the salmon and eel of the Bann fed the
> O'Neill clan when their crops and stock were burned
> or destroyed by the invader.

With the sway of the O'Neills broken, the officers of
the new King, James I, set about the subjugation of this
troublesome land. They devised the system of colonisation
which they called the Plantation, and one of the inducements to the City of London to fund it was the promise of
the valuable fishing rights on the Bann and Lough Neagh.
The institutions were thwarted, though, by the very man
sent to implement the Plantation – the Lord Deputy, Sir
Arthur Chichester. Timothy Healy called Chichester the
'ablest of the able men who wrought the overthrow of
Celtic power in Ireland', but also showed him to have
been among the most unscrupulous, devious, vindictive and
avaricious; well able to combine the energetic prosecution
of the political objective with self-enrichment on an epic
scale. The securing to himself of the fishing rights to the
river and the lough by forged letters patent purporting to
convey royal assent was but one of the acts of fraud and
coercion by which he made himself the most powerful and
hated man in Ireland.

Chichester died in 1625, leaving his estate to his brother
Edward. In 1632 Charles I appointed as Lord Deputy
of Ireland someone even more adept than Chichester at
arousing fear and loathing: Sir Thomas Wentworth, Black

Tom Tyrant, later Earl of Strafford. Wentworth's task was to quell disturbance and extract much-needed revenues. He was mercilessly efficient in its discharge, alienating Catholics, Protestants, lords, commoners, landlords and officials alike. One of Wentworth's most lucrative areas of prosecution was the thicket of fraudulent titles that had sprouted through the Plantation – among them the rights to Lough Neagh and the Bann. In 1638 Edward Chichester, under severe pressure, gave back the 'Stolen Waters' to the Crown.

Wentworth's service availed him little, for in 1641, on Tower Hill, he paid the ultimate price for his genius in making enemies. Among those charged with managing – or, rather, mismanaging – the impeachment proceedings against him was an Antrim landowner, Sir John Clotworthy, later Viscount Massereene. Clotworthy had long cast envious eyes on the fishing rights, and in 1656 – despite having served a term of imprisonment for embezzlement – he was rewarded for his loyalty to the Cromwellian cause with a ninety-nine-year lease to the fishing on Lough Neagh. Unknown to the Lord Protector, he simultaneously induced the Commonwealth Council in Dublin surreptitiously to grant him the lease to the Bann – which Cromwell himself had promised to restore to the City of London.

Clotworthy's title was, at best, dubious, and quite possibly unlawful. Nevertheless, within a few months of the Restoration of the monarchy in 1660, he had successfully petitioned Charles II to confirm his prerogatives over lough and river, and was made a viscount for his pains. As Healy puts it, with tremendous scorn: 'While Cromwell's skull bleached in Westminster Hall the brows of his bantlings were decked with coronets.' But the new Lord Massereene's success was short-lived. Manoeuvring against him was one Arthur Chichester, nephew to that first thief of the title and son of the Edward Chichester who had inherited the estate. This Chichester, who had been ennobled as Lord Donegal in 1647, persuaded the King that his father had renounced the rights only as a favour to oblige Charles I, that the promised compensation had never been paid, and that the injustice should be remedied by restoration on the expiry of Clotworthy's lease.

That reversion became operative in 1755. For a century and a half after that, ownership passed unchallenged to successive earls of Donegal, who were generally content to secure what income they could by subletting the rights while staying far away from Lough Neagh and its unappealing surroundings. The value of the fishery – which in 1700 provided a revenue of £1600 – lay with the salmon, and the Donegals and their lessees and agents saw no reason to trouble themselves with the eels. These were left to the impoverished Irish, who did as they had always done, setting their traps on the Bann and their nets on the lough, filling their sod huts with the smells of eels fried, roasted, salted, and pickled. Without the eels, the fishermen of Neagh would have faced the starvation that was becoming a fact of life throughout the island.

The Irish naturalist, William Thompson, recorded his impressions of a visit to Toome during the 1830s, where he was told of a catch of seventy thousand eels in one night from the weir below the village. He visited Coleraine, to watch the elvers fighting their way over the salmon weir known as The Cutts – 'it is an interesting sight to mark the thousands of young eels ascending. Hay ropes are suspended over the rocky parts to aid them. At these places the river is black with the multitudes of young eels.' (Thompson had other good eel stories. One, lifted from a seventeenth-century history of Iar Connaught, concerns a fisherman called William M'Ghoill of Cong, at the northern end of Lough Corrib, who, having caught one good eel and 'being busie about catching more', thrust his girdle through its gills; whereupon the eel broke free, escaping with the girdle, M'Ghoill's knife, and his purse with thirteen shillings and fourpence in it, only to be recaptured with its booty in the Galway River which flows out of the southern end of Corrib. Thompson also relates how a hose being used to fight a fire in Belfast burst 'in consequence of an eel about 18 inches in length completely stopping it . . . A portion of the eel's head which projected from the aperture of the pipe was caught by a man in his teeth and the creature thus removed.')

Until the middle of the nineteenth century the trade in Lough Neagh eels was purely local, the price, according to Thompson, varying between one and two pence a pound. But with the development of the rail network in England, the merchants at Billingsgate began to show an interest in Irish eels. They found that it was viable to ship them alive from Coleraine to Liverpool, and then by train to London. They were prepared to pay top prices, and suddenly the owners of the ancient and dubious rights began to pay the eel closer attention.

Their solicitude was heightened by an accelerating decline in the revenues from salmon, blamed on pollution of the spawning streams by flax, bleach and dye works, the enormous losses of fry in the nets and traps, the depredations of cormorants, mergansers and other feathered predators, and rampant poaching. Arthur Grimble, in his authoritative *The Salmon Rivers of Ireland*, described this as being 'of a desperate character', carried out by a 'desperate bad lot of men', who on one occasion had set fire to a house in Toome where a party of police officers was being held.

It became an urgent imperative for the gaggle of lessees and sub-lessees to enforce their claims upon Lough Neagh. 'Casting greedy eyes upon its great expanse,' wrote Healy, 'they sought to make believe it was theirs ... Naboth's vineyard was not more keenly coveted.' A war of attrition broke out between the fishermen and those they regarded as the thieves of their birthright, which was waged in the courts and on the water. In 1874 the lessees won a legal action in Belfast, but it was reversed by a higher court. In 1878 the case went to the House of Lords, where the judges ruled that the Donegall family's claim was unproved and unsound, and that the right of public fishing should be upheld. But the matter did not rest there. The Marquis of Donegall's grandson and heir, Lord Shaftesbury, granted a lease in 1905 that included the right to catch eels in the Bann and Lough Neagh. Two years later the lessees issued a writ to restrain fishing on the lough. This case was heard in the Dublin High Court by Mr Justice Ross. He found that the fishermen – among whom was named Richard Johnston, one of the Johnstons of Annaghmore – were trespassers; and rejected the argument proposed on their behalf by Timothy Healy MP that the lough had been 'from time immemorial ... a public and navigable inland sea, and that every subject of the realm had ... the right to fish upon the lough.'

Mr Justice Ross had, in effect, concluded that the rights to the Bann and Lough Neagh had been lawfully appropriated by Sir Arthur Chichester, lawfully obtained by Sir John Clotworthy, lawfully passed to Chichester's nephew Lord Donegall, and lawfully assigned by Donegall's descendants to an assortment of profiteers. His opinion aroused fury and dismay. Guerrilla warfare broke out on the lough as the bailiffs, supported by armed police, endeavoured to assert the bosses' writ. Nets were seized and burned, boats holed, heads knocked together and some bones broken. The fishermen vowed to fight on. At a public meeting in Toome – called after the failure of an appeal against Mr Justice Ross's ruling – a well-known Belfast antiquary and nationalist, Francis Biggar, stoked the flames with these words:

> One by one, unworthy men wanted to oust them from the eel fishery ... and even the bed of the lough itself. Who owned the bed of the lough? The fishermen and their fathers for hundreds of years utilised it and will utilise it. [Cheers.] They were driven from the good lands to the lake, and they would not be driven from the lake to give place to London merchants and Dublin brewers to fish it at so much per head. [Cheers.]

Acts of defiance and sabotage persisted as preparations were made to take the fishermen's case to the House of Lords. The Bishop of Down and Connor, various priests, justices of the peace and local notables of Catholic and nationalist persuasion lent their financial and moral support to what had become a minor cause célèbre. In 1911 judgement was delivered. It went, by a margin of four to three, against the fishermen. Among the dissenters was the Lord Chancellor, who gave as his opinion that the words in a lease granted by Lord Donegall to his brother-in-law in 1805, which extended the rights to embrace the whole lough, had been forged.

Tim Healy, who had striven so long in the cause, exploded in bitter eloquence: 'To toil for one's daily bread in a perilous and precarious calling,' he wrote,

> is no enviable birthright. Since the world was young this craft had been freely plied by the longshoremen of Lough Neagh. To be bereft of one's living and see a scanty patrimony decreed to strangers is ill to bear; but the blow is made harder when the pretext for confiscation is alleged to be some musty letter from Cromwell, or reckless 'fairing' of the worthless tyrants. Well may it be asked why the welfare of the fishermen of five counties should count as naught against the parchments of ancient rascaldom?

The people of the lough had no choice but to give up the legal fight. None, however, believed justice had been done. The case was added to that long list of injuries done to the native Irish by their foreign oppressors, another festering sore, another wrong waiting to be righted. In the meantime they had to live; so, resentfully, they bowed the shoulder and went fishing. Demand for eels up to and during the Great War was buoyant, and catches had been bolstered by the adoption of the technique known as 'long-lining', the setting of lines with as many as two thousand baited hooks.

The 1920s saw hard times, with prices depressed and the management – the Old Company, as it was known –

intensifying its efforts to control the fishing. Many long-established fishing families gave up and emigrated, and the number of boats fell by half, to about a hundred. Some of those remaining bought licences from the Old Company, some did not. Some sold their eels through the company, some to local dealers or straight to Billingsgate. Whatever the arrangement, the living they were able to make was exiguous and precarious, and they remained – even by the standards of the times – conspicuously downtrodden and impoverished.

In 1959 a consortium of Billingsgate merchants bought the lease. It was headed by Hans Kuijeten, whose distribution company at Maldon was already the major customer for the Lough Neagh eels. Kuijeten was well aware that the full potential of the fishery was nowhere near being realised. He and the Billingsgate wholesalers – mainly of Danish and Jewish origin – were determined that much closer attention should be paid to the migrating silver eels. These could be caught in very large numbers with comparatively little effort on the weirs along the Bann, and – once transported to the storage barges at Maldon – could be kept in good condition through the winter, the supply being carefully controlled to keep prices high. The merchants were much less keen on the brown (or yellow) eels caught on the lough in dribs and drabs over the summer months, which came with nasty, rusting hooks in their mouths and gullets (extricating a hook from an eel is a tricky and often impossible operation, so the long-liners cut them and leave them in the fish), and could not be kept in prime condition for more than a few days. For the fishermen, of course, the preference was the other way round, since very few of them could hope to find work on the traps, and they needed to be able to sell their staple, the brown eel, over a six-month season to survive.

But the bosses had the whip hand. They told the fishermen that the days of making separate deals with different dealers were over. From now on all eels must be sold to the Toome Eel Fishery at a price fixed by the company. More to the point, the company decreed how many it wanted, and it had already decided that it would have more of its own silvers, and fewer of the fishermen's brown eels. The efficiency with which this strategy was pursued can be gauged by the fact that within a year or two of Kuijeten and his comrades taking over, shipments of silver eels had increased sevenfold, to about seven hundred tons a year, and catches of brown eels had been slashed in proportion.

Faced with what they regarded as monopolistic oppression, the fishermen resorted to desperate measures. Smuggling became rampant, the eels being dispatched on the quiet across the border via Dublin, Dun Laoghaire or Rosslare to dealers in London who were outside the cartel and not at all particular as to where their supplies might be coming from. As much as a third of total production was being siphoned away through illicit channels, a haemorrhage Kuijeten and the rest regarded as intolerable. It was time to go to law again.

In the longest civil action in Northern Ireland's legal history – lasting for eight weeks towards the end of 1962 – the Toome Eel Fishery sought a declaration that it enjoyed the exclusive right to fish over the whole of the lough, as well as the river, and orders restraining four named individuals from fishing or marketing fish, and the Billingsgate firm of Jangaard and Butler from buying fish. Evidence was heard from two former Scotland Yard detectives who had followed the devious routes taken by the boxes of eels between the shores of the lough and the premises of Messrs Jangaard and Butler. All that ancient history was exhumed once again, the old parchments and title deeds and leases were pored over, the familiar arguments were rehearsed, and the familiar judgement was delivered. Mr Justice McVeigh took three hours to express his view that right lay with the Stuart kings and with Mr Kuijeten, Mr Salomensen and their colleagues, and that the fishermen whose livelihoods were at stake had no rights at all.

The cartel may well have applauded Mr Justice McVeigh for his wisdom. But if they thought the matter was now settled, they miscalculated. Within a few weeks of the judgement a new factor had entered the equation. It took the form of Father Oliver Kennedy, parish priest of Toome, a man with no particular knowledge of or previous interest in eels, but possessed of a keen concern for the welfare of his parishioners. Kennedy was asked to help, and he advised that the existing Lough Neagh Fishermen's Association should be reorganised and registered as a trade union; that it should become, in effect, a campaigning force. Against a background of continuing and worsening local opposition to its hegemony, the cartel began to come apart at the seams. Kuijeten was deposed as chairman. Subsequently he attempted a comeback, by buying the twenty per cent holding of Salomensen. To forestall this, the shareholding was offered to the Fishermen's Association for £83,000. Just over half was raised locally, the rest in the form of a bank loan.

With a voice at the directors' table, and a fifth share in the profits, the association sought to press home its advantage. The sense of injustice that had burned so long was now channelled into a purpose. Political tensions were increasing across the province, and the band of fish merchants which had so opportunistically attempted to lay its hands on the wealth of Lough Neagh found it ever more difficult to exploit the right enshrined by Mr Justice McVeigh. As Father Kennedy had calculated, they wearied of the struggle. In 1971 the Fishermen's Association – by now reincarnated as a cooperative, owned by its members – acquired the remaining eighty per cent of the company's shares. 'By that achievement,' Kennedy wrote, 'the co-operative succeeded in bringing to reality the dreams of previous generations of fishermen.'

A celebratory lunch was held at Toome on 27 January 1972. A photograph in the *Irish News* shows Father Kennedy flanked by the Bishop of Down and Connor, the most Reverend Dr William Philbin, and the Right Reverend Monsignor P. J. Mullaly. The Bishop is quoted as telling the fishermen: 'I am confident you are not going to look upon what has been gained merely as an asset or source of income. More than that, it is an opportunity of utilising a great gift of God.' Be that as it may, the stolen waters had at last been restored.

Thirty years on, the sign stands proudly at the entrance to the fishery, where the Derry–Belfast road crosses the Bann: 'Lough Neagh Fishermen's Cooperative Society Ltd'. It is adorned by a fat eel, curved in the shape of a C – which may just be a coincidence, though they are mostly

Catholic hereabouts. As befits the biggest wild eel fishery in the world, an imposing building stands by the weir, with spacious offices, loading bays for the eel-bearing trucks, a cavernous hall for the creatures to be sorted, a staffroom as big as a gym for the lads to munch their sandwiches and swallow strong tea. Outside the windows, the waters of the river tumble through the weir, hastening to the sea. On top of the structure sit the herons, like the Swiss Guard at the Vatican. I counted at least twenty of them on the weir itself, and more swaying in the alders on the far side.

Father Kennedy's Christian names are Oliver Plunket. Archbishop Oliver Plunket of Armagh was a recipient of English justice towards the end of King Charles II's reign – seized during the anti-Catholic frenzy unleashed by the 'discovery' of the bogus Popish Plot, tried for treason on evidence acknowledged even by Protestant fanatics as false, hanged, drawn and quartered on Tyburn. Ancient history, but not forgotten. Although Father Kennedy is far from anxious to talk politics, fragments are revealed: a quiet contempt for the old guard of Unionism, a quiet admiration for the leaders of Sinn Fein, a quiet, contemptuous hostility to the workings of the British government as represented by the Northern Ireland Office – 'they'll do nothing for us down here, they regard us as nothing more than a nest of nationalists' – a quiet, constant awareness that he speaks for a community but recently rescued from institutional oppression.

He looks remarkably like a rounder, more substantial version of Alec Guinness – a subtle, quizzical face sandwiched between two large ears made more noticeable by the flaring lobes. He rarely laughs, yet sounds as if he were constantly on the verge of doing so, his face creased in the enjoyment of some deeply private joke. The voice is soft, never rising above *piano*, soothing in its easy flow, the consonants picked out with fastidious clarity. To hear Father Kennedy refer to the 'fat content' of his eels – which in the course of any protracted conversation he will surely do – is one of the incidental pleasures of visiting the fishery.

Yet there is something formidable in his manner, too. He is, they say, capable of remarkable and frightening rudeness, with a temper that commands awe. I found him friendly, occasionally almost genial, humorous, informative, beguilingly fluent. There was no sign of that temper. But there was an unconcealed impatience with those who might be inclined to try to tell him his business or get the better of him in a commercial dealing, to waste his time, or challenge his expertise. The name of a Billingsgate merchant came up, the main eel buyer in London, renowned for his less than refined manners. 'He thinks he's the big man,' Father Kennedy said of him, voice dripping with disdain.

Having warned me several times over the telephone and on my arrival that he might well be too busy with the eels to talk to me at all, the priest discoursed for two hours. Much of what he told me I knew already, from a copy he had sent me of an address he had given at a workshop on eel management. The annual catch is about seven hundred and fifty tons, of which slightly over two thirds are brown eels caught in the lough over the summer, and the rest silvers taken in the traps in the autumn. About fifteen per cent go to London. The rest are exported live, by air, from Belfast to Holland, where they are sent out to Dutch smokers or sold on to other European markets. At the height of the summer season, the Toome fishery processes between six and seven tons of eel a day, around seventy thousand fish. The night before my arrival they had taken four tons in the traps.

The figures, the sheer fecundity of the lough, are staggering, and occasionally you have to remind yourself that this enterprise, turning over £6 million a year, is run not by some youthful, sharp-suited technocrat but by a portly, white-haired priest in a black shirt and comfortably shapeless old cardigan who should, by rights, be slipping into agreeable retirement instead of working a thirteen-hour day. He explained his initial involvement in a matter-of-fact fashion: 'I knew nothing about eels and I didn't want to. I was the curate, and here was a social problem, of a deprived community being manipulated by money people. When the fishermen lost the case, it was the end of the road legally. It was a bad law, but there was nothing we could do about that. We had to use other means.'

But all that was long ago. Why, into his seventies, was he still in charge? Father Kennedy smiled his self-deprecating smile, looking as if he were about to burst out laughing at some old joke between him and his God. 'I failed to extricate myself,' he said. 'Yes, it's high time I retired. I would like to find someone younger to take it on.' And suddenly he looked tired, and a little wistful.

The fishermen have known bosses in the past, and not liked them. In Father Kennedy's business strategy, the profit motive is down the list of priorities, well below the welfare of the community. But it is he who defines wherein that lies. His role is that of a patriarchal despot, allying benevolence of intent with intolerance of opposition. He speaks of the fishermen as if they were children, who must be helped despite themselves. 'The only time a Lough Neagh fisherman tells the truth,' he says in affectionate, condescending tones, 'is when he calls another fisherman a liar.' Left to themselves, the assumption goes, they would poach, overfish, cheat, quarrel, squander their money and the resource that sustains them – and, to be fair, there are many among the fishermen prepared to concede the justice of that view.

So they let their parish priest decide how many eels they should catch, by what method, how much they should be paid, and when. They grumble and criticise, and get round the rules when they can. But they do not challenge the system. The collective memory and historical awareness of the wretchedness and injustices of the past bind them in a strong, if grudging, appreciation of the present. It is difficult to see how this patriarchal, individualistic, indulgent structure would survive were the profit imperative to take charge. As it is, the cooperative continues only by courtesy of the lough. And here chill winds are blowing.

For a great many years the stock of eels in Lough Neagh has been sustained by human intervention. The run of elvers into the Bann has been intercepted at Coleraine, the little creatures then being transported overland and consigned to the broad waters of the lough to grow at their leisure into eels of harvestable size. It stands to reason that if upwards of three million grown-up eels are removed from the lough each year, the same number must mature for stocks to be maintained. The scale of the elver run has always varied wildly. In 1933 ten million were caught, in 1941 thirty million, in 1963 twenty-seven million, in 1967 five and a half million. Generally there were enough to supply the lough, and when there weren't, it was possible to buy in elvers from the Severn in England. Thus in 1985, when fewer than one and three quarter million Bann elvers were caught, more than ten million were brought in from outside.

Over the past ten years Lough Neagh – in common with every other eel fishery in Europe – has suffered a steep decline in elver recruitment. At the same time the soaring demand for them has lifted the price to a level that makes large-scale stocking from other sources prohibitively expensive. The fishermen are now catching the eels introduced perhaps seven or eight years ago. In the year 2000 a meagre one and a half million elvers were brought from Coleraine to the lough. That was the lowest figure for twenty years, but 2001 was even worse – 'a disaster', Father Kennedy called it. And in neither year was it possible to obtain fish from the Severn to supplement local supplies. The question asks itself insistently: in seven or eight years' time, how many eels will be left to be caught in that vast basin created – according to legend – when the giant Finn MacCool picked up the rock that was to become the Isle of Man and hurled it into the Irish Sea? No wonder Father Kennedy looks a worried man.

That night, on the weir, I listened to warm words about the priest – spontaneously uttered, I believe. I was in the company of two Conlon cousins: the younger, Seamus, the elder, Joe. They were there for the night fishing, as was I. But it was not a great night for the silvers to run. It was dark enough and the water high enough. But you need a good wind from the south to usher the fish from Toome

Bay into the river, and with the coming of darkness it had dropped to a gentle breeze. So there was plenty of time for sitting by the glowing coal fire in the snug little cabin above the black, rushing water of the Bann, smoking, drinking tea, telling and hearing fishermen's tales.

Initially the conversational running was made by Seamus, thirty-six years old, with nineteen years of fishing on the lough. I felt that Joe, twenty years older, viewed me with suspicion; and why should he not? I steered the chat towards Father Kennedy, and suddenly Joe became eloquent, going through the history of how the cooperative had been fashioned. Sure, the priest was sharp sometimes, even rude. But that was his shyness. He was a man who would do anything for you.

Unlike his cousin, Joe had been a fisherman under the old regime. Drive around the lough, he urged. Look at the houses the fishermen have, look at their cars. Their lives had been transformed, they were lives their fathers could only have dreamed of. The trouble was, Seamus interjected, that they expected the good times to go on getting better.

Every half-hour or so they left the warmth of the cabin to lift the nets. In the old days, the weirs consisted of Vs made of woven sections of hazel or willow known as *skeaghs*, fixed to piles driven into the bed of the river. Hemp nets twelve feet long were set at the apex from flat-bottomed boats called cots. The timber and wattle weir at Toome was dismantled in the 1930s when the Bann was being dredged, and a new structure, of metal and concrete, was installed soon after the Second World War. These days the nets are of nylon, and instead of having to be positioned from boats, their front ends are permanently attached to gates at the head of the weir, which are lowered when the night's fishing is to begin. There are four channels through the weir, each carrying two nets. At the downstream end of each net is a tail, which is detached for the eels to be landed. By law the weir can only extend across nine-tenths of the river, a channel known as the Queen's Gap being left unimpeded.

I watched the cousins by pale lamplight as they hauled in the tail, hand over hand, bent over the foaming torrent in their glistening waterproofs. Up it came, onto the greasy decking, a bulge of twisting shapes, slime frothing through the mesh. They tipped the eels into a plastic bin, reattached the tail to the main net and dropped it back into the channel, then lugged the bin across to the holding tanks, lifted a hatch and tipped them in. We returned to the cabin for another brew, and watched a television programme called *Who Wants To Be A Millionaire?*, perfect dream fare for men fated to spend chill autumn nights heaving eel nets and summer dawns lifting eel lines. Joe and Seamus were held by the drama of the quiz, by the ordinariness of these people gambling a year's earnings on a question. The lottery, the TV quiz, the pools, the horses – it was good to glimpse an existence free from toil, free from eels. But it was someone else's existence, for here was Father Kennedy on the blower, wanting to know how they were doing.

It was a slow night, a measly hundred and thirty stones. You should have been here, Joe Conlon said, that night back in the 1980s, the best night there ever was. They took six thousand stones, forty tons of eel, eight men at it without cease from dusk until dawn, the volume of silvers coming down so great that as soon as the last net had been emptied, the first was bursting again. I bid them goodnight and walked back across the bridge to the O'Neill Arms, where, yet again, my dreams were filled with images of pale-bellied, black-backed water serpents.

After breakfast I went back. Under the gaze of the herons, the men were transferring the catch from the holding tanks to the main building for sorting. As they dipped the nets into the tanks and lifted the fish, slime cascaded like melting sugar. I felt that I had had almost enough of eels, for the time being. I said farewell to a thoroughly amiable and decent body of men and thanked Father Kennedy, while attempting to stem a renewed panegyric to the Lough Neagh eel and its exceptional fat content.

I walked up towards the lough, past the derelict bridge which once carried the railway from Belfast to Derry, past a scattering of burned-out cars, past deserted lock gates and the giant sluices which control the flow from the lough down the river. I came at last to open water, stippled grey under a benign grey sky. There was nothing much to look at: a flat shoreline of scrubby trees and soggy fields, rocks, a great many waterfowl swimming and flapping about, quacking and clucking and taking to the air for no very obvious reason, water stretching away to meet the sky. I tried to picture the life beneath the ripples: snouty, beady-eyed fish in their silvery travel garb, snaking their way in my direction, bellies against the mud, answering the age-old call.

I was back the following July to see the netting and long-lining on the lough itself. I went out with Paul Wiley and his father Charlie, who lived among a good many other Wileys a little way out of Arboe on the western shore. Charlie, who was in his sixties and had been a fisherman all his adolescent and adult life, preferred the lines because they caught more fish. Paul, a tall man with a gentle way of talking, favoured the nets, while his wife, Antoinette, would have liked him to have got out of the fishing altogether and stuck with the painting and decorating.

We headed well out to set the lines. The process took a good three hours, Paul steering the big fibreglass boat while his father and his regular helper, John O'Neill, perched side by side at the stern, baiting the hooks alternately with red worms dug from the local dump, and mealworms imported from England. The lines, with the hooks and the smooth flat stones used to keep it down, were heaped in trays, looking like mounds of slender pasta. The line snaked out between and behind the two men, the best part of a mile of it by the time we had finished, not far short of two thousand baited hooks.

That night I went out with Paul and his brother Martin. The lough was getting itself into a boisterous mood, the wind coming from the south-east, where the Mountains of Mourne formed a dark hump on the horizon. Behind us, as the boys cast the net, the sun set in streaks of fire behind a fat tongue of grey cloud. It was hard, constant work, placing the mesh in a horseshoe behind the boat, the two of them dragging it in fast hand over fist, tipping the eels on the deck, sorting out the rubbish and turning the decent fish into the barrel; then again, over and over again, often for six hours or so until dawn showed its face. But it didn't have the fiddly, mucky monotony of the hooks, and Paul said they got better eels.

Each time the net came up the gulls appeared as if by

magic, twisting and wheeling feet above the stern, then diving at the discarded roach, bream and pollan. The herons followed, with heavy, slow wing-beats, catching nothing that I could see. On the far side of the lough the planes moved deliberately through the night sky, yellow lights over the orange lights of Aldergrove Airport. For a couple of hours the eels came in steadily, and I could hear their tails slapping lightly against the side of the black bin as the net was paid out. I sat down on the box in front of the wheelhouse, and, despite the jerky motions of the boat, I fell asleep. I awoke as we nosed back into the mooring. The brothers said they had decided to pack up early. The eels had gone elsewhere, and the last few draughts had produced only roach, in vast shoals that clogged the netting with a porridge of silver scales. They weighed in about six and a half stones of eels, which was not bad, not great.

Three hours later we were back, to take up the lines. We had to go a couple of miles out, searching for Charlie's blue buoy under a crescent moon that hung in the paling sky. The wind was blowing insistently, the waves coming foam-crested and fast, making the boat leap and corkscrew. In the east an angry crimson glow presaged sunrise. Paul scooped up the buoy, then took the helm while John O'Neill pulled in the line with his hard, stained hands. Whenever there was a keepable eel on the hook, he would flip it in an arc so that the nylon just above the hook was cut by the blade of a knife stuck upright in a wedge of wood fixed to the lip of the bin. The little eels, perch and other fish went into another bin to be returned. Charlie watched, intervening to sort out tangles and cut free fish strangled in the lines.

Even with three men (normally the whole operation

is done by two) it was gruelling work on that heaving water. Twice they found that the lines had been cut, then just thrown back, by other fishermen who had pulled up Charlie's gear with their own. On one occasion we came upon the culprits, who had got the line caught around their propeller. Each time we had to drag the bottom for it, using a coronet of barbed wire weighted with a steel chain. They told me that this happened all the time, and – whereas the fishermen used to be as careful of another's lines as their own, pausing to disentangle them and return them intact – these days no one bothered. They just cut them and chucked them away, and too bad if it was done to you. It was a sign of the times, Charlie said, another sign of the times.

They weighed in nine stones, a hundred and thirty pounds of good eels, and Charlie was well enough pleased. I asked if he would be baiting again that afternoon in the usual way, but he scowled at the wind, which by now was setting the trees to a wild dance, and said probably not: a day of enforced idleness, a day earning no money. Although he had had a reasonable catch, the talk was unrelievedly gloomy. The number of boats was down to below one hundred, half what it was two or three years back. Even so they were struggling to get their quotas, struggling to get a decent price for them. And there was something wrong with the lough and with the eels. If you tried to keep them in the sunken storage barrels for more than a couple of days they sickened and developed red lesions.

At the fishery Father Kennedy was not exuding cheery optimism either. He was as courteous as I remembered, and was wearing the same – or an identical – blue cardigan. But he seemed more subdued, as if the worries were getting to him. The elver run had failed, and all his efforts to buy in supplementary stocks had come to naught. The lough was not in a good condition, but no one would do anything about it. The fishermen no longer looked out for each other, it was every man for himself, and every warning he gave about handing in undersized or sick fish went unheeded. No, he still had not found anyone to take over from him.

I went to look at the old cross at Arboe, where St Colman once fished. Between the cross and the shore is a ruined church and a graveyard. The beauty of the spot is somewhat diminished by the huge, gleaming monuments, engraved in shining gold, the stones vertical in rectangles of coloured chippings. With my back to the excesses of the monumental mason, and the wind from the water in my face, I looked out over that foamy, restless inland sea, and thought about that long history of monks and scribes, of invaders and oppressors, of the generations of fishermen and their fishing, the lough sustaining its people.

EPILOGUE

A lament

It is the strangest of seas: without shores, without waves, without currents. Its bottom is two, sometimes three miles down, a place of utter darkness where starfish and sea cucumbers creep. Above is the blackness of the abyssal deeps, relieved only by the occasional pinprick of bioluminescence from the tail of a gulper eel and the unearthly glow from the comb jellies, where pteropods, jellyfish, scalps, and other blobs of bathypelagic tissue float in lifelong lightlessness.

Held up by that dense, frigid mass is an oval lens of warmer, saltier water three thousand feet deep. Those who sail across this lens are startled and unnerved by the deep electric blue of the element below them, and its clarity, so intense that a white disc six feet across is visible at a depth of two hundred feet. That transparency is a measure of its barrenness. Its rate of planktonic production is paltry, its plant content one two-thousandth of the average in the English Channel. It is the cleanest, clearest, purest, most biologically impoverished sea on the planet.

The great depths of the Sargasso Sea and the shallow ellipse at its surface together form an immense eddy, moving clockwise with extreme slowness. It is kept in place by the ocean currents which drive around its perimeter: the Canaries Current to the east, the North Equatorial Current to the south, the Gulf Stream to the west, the North Atlantic Current to the north. Energised by the heat of the sun, the pull of the moon, and the turning of the earth, the motion of these currents is urgent. But within and above the eddy of the Sargasso is an epic stillness. The sky is blue or monochrome light grey, the winds are light, atmospheric pressure is high and constant. The surface, greasy with a slick of organic matter, shifts to no perceptible rhythm. The clumps of yellow sargassum weed hang in lines, motionless. Rubbish collects here – sheets of plastic, styrofoam cups, fluorescent tubes – and drifts with infinite slowness. In an experiment carried out in the 1920s, 355 bottles weighted with sand to float low in the water were dropped into the Sargasso. Only seven ever escaped to reach land.

It was inevitable that a sea so unlike other seas should have stimulated the mariner's affection for the telling of tall tales which were generally told by men who had never been near it. Those who did found they had little to fear. Columbus, in the *Santa Maria*, crossed the Sargasso in a matter of ten days in September 1492, commenting that the conditions reminded him of Andalusia in April, nothing being wanted except the song of the nightingales. But Columbus knew what to expect. Before sailing west from the Canaries into the unknown, he had taken the trouble to drop in on an ancient mariner of Palos, Pedro de Valasco, who, forty years before, had sailed south from the Azores into the sea of weed. De Valasco told Columbus that, although the winds were light, they blew, and the weed would give way before the keel of the *Santa Maria*.

He was right. But Columbus' men had heard other accounts, and when they first encountered the floating islands of sargassum, the nervous seamen cried out, imploring the Admiral to turn back or condemn them to perish. He did neither, but pressed on, reaching the West Indies after a remarkably uneventful journey. One presumes his men told their own stories of surviving the Sargasso. But somehow the other tales held sway, and were elaborated until a complete mythology about the place became accepted. Its chief elements were the weed – which choked ships and harboured sea monsters – and the calm, which rendered escape impossible.

So, when Jules Verne's Captain Nemo traversed it, he kept the *Nautilus* several yards down 'not wishing to entangle his screw in that herbaceous mass'; while the narrator of *Twenty Thousand Leagues Under The Sea* looked fearfully up at the trees 'torn from the Andes or the Rocky Mountains and floated by the Amazon or the Mississippi' and the 'numerous wrecks', and gratefully ahead to the time when all this driftwood would have been petrified into coal and mined to keep future generations warm. The nightmare of the Graveyard of Ships took a firm grip on the seafaring imagination – 'a vast, ruinous congregation of wrecks . . . as though all the wrecked ships in the world were lying huddled together in a miserably desolate company . . . the dross of wave and tempest which has been gathering slowly and still more slowly wasting in the fastness of the Sargasso Sea', wrote an American spinner of nautical nonsense, Thomas Janvier. At about the same time, the supposedly sober and factual *Chambers Journal* of 1897 warned all prudent skippers against attempting to enter the sea 'for it certainly will not be long before the tangling weeds would altogether choke up his screw and render it useless'.

The reputation lived on. *Wide Sargasso Sea*, Jean Rhys's haunting novel about love, betrayal and madness on a Caribbean island, actually makes no mention of the place. But in a poem written at the same time, 'Obeah Night', she touched on that enigmatic title:

> Perhaps Love would have smiled then
> Shown us the way
> Across that sea. They say it's strewn with wrecks
> And weed-infested.
> Few dare it, fewer still escape.

And – more prosaically – as recently as 1952, a French doctor and adventurer, Alain Bombard, declared before setting sail across the Atlantic on a raft his determination to avoid 'the terrible trap . . . where plant filaments and seaweed grip vessels in an unbreakable net'.

In fact, long before Dr Bombard began paddling, the innocuous reality of the Sargasso had been thoroughly revealed, and the popular hunger to believe in sinister forces at sea had been transferred to the more seductive mythical properties of a neighbouring death trap, the Bermuda Triangle. William Beebe took the *Arcturus* into the depths off Bermuda in 1925, and found no sea monsters, little weed, and nothing else to cause alarm; while Johannes Schmidt scoured the southern Sargasso for weeks on end without encountering anything more intimidating than eel larvae three inches long.

One of the attractions of the hypothesis about the evolution of the freshwater eel, and the separation between the two Atlantic species, and those of Africa, Australasia and the Pacific, is that it offers a possible explanation of the enduring loyalty of *A. anguilla* and *A. rostrata* to the Sargasso Sea. Louis Bertin expressed it elegantly half a century ago:

> It is because the temperate eels have a sub-tropical origin that they continue to go to the warm waters to spawn and make long journeys to reach them. Having become, in the adult state, able to live in the most varied climes, they have remained faithful to the conditions of their ancestral life in the matter of reproduction.

It is a beguiling proposition, that the eels of Europe are programmed to swim three thousand miles in order to find the closest contemporary equivalent in terms of warmth and saltiness to the gigantic proto-Mediterranean ocean where their ancestors struggled into existence. It gains support from the theory of continental drift, put forward by Alfred Wegener early in the twentieth century, which Bertin dismissed as 'highly debatable', but which is now widely accepted. The stretching of the Atlantic that accompanied the movement of the American landmass to the west would account for the most immediately striking aspect of the migration, its extreme length.

They come from the north, following routes we know nothing of, passing Bermuda and the thirty degree latitude line. There the character of the Sargasso begins to change. Located between 30°N and 22°N is a narrow band, about three degrees wide, known as the subtropical frontal zone, which is like a ribbon laid from west to east; but slackly, so that its course wanders, varying seasonally and even from day to day. Within it, temperature and salinity rise markedly. There is something in that ribbon that the eels recognise – some sort of cue, possibly imprinted on them as infants, possibly a bouquet released from dissolved amino acids or by the weed, similar to that which guides salmon back to their home rivers to spawn. It, whatever it is, acts as a behavioural trigger. They know they are there, that they are summoned.

In the shadows below the floating weed, a fantastic silent drama is enacted. They gather in that half-lit meeting place, the eels of America and Europe, feeling the warmth against their skins and tasting the salt. All around others are joining them, long shapes, dark and silver, twisting through the blue water, seeking company. The stage is dominated by the females, their bellies hugely distended by their load of eggs. They stop and remain still, waiting, their little black heads protruding in front of their pale, swollen bodies. The much smaller male, still slender but with eyes as big as buttons, swims hesitantly, as if searching for the pheromone that tells them that a female is of their species, and is ready. He approaches, rubs his head along that tight, bulging stomach.

He pushes her slowly through the water, arching his back to fit the curve of her bursting ovaries, almost clinging to her. After a few minutes he releases the first cloud of sperm, as the eggs stream from his partner. Over the next twenty minutes he ejaculates several more times, male and female almost glued together as they are carried through the twilight. To imagine one pair, locked in that climactic embrace, is to picture – however imperfectly – an event of poignant grace. Multiply that a thousand times, and who knows how many more times; imagine a sea alive with twisting, quivering forms, the clarity of the water cloudy with emissions as egg and sperm mix. The imagination falters.

And then? Spent and exhausted, the fire of life and desire that sent these creatures away from their home waters and impelled them across the ocean until they reached this place of fulfilment, goes out. The bodies of the eels spiral into the abyss, while the fertilised eggs – 'slicks of orphaned spawn' in Seamus Heaney's words – ascend towards the sun. As they drift down, the corpses are set upon by the strange denizens of the blackness: viperfish, dragonfish, hatchetfish, the blind, jawless hagfish which drills into tissue and consumes from the inside out. Deeper and deeper they sink, until – three miles down – they reach the soft seabed, where the swarming hordes of scavenging crustacea known as amphipods feast upon whatever meat is left, and the excrement of the amphipods becomes food for the slimy holothurians. Thus is the life that began in the sunlit world far above and followed its path through the estuaries, rivers and lakes of two continents reduced in the end to the sludge at the bottom of the world, extruded by a creature that breathes through its anus.

Here, in this quiet, wonderful sanctuary, the cycle of life, death and burial ends, and begins again. For all its singularity, it has proved over many thousands of years to be a reliable system for sustaining two remarkably abundant and widely distributed species of fish. But for how much longer?

To try to assess the plight of the European and American eels and the extent to which the mechanisms for supporting them have been degraded, I have re-examined the mountains of statistics and learned speculations, and I have asked the scientists some simple questions. There is, and can be, no complete picture. But almost all the figures point to steep and continuing reductions in stock levels, and the eel watchers are of pretty much one mind. Some judge the decline to be critical, others prefer 'significant' or 'dramatic'. Some speak of stocks collapsing. Suffice it to say that the situation is bad and getting worse, or – in the measured words of a recent report on the European fishery from the International Council for the Exploration of Seas (ICES) – 'the eel stock is outside safe biological limits'.

Having reached that conclusion, it is hardly radical of the ICES panel to agree that 'the current fishery [in Europe] is not sustainable.' The element of ambiguity – over whether there are already insufficient eels to sustain commercial exploitation at its current level, or whether exploitation at its current level is close to pushing stock levels into a spiral of depletion – is left hanging. Are we on the edge of the precipice, or have we fallen over it?

No one knows what impact eel fishing is having, because

no one knows how many eels there are and how many are being caught. Anyway, the effect of fishing is but one of the factors determining population dynamics. Others include the creeping advance on both sides of the Atlantic of the parasitic nematode *Anguillicola crassus*, which destroys the fish's swimbladder, the spread of a herpes virus which attacks blood-forming tissue, contamination by PCBs and other pollutants, and the loss of habitat due to the draining of wetlands and the construction of dams.

There is one mighty imponderable in this complex equation, and it is hidden far out at sea. The Sargasso itself has been given a generally clean bill of health. International agreements on restricting the dumping of oil at sea have cut the concentrations of petroleum residue which – twenty years ago – resulted in the surface being spotted in black balls of tar. Concentrations of toxins such as pesticides and PCBs are calculated to be well within safe limits, and overall, there is no reason to suspect that the eels find anything intolerable in their ancestral breeding place.

But there is deep concern about the transport system that delivers the baby eels to the shores of Europe and North America, and in particular that the great alliance between the Gulf Stream and the North Atlantic Current may be faltering. It was voiced in the early 1990s by a group of biologists – including the Canadian eel experts Martin Castonguay and Brian Jessop, and Christopher Moriarty of Ireland – who speculated that declining recruitment of elvers might be attributable to a weakening in the currents. Since then there has been a trickle of more or less substantial research, suggesting that the warming of the Arctic Ocean might be eroding the vigour of what media-conscious ecologists have dubbed the 'global conveyor belt'. The hardest and most alarming evidence was presented in the summer of 2001. A team of British and Norwegian observers had spent five years monitoring the Faroe Bank, a flow of dense, cold water from the Arctic, which sinks to help fuel the western counter-current to the Gulf Stream. Oceanographers believe that the motor of the global conveyor belt is formed by the counter movements of warm and cold water, and without an ample infusion from the Arctic, the Gulf Stream – the 'river in the ocean', as Matthew Maury famously defined it a century and a half ago – is doomed to slacken. According to the team stationed off the Faroes, the volume of the outflow is declining at an accelerating rate of between two and four per cent a year. They calculated that since 1950 the contribution had diminished by a fifth.

To say that such research raises more questions than it answers is one truism. Another is that our understanding of the forces that shape climate – of which the behaviour of the oceans is the most potent – is incomplete. The measurements of the frigid, dense water piling south past the Faroes, once arranged into a form capable of supporting a hypothesis, then simplified by the scientists to assist the understanding of journalists, and dressed up by journalists to startle and entertain the public, inspired a lurid scenario. It was focussed on the 'possibility' that 'within a decade' Britain – chief beneficiary of the Gulf Stream's warmth – could be 'plunged into a new Ice Age', with London exposed to the same extremes of temperature as Moscow, Spitzbergen or Saskatoon. In vain did the professionals caution that this was merely one of a series of 'projections', and that it was just as likely that the Gulf Stream would merely alter the direction of its flow by a few degrees as shut down altogether. It was too late. The previous dreamworld favoured by the climate soothsayers – of a Britain bathing in Mediterranean heat, its hillsides blanketed in vineyards – was pushed aside. Olive groves gave way to icefields and glaciers.

The scientists have good reason to suspect that the Atlantic current system has flagged periodically in the past – long before the concept of artificially induced global warming was born – and they think it may be happening again. If so, it could certainly explain the drastic reductions in the numbers of thin-heads being delivered to Europe and Canada. The eel watchers have also been studying some less apocalyptic data relating to water circulation. The North Atlantic Oscillation Index records the difference in atmospheric pressure between Portugal and Iceland, and – without elaborating the daunting technicalities – is regarded as a sound measure of the behaviour of the Gulf Stream and the North Atlantic Current. High values correspond with periods of strong winds and greater mixing of cold and warm water in the surface layer, reducing the strength of the Gulf Stream and pushing it on a more easterly path. Between 1900 and 1925 the index was high, between 1925 and 1955 average, between 1955 and 1970 low, and in recent years high again. There is a distinct correlation between the level of the index and the abundance of elver recruitment. Low is good, high is bad.

The mystery of what is happening in the oceans is endlessly intriguing, and will doubtless nourish a mighty expenditure of research effort, a flood of worthy papers, an infinite succession of seminars and conventions replete with scholarly talk. But the guesswork does nothing for the eel. Even if we knew what the currents were up to, we are a very long way from being able to direct them. But we could – in theory at least – refrain from poisoning our waters and blocking our rivers with mincing machines hidden in concrete. We could stop the international trade in live eels, which has spread disease and parasitic infestation from one side of the world to the other. And we could stop fishing for eels altogether. It is, after all, exploited in uncontrolled and unmonitored fashion at all the accessible stages of its existence, and is the only species of fish expected to face such exploitation in infancy.

Here, expert opinion divides sharply. The indefatigable Dutch eel champion, Willem Dekker, considers that 'economically optimised' eel fisheries have depleted spawning escapement to unsustainable levels, and that 'there is an argument' that all commercial exploitation should be stopped. The American expert, Jim McCleave, argues that – certainly for the European eel – it is time to invoke the 'precautionary principle', and ban all fishing. He points to the decision of the Canadian government to shut down the cod fishery, and to signs that stocks of cod are beginning to recover. Others – notably Christopher Moriarty, and Brian Jessop of the Canadian Department of Fisheries and Oceans – contend that such a move would be self-defeating, and that what is needed is 'better management'.

It is notable that the eel states of the US – in the form of the Atlantic States Marine Fisheries Commission – have got together to put in place a management plan which requires state governments to monitor stocks and catches, improve habitats, and restrict the number of licences and types of fishing gear. Canada is going the same way. But Europe – where the eel fishery is much more valuable and the problems much more acute – has entirely failed to progress beyond the pious hope stage. This collective feebleness is vividly and depressingly illustrated by the imposingly titled National Eel Management Strategy, which was published early in 2001 by the Environment Agency of England and Wales after years of consultation with the gaggle of competing interests. I have no wish to be unkind to the authors of this well-intentioned but useless document, knowing them to be moved by the best intentions themselves, and hamstrung by financial and political constraints entirely beyond their control. The fact remains that, having recycled a ragbag of stale old news about declining stocks, all the agency is able to do by way of addressing the situation is to promise a 'national eel recovery plan' for 2001, and an 'eel monitoring programme' for 2002 – both 'subject to available funds'. The possibility of eel or elver fishing being restricted or phased out is not even raised. Instead the agency seeks to disguise its impotence behind vacuous platitudes about the need for a 'comprehensive management system' whose 'key element' is 'likely to be the establishment of targets of silver eel escapement'.

To be brutal, it does not really matter what those interested in the fate of the European eel think about the wisdom or otherwise of limiting or banning fishing. In the short term it is not going to happen. No one country will act on its own to protect a fish of such marginal economic significance whose offspring insist on offering themselves promiscuously to a dozen others. And the notion that the European Union which has shown itself powerless to arrest the plunder of its seas or to correct the scandal of its agriculture – would pause to consider the welfare of the humble eel is laughable.

It is much more likely that economic, sociological and biological imperatives will, in their crude, destructive way, achieve a resolution. Already, all over Europe and North America, the fishing way of life is withering away. Stocks are hammered into scarcity, officialdom steps in with quotas and inducements to stop fishing, the communities decay, the old skills are lost, and the tradition is dumped in the heritage museum. Eel fishing represents a minute sliver of this industry, and it, too, is quietly fading away. A mere handful of men work the surviving traps on the great lagoon of Comacchio, where thousands once sweated to bring in the writhing harvest. Ten years ago there were half a dozen eel catchers on the Thames Estuary. Now there is one. Ten years ago there would have been half a dozen boats out on Jamaica Bay, New York. Now there is one. Forty years ago there were eight hundred fishermen catching eels along the St Lawrence. The figure today is a tiny fraction of that. On Lough Neagh, the number of fishermen is half what it was three years ago.

Several factors have locked arms to engineer this slow death. One is the diminution of stocks. Another is the downward pressure on prices due to increased production from eel farms. A third – the hardest to pin down, and possibly the most significant – is the decline in the desire to fish. In an ever more affluent and comfortable society, fishing remains as hard, as uncomfortable, as uncertain as ever it was. Who, today, seeks a hard life?

The survival of the two species of Atlantic eel is not at

stake. They are too widespread, too adaptable, too resilient to be under threat. What is at stake, what is being surely lost, is something more precious and entirely irreplaceable: the interaction between the eel and humankind. A Canadian scientist, John Casselman, who has charted the virtual disappearance of *A. rostrata* from the upper St Lawrence, expressed the loss thus: 'I'm not really very concerned with the survival of the species. I believe it will survive. What we are losing is the resource. And especially important, we are losing the ability to use that resource. We are losing eel fishermen. A generation after we have lost these fishermen, there may be little interest in dealing with resource issues.'

Without fishermen seeking to catch and kill it, the eel is just another fish, another animal: curious in its appearance, singular in its habits and life cycle, but no longer important to anyone. Fishermen perceive and understand fish in a way inaccessible to biologists or environmental campaigners, because they depend on them. The man who lives from eels must be at ease with darkness and silence and must be attentive to the phases of the moon and the moods of the weather. He must be able to sense what his hidden prey is about. He has sharpened and refined his instinctive responses to that other world, because he has had to, to live. With his knowledge comes respect, even love. His relationship with the fish has a depth, a value, a beauty to it that no observer can aspire to. An American ecologist quoted to me a remark made to him: 'There'll always be an eel.' That is true, but it is only half the story.

A SELECTIVE BIBLIOGRAPHY

Alexander Boyd *England's Wealthiest Son: A Study of William Beckford* 1962

Aston Michael (ed) *Medieval Fish, Fisheries and Fishponds* 1988

Badham Rev. David *Ancient And Modern Fish-Tattle* 1854

Bertin Louis *Eels: A Biological Study* 1956

Boetius Jan and Harding Edward A re-examination of Johannes Schmidt's Atlantic Eel Investigations, in the *Dana Journal of Fisheries and Marine Research* 1985

Boosey Thomas *Anecdotes of Fish and Fishing* 1887

Bruun Anton The Breeding of the North Atlantic Freshwater Eel, in *Advances in Marine Biology* 1963

Buckland Frank *The Natural History of British Fishes* 1881

Cairncross David *The Origin of the Silver Eel* 1862

Chalmers Patrick *At the Tail of the Weir* 1932

Couch Jonathan *A History of the Fishes of the British Isles* 1878

Crewe Quentin *Foods from France* 1993

Davidson James *Courtesans and Fishcakes* 1997

Donnelly Daniel J. *On Lough Neagh's Shores* 1986

Eales J. Geoffrey *The Eel Fisheries of Eastern Canada* 1968

Englefield James *The Delightful Life of Pleasure on the Thames* 1912

Falkus Hugh and Buller Fred *Freshwater Fishing* 1975

Francis Francis *A Book on Angling* 1880

Grey Zane *Tales of Freshwater Fishing* 1928

Grassi Giovanni Battista The reproduction and metamorphosis of the Common Eel, in the *Proceedings of the Royal
Society of London* 1896

Grigson Jane *Jane Grigson's Fish Book* 1993

Grimble Augustus *The Salmon Rivers of Ireland* 1903

Hagen Ann *Anglo-Saxon Food and Drink* 1995

Harden-Jones R. *Fish Migration* 1968

Healy Tim *Stolen Waters* 1913

Herd Andrew *The Fly* 2001

Hornell James *Fishing in Many Waters* 1950

Houghton Rev. W. *British Freshwater Fishes* 1879

Jenkins J. Geraint *Nets and Coracles* 1974

Jesse Edward *Gleanings from Natural History* 1838

Jordan David S. and Evermann Barton W. *American Food
and Game Fishes* 1902

Mabey David *In Search of Food* 1978

Mitchel N.C. The Lower Bann Fisheries, in *Ulster Folklife*
1965

Moriarty Christopher *Eels: a Natural and Unnatural History*
1978

Root Waverley *Food* 1980

Rostlund Erhard *Freshwater Fish and Fishing in Native North
America* 1952

St John Charles *Wild Sports of the Highlands* 1847

Schmidt Johannes The Breeding Places of the Eel, in the
Philosophical Transactions of the Royal Society Series B 1923

Speck Frank G. *Penobscot Man* 1940

Storer David H. *A Synopsis of the Fishes of North America*
1848

Swift Graham *Waterland* 1983

Teal John and Mildred *The Sargasso Sea* 1975

Tesch F-W. *The Eel* 1977

Tsukamato K. and Ayama J. The Evolution of Freshwater Eels, in *The Environmental Biology of Fishes* 1998

Tucker Denys A New Solution to the Atlantic Eel Problem, in *Nature* 1959

Walker Richard *Still-Water Angling* 1953

Walton Izaak *The Compleat Angler* 1653

Waters Brian *Severn Tide* 1947

Watson John *The English Lake District Fisheries* 1925

Yarrell William *A History of British Fishes* 1836–9

Other Works Referred to in the Text

Bartram Bartram's Observations on his Travels from Pennsylvania to Onandago, Oswego and the Lake Ontario 1751

Bede *Ecclesiastical History*

Bonaveri Giovanno *Della Citta di Commachio, Delle sue Lagune e Pesche* 1761

Dante *Purgatorio Canto XXIV*

Davy Humphry *Salmonia* 1828

Heaney Seamus From 'Up the Shore', one of the poems in a Lough Neagh sequence from *Door into the Dark* 1969

Janvier Thomas *In the Sargasso Sea* 1898

Jordan David Starr *Fishes* 1907

Leland *Leland's Itinerary 1* 1710

Prescott William Hickling *History of Philip II*

Rafinesque, Jordan and Everman *Ichthyologia Ohiensis*

Smith Delia *The Complete Cookery Course* 1983
Smyth John *Description of the Hundred of Berkeley* 1639
Spallanzani Lazaro *Journey to the Two Scillies* 1792
Thompson William *A Natural History of Ireland* 1849-56

INDEX

HQ Moorside

LL - Lancashire